Rebound 2001

Childhood and Chemical Abuse: Prevention and Intervention

The *Journal of Children in Contemporary Society* series:

Childhood and Chemical Abuse: Prevention and Intervention

Edited by
Stephanie Griswold-Ezekoye, MEd, MPH
Karol L. Kumpfer, PhD
William J. Bukoski, PhD

The Haworth Press
New York • London

Childhood and Chemical Abuse: Prevention and Intervention has also been published as *Journal of Children in Contemporary Society*, Volume 18, Numbers 1/2, Fall/Winter 1985.

The Haworth Press, Inc., 12 West 32 Street, New York, NY 10001
EUROSPAN/Haworth, 3 Henrietta Street, London WC2E 8LU England

Library of Congress Cataloging in Publication Data

Childhood and chemical abuse.

"Has also been published as Journal of children in contemporary society, volume 18, numbers 1/2, fall/winter 1985"—T.p. verso.
Includes bibliographies and index.
1. Youth—United States—Substance use. 2. Substance abuse—United States—Prevention. 3. Children—United States—Drug use. 4. Drug abuse—United States—Prevention. I. Griswold-Ezekoye, Stephanie. II. Kumpfer, Karol L. (Karol Linda), 1943- . III. Bukoski, William J. [DNLM: 1. Substance Abuse—in infancy & childhood. W1 J0584T v.18 no. 1/2 / WM 270 C5365]
HV4999.Y68C47 1986   362.2'9   86-14956
ISBN 0-86656-580-9

Childhood and Chemical Abuse: Prevention and Intervention

Journal of Children in Contemporary Society
Volume 18, Numbers 1/2

CONTENTS

PART I: ETIOLOGY

PART II: PREVENTION

PART III: INTERVENTION

SELECTED READINGS

About the Editors

STEPHANIE GRISWOLD-EZEKOYE has been a private design and training consultant for eight years. She has developed prevention projects for youth and communities for both the public and private sector and is author of *Who am I? A comprehensive personal growth and development program.* Mrs. Griswold-Ezekoye has also designed and implemented chemical abuse training programs for both lay volunteers and professionals. She is Vice-President of the Pittsburgh Coalition to Promote Multicultural Substance Abuse Prevention, an active member of the American Public Health Association's Drug and Alcohol Forum, and National Secretary of the African Heritage Federation (of The Americas). Mrs. Griswold-Ezekoye is currently executive director of the Addison Terrace Learning Center of Pittsburgh, a chemical abuse prevention/intervention agency, and she is a certified drug and alcohol trainer for the Pennsylvania Department of Health.

KAROL L. KUMPFER is currently Visiting Assistant Professor and Research Associate at the Social Research Institute of the Graduate School of Social Work of the University of Utah, Salt Lake City, Utah. She is Principal Investigator on a NIDA prevention research grant in which prevention strategies for children of substance abusers are being evaluated. Her prior experience includes administration in substance abuse as the Deputy Director of the Utah State Division of Alcoholism and Drugs, and direct clinical work in community mental health. She received her doctoral degree in experimental and counseling psychology in 1971 from the University of Utah Psychology Department and completed post doctoral training at the Institute of Child Development at the University of Minnesota in 1975. She has taught at several colleges and universities in the USA and has written extensively on the topic of substance abuse. She is currently President of the

Utah Psychologists in Private Practice and serves on the NIDA/NIAAA Prevention Planning Council.

WILLIAM BUKOSKI has worked as an education and health researcher and program evaluator for the past 15 years. In his current position as Research Psychologist at the National Institute on Drug Abuse, he provides technical guidance and direction for a national program of school and community based substance abuse prevention research. He has published on this topic in a number of prominent scientific journals and has presented technical papers at seminars and at a variety of professional state health conferences. He is a member of the American Educational Research Association, a service provider for the Southern Maryland Health Systems Planning Agency and serves as the Vice-Chairman of the Plan Development Committee. He is active at the local level as a member of a parent group for drug free youth, as a PTA Board representative, and as a member of the local county Mental Health Advisory Committee. He co-edited this monograph in his private capacity. No official support or endorsement by the National Institute on Drug Abuse or of the Department of Health and Human Services is intended or should be inferred.

Foreword

Dear Friends:

Over the past several years, I have met with many wonderful concerned parents, dedicated youth and skilled health professionals who all share my profound concern about the harmful effects of drug abuse on our nation's youth. In our discussions, we agreed that the prevention of this serious problem will require that each of us play an important role.

This special Journal issue focuses upon childhood and adolescence and the problems of chemical abuse from a prevention perspective. The authors, each writing from their own rich experience in research and services, state that drug abuse must and can be stopped. Prevention tools are available to build a drug-free society.

By working together, I hope we will soon see an end to the personal and national tragedy of drug abuse.

Sincerely,

Nancy Reagan

Nancy Reagan

Preface

This special edition is dedicated to the positive development of youth, especially those who are impacted either directly or indirectly by chemical abuse or dependency. Since the traditional audience of *JCCS* includes educators, therapists, counselors, psychologists and psychiatrists, Haworth Press and the *Journal of Children in Contemporary Society* were compelled to address the issues of chemical abuse and children as one which impacts the total spectrum of professional human services.

In all of human experience, there is not a more joyous or ecstatic moment than the birth of a child. For those fortunate to experience that moment in the delivery room, the emergence of the child from the birth canal brings forth from the mother and father, a heartfelt shout of joy, tears of gladness, and an abundance of warm feelings. This moment of joy is shared equally by all present. For that one moment, personal problems are forgotten and this new life is celebrated by family, friends, and the community. The newborn becomes the proud possession of not only the parents, but of all mankind.

The death of a child has the reverse effect. No human experience is more tragic and felt more deeply by more people than the loss of a child through illness or accident. The death of a child steals from each of us a ray of hope, the precious optimism for the future and the gladness that life will continue. Intense grief is felt by all, and not by just the parents and immediate family. The death of a child shakes for a moment, the very soul of mankind.

Each year chemical abuse either directly or indirectly strikes at the life of children. Accidents or injuries due to chemical abuse, and suicide related to alcohol or drug abuse impact the lives of children directly or through the loss of a parent, guardian or sibling.

Since the trafficking to youth of both licit and illicit chemicals has become an uncondoned but organized business within

xv

the United States, the question of prevention is proving to be the most cost-effective and efficient method of addressing the problem. The increasing availability and accessibility of chemicals to youth along with the decrease in age at onset of use make it very clear that prevention strategies must begin as early as possible, and the pervasive nature of this phenomenon also suggests that prevention should be addressed comprehensively to include the significant individuals and systems (family, culture/community, school) which influence a child's development. The issues of chemical abuse are generally complex and very rarely are attributed to a single causal factor, yet in many instances use and abuse among youth correlates with their understanding of themselves and the supportive links and skills they have to resist use. Since those supports are usually lacking in a household where a parent or guardian is dependent, the most vulnerable population among youth are the offspring of these parents. The implications of this for human services is significant. It will impact on the diagnosis of childhood behavioral disorders along with the treatment plans implemented within education, health and human service institutions throughout the nation. There is a growing consensus within the chemical abuse field that many of these youth have reoccurring problems in behavior which can lead to problems in school, involvement with chemicals, and eventually involvement with the juvenile justice system if the issues of coping with the distortions of a chemically dependent household are not resolved.

Overall, the greatest threats to the life of our children appear to come from areas of human experience where we have the most control, human behavior, rather than from the indiscriminant attack of infectious disease or illness. Because of the nature of the problem, it is the hope that preventive interventions can be designed, tested and implemented to halt this trend.

Beyond affecting the lives of children directly, chemical abuse related injury and death also attacks children who have lost parents or guardians due to this problem, and who must now make major adjustments in their own life conditions. According to a recent epidemiological assessment (Ravenholt, 1984), mortality resulting from addiction to alcohol, tobacco, and other drugs accounted for (using 1980 data) the loss of 485,000 lives due to smoking, 99,547 lives due to alcohol, and 30,245 lives due to other drugs. These estimates include death caused directly by the use of the substance (such as drug overdose) and death that is related to the use of a substance, such as alcohol related motor vehicle deaths. The most profound tragedy is that morbidity and mortality resulting from chemical abuse can be prevented. Children's lives can be saved, lost futures can be restored, and the pain and suffering concomitant with chemical abuse can be avoided.

To address this pervasive problem, this issue is structured to discuss the most recent research in the field along with prevention strategies as they relate to child development. In the first section, the first article includes an extensive review of the causes and correlates of chemical dependency in children and youth. In a companion article, the author discusses family, environmental, and genetic influences.

The second section discusses the current primary approaches to prevention in the wide variety of primary sites of intervention: the family, the school, the local community, and society in general. Interventions which target changes in the child (the host) directly may occur in the family by teaching the parents to intervene with the child, in the school by training teachers to deliver prevention intervention, in the local community by having local volunteers or prevention specialists involve children or youth in prevention activities, or by making societal changes such as revising public legislation, mass media, and advertising practice.

The final section covers multicultural issues, treatment possibilities for chemically dependent youth and promising directions for prevention in the future as well as emerging issues in control of drugs when new drugs are being created daily.

Haworth Press and the *Journal of Children in Contemporary Society* are to be commended for furthering the important effort to disseminate timely information on the prevention of chemical dependency in youth. The editor, guest editors, and contributors to this issue are all well-known experts and researchers. Their substantive articles reflect the state-of-the-art in this young but complex field. Special acknowledgement is given to Mrs. Nancy Reagan, the First Lady, for her opening words in the Foreword of this issue and her ongoing contributions and support in the efforts to combat chemical abuse.

Stephanie Griswold-Ezekoye
Karol L. Kumpfer

Introduction

Donald Ian Macdonald, MD

This special issue offers readers a useful account of the most recent knowledge about prevention of substance abuse in children and adolescents. It addresses several major questions: What are the causes and correlates of chemical dependency in youth? What are some of the most effective prevention strategies? And what are some promising new directions in the prevention of chemical dependency?

American youth have the dubious honor and hold the unfortunate record of leading the world's industrialized nations in use of drugs. The phenomenon is of growing societal concern. Alcohol and polydrug use is increasing and there is evidence that substances of abuse have greater health and psychological effects than previously believed. It has been estimated that the annual cost to our society of chemical dependency is approximately $205 billion, of which $140 billion is attributed to alcohol abuse and $65 billion to drug abuse. This includes lost productivity, crimes, accidents, fires, treatment cost, and various indirect costs. Although these figures may seem incredibly high (and contribute significantly to the national debt), they cannot reflect the highest cost of all, and that is the personal and emotional suffering experienced not only by the abuser, but by family, friends, employers, and co-workers. Studies described in this issue clarify the negative impact one substance abuser can have on the health, welfare and productivity of others, as well as the increased risk that children of substance abusers will become substance abusers themselves.

Donald Ian Macdonald, Administrator, Alcohol, Drug Abuse, and Mental Health Administration, 5600 Fisher's Lane, Rockville, MD 20857.

1

INCIDENCE AND PREVALENCE

In the last decade, more teenagers have used alcohol and a variety of psychoactive drugs, and first use has been at younger and younger ages. Their use of tobacco, alcohol, and marijuana are seen as "gateway" drugs to later use of a variety of substances, and to chemical dependency. Through prevention efforts, cigarette smoking and marijuana use are decreasing among youth. Alcohol, after years of stable use, is also showing signs of decreasing use (Johnston, O'Malley & Buchanan, 1985). This good news of high school senior surveys must be tempered by a realization that the incidence is still unacceptably high and that high school surveys do not count the 15–20% of young people who do not get to be high school seniors.

CONSEQUENCES OF ALCOHOL AND DRUG USE

Alcohol and other drugs may cause problems associated with acute use (e.g., auto accidents), chronic use (e.g., cirrhosis), and a behavioral pattern of chronic use called dependency.

Associated with use of drugs and alcohol is a significant increase in the death rate of 15- to 24-year-olds. Alcohol is associated with more than 50% of the reported cases of the three major causes of death for youth: accidents, homicides, and suicides. In 1982 alone, 9,263 teenagers died in alcohol-related auto accidents. Alcohol and tobacco greatly increase a youth's risk for a broad range of health problems, including cardiovascular disease and cancer. Cigarette smokers have a life expectancy seven years shorter than nonsmokers. Recent studies have linked marijuana use to chronic cough, emphysema, and lung cancer (Tashkin & Cohen, 1981), endocrine problems such as decreased testosterone and gynecomastia (Harmon & Aliapouluis, 1972; Copeland, Underwood, & VanWyk, 1980), immune system suppression (Munson & Fehr, 1982), ophthalmological problems (Hepler, Frank, & Ungerleider, 1972), alterations in blood pressure, and tachycardia (Tennant, 1982).

One of the chief concerns about marijuana is the drug's

effects on the youth's personality, cognitive capacities, and behavior. The active ingredients in marijuana, such as delta-9-tetrahydrocannabinol (THC), are reported to be 25 to 50 times more potent now than in the mid-60s. THC produces short-term memory loss, decreased attention span, and perceptual changes that can lead to school and driving problems (Moskowitz & Peterson, 1982). Studies in primates show increased aggression and irritability, and brain cell alteration and destruction in monkeys who used marijuana for six months. Changes in brain structure persisted in primates for up to two years. Because of the long half-life of the drug, marijuana is capable of directly sustaining these cognitive and personality changes for up to 30 days (Turner, 1981).

IMPORTANCE OF PREVENTION

Many Americans are having to change their personal views of chemical dependency from considering it a moral issue to acknowledging that it is a medical and social problem. Chemical dependency has a characteristic clinical course that needs to be understood and recognized to be prevented and treated. Prevention of chemical dependency is widely accepted to be the most cost effective method of dealing with alcohol and drug related problems. The Rand Report on Strategies for Controlling Adolescent Drug Use (Polich, Ellickson, Reuter & Kahns, 1984) concluded that prevention is the most promising strategy for the control of substance use. Prevention, historically neglected as a complex and difficult favored strategy, is only recently receiving national priority. One salient side effect of the health/wellness movement in this country has been the increased interest in substance abuse prevention.

IMPACT OF CHEMICALLY DEPENDENT YOUTH ON MANY PROFESSIONS

The many helping professions that deal with youth who are chemically dependent need no convincing that prevention is of paramount importance. Educators face students in their classrooms daily who are under the influence of some psycho-active drug. According to the annual high school survey for the National Institute on Drug Abuse (NIDA), (Johnston, O'Malley, & Buchanan, 1985), 5% to 7% of high school students report daily use of alcohol and marijuana. It is difficult enough for students to learn in often overcrowded schools, but even harder when mentally handicapped by decreased motivation, short-term memory loss, lack of concentration, tardiness, and truancy. A recent prospective study of 9th, 10th, and 11th grade students found that significantly more of the students involved with drugs failed to graduate from high school, and the more severe the drug use the greater the probability of not graduating and dropping out of school (NIDA Clinical Research Notes, January 1985).

Mental health professionals should be aware of the high prevalence of chemical dependency in the adolescents they treat. Youth involved in alcohol and drug abuse often have suicidal tendencies, severe depression, and problems with anger and impulse control. Many community mental health professionals face the problem of where to find detoxification facilities and appropriate treatment for these youth.

From their experience, juvenile delinquency specialists and probation officials should be well aware of the high correlation between crime and substance abuse. Drug use is not an isolated behavior, but part of a multiple problem syndrome that often involves feelings of parental and peer rejection, lack of social skills, decreased academic ability, precocious sexuality, and health and behavior problems. Until the chemical use is stopped, it is not possible to understand in any one youth whether these problems predate the substance abuse or are caused by it.

Health care professionals are becoming more aware of the signs and symptoms, as well as the predictable stages of this progressive disease. Pediatricians and other physicians can better diagnose the child at highest risk for abuse when they understand the etiology of chemical dependency and the four stages of drug use (Macdonald, 1984). In *Stage One*, the youth is willing to try drugs when offered socially in order to belong to the group, feel mature, have a new experience, or enjoy the feeling of being high. In *Stage Two*, the youth begins to seek out reliable sources for psychoactive drugs and starts trying stronger forms of drugs. Diagnostic clues include deterioration in school performance, change in social group to older friends or nontraditional friends, increased irritability and dramatic mood swings, argumentative behavior, and family alienation. *Stage Three* drug-involved youth are easier to recognize as they often dress in nontraditional ways. In addition to problems at home and at school, they may begin to experience problems with the law, including shoplifting, truancy, broken curfews, traffic citations, and vandalism. Use of harder and more costly drugs occurs. These youth spend an average of $50 to $60 per week on drugs. *Stage Four* youth would be easiest to diagnose, but have often left home and move beyond traditional support systems and family medical care. In this stage, drugs are used to ward off withdrawal, guilt, and depression, basically to just feel OK since it is progressively more difficult to produce sustained euphoria. Physical signs of weight loss, sore throat, fatigue, and poor nutrition are common. These youth may appear in hospital emergency rooms because of overdose, suicide attempts, or drug-and alcohol-related accidents.

ISSUES IN PREVENTION OF CHEMICAL DEPENDENCY

Like any young science, prevention of chemical dependency faces a number of critical issues. Among these are:

1. What are we trying to prevent? In my view, any use of psychoactive drugs by adolescents, except under strict medical supervision, is misuse. Drug use is a potentially progressive phenomenon in which experimentation is often but an early stage.

2. How do you measure effectiveness of prevention interventions in children before the typical age of onset of use? Valid theoretical models are needed, based on developmental milestones in a child's growth which can highlight the early indicators of subsequent chemical dependency. Longitudinal studies are needed to test the effectiveness of these theoretical models and prevention strategies that have demonstrated positive alterations in the child's cognitions and behaviors linked to future chemical dependency.

3. What are the major causes of chemical use in children and youth? To be effective, prevention programs must be grounded in the etiology of chemical dependency. More research is needed to identify the factors most highly correlated to future substance use and abuse.

4. Who are the youth most at risk of chemical dependency? One promising approach to prevention is to target intensive interventions at high-risk children and youth. More research is needed in this area, but preliminary evidence suggests that children of chemically dependent parents are probably the highest risk population (Goodwin, 1985; Kumpfer & De-Marsh, in press). Children from disadvantaged and socially isolated families, including many minority children, are also at high risk for chemical dependency.

5. How can we make prevention intervention cost-effective? We must demonstrate that they are cost-beneficial and also that the most cost-effective strategies are being used. The life-time cost of a single drug abuser is currently estimated at $85,000 in lost productivity and direct economic burden on society, hence prevention of drug abuse in even one youth can have ample economic returns.

The search for answers to these and other questions is on the scientific agenda in this country's national strategy against drug abuse. While we are attempting to cut down the supply of drugs entering this country, we are intent upon reducing demand, and nowhere in our society is it more important to start than with our youth.

REFERENCES

Copeland, K. C., Underwood, L. E., & VanWyk, J. J. (1980). Marijuana smoking and pubertal arrest. *New England Journal of Medicine, 96*, 1079–1080.

Goodwin, D. W. (1985). Alcoholism and genetics: The sins of the fathers. *Archives of General Psychiatry, 6*, 545–549.

Harmon, J., & Aliapouluis, M. A. (1972). Gynecomastia in mariguana users. *New England Journal of Medicine, 287*, 936.

Hepler, R. S., Frank, I. M., & Ungerleider, J. T. (1972). Pupillary constriction after marijuana smoking. *American Journal of Ophthalmology, 74*, 1185–1190.

Johnston, L., O'Malley, P., & Bachman, J. (1985). *Use of licit and illicit drugs by America's high school students, 1975–1984* (DHHS Publication No. ADM 85–1394). Washington, DC: U.S. Government Printing Office.

Kumpfer, K. L., & DeMarsh, J. P. (in press). Prevention strategies for children of drug-abusing parents. *Proceedings of the 34th Annual Congress on Alcoholism and Drug Dependence*, Calgary, Alberta.

Macdonald, D. I. (1984). Drugs, drinking, and adolescence. *American Journal of Diseases of Children, 138,* 117–125.

Moskowitz, H., & Peterson, R. (1982). *Marijuana and driving: A review.* Rockville, MD: American Council for Drug Education.

Munson, A. E., & Fehr, K. P. (1982). Immunological effects of cannabis. In K. O. Fehr, & H. Kalant (Eds.), *Cannabis and health hazards: Proceedings of the ARF/WHO scientific meeting on adverse health and behavioral consequences of cannabis use* (p. 257). Toronto, Canada: The Addiction Research Foundation.

Polich, J. M., Ellickson, P. L., Reuter, P., & Kahan, J. P. (1984, February). *Strategies for controlling adolescent drug use.* Santa Monica, CA: The Rand Corporation.

Tashkin, D. P., & Cohen, S. (1981). *Marijuana smoking and its effects on the lungs.* Rockville, MD: American Council for Drug Education.

Tennant, F. S., Jr. (1982). Clinical toxicology of cannabis use. In K. O. Fehr, & H. Kalant (Eds.), *Cannabis and health hazards: Proceedings of the ARF/WHO scientific meeting on adverse health and behavioral consequences of cannabis use* (p. 69). Toronto, Canada: The Addiction Research Foundation.

Turner, C. E. (1981). *The marijuana controversy.* Rockville, MD: American Council for Drug Education.

PART I: ETIOLOGY

Introduction

An understanding of the nature and scope of a problem serves to provide reliable foundations for developing effective strategies to combat it. This section includes a discussion of the factors that serve to impact the susceptibility or non-susceptibility to chemical abuse. Hawkins et al. provide an indepth discussion of the childhood predictors of chemical abuse which include antisocial behavior, school acquiescence, peer influence, and age at onset of use. Kumpfer and De-Marsh cover family environment and genetic influences which impact on youth chemical abuse. They discuss the susceptibility of children of chemically dependent parents, genetic transmission, family structure and management, socialization and cognitive family characteristics in relation to their predictability to future abuse in youth.

Childhood Predictors of Adolescent Substance Abuse: Toward an Empirically Grounded Theory

J. David Hawkins, PhD
Denise M. Lishner, MSW
Richard F. Catalano, Jr., PhD
Matthew O. Howard, MA

ABSTRACT. This article reviews the etiology of chemical use and abuse among children and adolescents as well as states the etiological pathways of youth drug behavior between initial, occasional and regular use. The authors also discuss determinants of the onset of chemical use such as the family; peers; early antisocial behavior; school; attitudes, beliefs and personality traits; and early initiation of use. They develop a theoretical premise based on the most current etiological research and offer a social development model that serves as a basis for prevention intervention.

This chapter examines the existing knowledge concerning the etiology of drug use and abuse among children and adolescents. It is important to distinguish between the behaviors of drug initiation, occasional use of drugs, regular use of drugs, and drug abuse, since each of these behaviors may be predicted by somewhat different etiological pathways (Hawkins & Weis, 1985).

J. David Hawkins, Denise M. Lishner, Richard F. Catalano, Jr., and Matthew O. Howard are members of the Center for Social Welfare Research, School of Social Work, JH-30, University of Washington, Seattle, WA 98195.

Preparation of this paper was supported in part by Grant #80-JS-AX-0052-(S2) from the National Institute for Juvenile Justice and Delinquency Prevention and by Grant #5-R18-DA03013-03 from the National Institute on Drug Abuse. Points of view or opinions in this document are those of the authors and do not represent official positions or policies of either institute.

Drug use initiation refers to an individual's first use of a particular substance. Occasional use refers to a pattern of use following initiation in which a designated frequency threshold is not exceeded for more than a specified period of time. Regular use refers to a pattern of use exceeding a designated frequency threshold for more than a specified period of time, regardless of whether this use is accompanied by overt problems in personal, social, education, or economic functioning. Drug abuse has been defined as a pattern of pathological use that persists for at least a month and that causes impairment in social or occupational functioning in the family, at school, or in a work setting (American Psychiatric Association, 1980).

There is evidence that different patterns of drug use at different developmental stages have different etiological origina (Kandel, 1982) and are associated with different patterns of current behavior. Robins (1980) found that the occasional use of drugs is not associated with antisocial personality. In contrast, drug abuse, especially in early and mid-adolescence, appears to be part of a general pattern or rebelliousness and nonconforming behavior (Johnston, O'Malley & Evelard, 1978; Segal, Singer & Huba, 1979; Segal, Huba & Singer, 1980) which criminologists have called a "deviance syndrome" (Elliott, Huizinga & Ageton, 1982; Hindelang & Weis, 1972; B. Jessor & S. L. Jessor, 1978) and mental health professionals have labeled antisocial personality (Robins, 1980).

The epidemiological statistics suggest the possibility that the occasional use of drugs by most adolescents is a different phenomenon from drug abuse which is associated with a deviance syndrome or antisocial personality. Annual surveys of high school seniors conducted by Johnston, O'Malley and Bachman (1985) have shown that 54.9% of the class of 1984 had initiated marijuana use and 62% had initiated use of other illicit drugs. These rates of lifetime prevalence of illicit drug use among high school seniors are far greater than the estimated rate of chronic antisocial behavior among boys, which ranges from 4% to 15% depending on the age of the subjects and the type of behaviors included (Loeber, 1982; Robins, 1979; Rutter, Tizzard & Whitemore, 1970). The rates of drug initiation are also far greater than the 5.0% prevalence of regular (daily) marijuana use found by Johnston in the class of 1984. It appears reasonable to hypothesize that behaviors with such different rates in the population may arise from somewhat different etiological roots. In sum, the etiologies of drug initiation, occasional drug use, regular drug use, and drug abuse well may be different (Robins & Przybeck, 1985).

These considerations suggest that the prevention of drug abuse among adolescents may require a different strategy than the prevention of experimental or occsional use of drugs. Strategies which are adequate for preventing experimentation among those at low risk of engaging in serious antisocial behaviors may be wholly inadequate for preventing initiation and use by those who exhibit a "deviance syndrome." On the other hand, well-founded strategies for preventing drug abuse among those at highest risk for abuse may be inappropriate for those at risk only of becoming occasional users.

With these considerations in mind, this chapter seeks to distinguish etiological risk factors as they relate to different outcomes of interest, especially as they appear related to occasional drug use among adolescents versus adolescent drug abuse.

There have been few studies that focus on childhood and preadolescent predictors of subsequent drug involvement. Though the age of onset for some drugs had been declining (Gersik, Grady, Sexton & Lyons, 1981), studies assessing precipitating factors for drug use generally have focused on adolescence. Those studies that do examine childhood predictors rarely differentiate drug-specific behaviors from general deviant, delinquent, or problem behaviors. One notable exception is the research of Bush and her associates (Ahmed, Bush, Davison & Iannotti, 1984; Bush, 1981; Bush & Davidson, 1982; Bush, Iannotti & Davidson, 1983a, 1983b) who are studying the development of attitudes and behaviors toward abusable substances in youths beginning at age five.

FAMILY FACTORS

- There is evidence that the use of drugs, including alcohol, has origins in the family. Parental drug use is associated with initiation of use by adolescents (Kandel, Kessler & Margulies, 1978; McDermott, 1984; Johnson, Schoutz & Locke,

1984). Similar findings have been reported for adolescent drinking habits (Rachal et al., 1980, 1982; Zucker, 1979). Bush and colleagues (Ahmed et al., 1984) have examined the effects of parental modeling of drug use on children's expectations to use drugs and on their actual drug use. In a study of 420 children in grades K-6, they found "salience," a measure of the number of household users of a drug and the degree of children's involvement in parental drug taking behavior, to be the best predictor of both expectations to use and actual use of alcohol. Salience was also a strong predictor of children's cigarette and marijuana use. The importance of number of household users varied across substance. As the number of family members who used alcohol or marijuana increased, so did the probability that the child used or expected to use these substances. Having one household member who smoked cigarettes almost doubled the probability that a child smoked or expected to smoke. This probability did not increase for additional smokers in the home.

_ A consistent correlation between adolescent drug abuse and parents' use of alcohol and other legal drugs also has been shown (Bushing & Bromley, 1975; Lawrence & Velleman, 1974). A review by Stanton (1979) showed that a disproportionate number of heroin addicts have fathers with a drinking problem (Cannon, 1976; Ellinwood, Smith & Valliant, 1966), that marijuana users frequently have fathers who use alcohol and tobacco and mothers who use tranquilizers (McGlothlin, 1975), and the parents of marijuana users have elevated rates of tranquilizer, barbiturate, and stimulant use (Smart & Fejer, 1972). Johnson et al. (1984) found that parental use of marijuana was strongly associated with adolescents' use of other illegal drugs including cocaine and barbiturates.

Reviews of the familial incidence of alcoholism (Cotton, 1979; Goodwin, 1971) similarly conclude that alcoholics are more likely than non-alcoholics to have a history of parental alcoholism or siblings with alcoholism. Cotton (1979) reports, in a meta-analysis of 39 studies selected for their methodological rigor, that nearly 30.8% of the alcoholics studied, compared with 7.1% of schizophrenics, 12% of psychiatric patients, and 4.7% of non-psychiatric controls had a history of parental alcoholism. Thus, a higher rate of parental alcoholism is characteristic of alcoholics.

The link between parental drug use and the initiation and abuse of drugs in children has generated controversy regarding the extent to which intergenerational transmission is due to genetic versus environmental factors. Virtually all the evidence regarding this question comes from research on alcoholism. Researchers have sought to assess the independent contribution of genetic factors to the development of alcoholism through twin and adoption studies. Kaij (1960) studied 174 male twin pairs born in Sweden and raised apart from birth. At least one member of each pair was a registered alcohol abuser. Using information from psychiatric clinic and governmental records in Sweden, each member of the twin pairs was placed in one of five drinking classifications, ranging from abstinent to chronic alcoholic. Fifty-three percent of the genetically identical (monozygotic) twins compared with 28% of the dizygotic twins were placed in the same classification. For the twin pairs with at least one chronic alcoholic proband, the concordance rates were 71.4% for monozygotic (MZ) and 32.3% for dizygotic (DZ) twins. Hrubec and Omenn (1981) have reported concordance rates for male alcoholism of 26.3% for monozygotic and 11.9% for dizygotic twins. While the rates in the Kaij and Hrubec studies were dissimilar, the concordance ratios were almost identical: monozygotic twins were over twice as likely as dizygotic twins to be concordant for alcoholism.

In contrast, Gurling, Clifford and Murray (1981) have reported concordance rates for alcoholism of 21% in monozygotic and 25% in dizygotic twins. Several factors are noteworthy regarding the Gurling et al. (1981) study. On the one hand, Gurling et al. (1981) determined zygosity by using serological markers in addition to the more commonly employed anthropomorphic measures of physical resemblance. The use of serological measures to determine zygosity constitutes a more rigorous procedure. Thus, it could be expected to *increase* the differences in MZ-DZ concordance rates from alcohol if there are genetic contributors to alcoholism (Schuckit, 1981). Yet, Gurling et al. (1981) found no significant differences. On the other hand, Gurling and associates studied both males and females, whereas Kaij (1960) and Hrubec and Omenn (1981) studied only males. Evidence supporting the hypothesis of a genetic link has been found only for male alcoholism in previous research. For males only, Gurling et al. (1981) report slightly higher, though not significantly different, concordance rates for MZ twins (33%) than for DZ twins (30%). Finally, 38% of the twins pairs studied by Gurling et al. (1981) were under 40 years of age and thus, may not have passed through the "age of risk" for developing alcoholism. If genetic contributions to the development of alcoholism are expressed later in life, the Gurling et al. (1981) study would underestimate them. Nonetheless, the Gurling et al. (1981) study does not support claims regarding genetic predisposition to alcoholism.

Adoption studies provide more consistent evidence for a genetic factor in the etiology of male alcoholism. Different rates of alcoholism between adopted offspring of alcoholics and adopted offspring of nonalcoholics would appear to implicate genetic factors in the pathogenesis of alcohoism. Goodwin et al. (1974); Goodwin, Schulsinger, Knop, Mednick, and Guze (1977a); Goodwin, Schulsinger, Moller, Mednick, and Guze (1977b) conducted a series of adoption studies in Denmark. They found that 18% of the adopted sons of alcoholics (N = 55) compared with only 5% of adopted males without a biological alcoholic parent (N = 78) were diagnosed as alcoholic. The rate of alcoholism among adopted sons of alcoholics (18%) was similar to the rate among their brothers raised by their alcoholic biological parents (17%). Length of exposure to the alcoholic parent was not associated with alcoholism, while the severity of parental alcoholism was positively associated with male alcoholism (Murray & Stabenau, 1982). In contrast, the 2% rate of alcoholism among adopted daughters of alcoholics (N = 49) was lower than the 4% rate among adopted daughters without a biological parent with alcoholism (N = 47), though the difference was not significant and both rates were quite low, inhibiting meaningful comparison. Bohman's (1978) adoption study in Sweden revealed similar evidence for a genetic component in male alcohol abuse. Twenty-seven percent of the adopted sons of registered alcohol abusers (N = 50) were themselves registered for alcohol abuse compared with 6% of a matched sample of 50 adopted sons of biological parents not registered as alcohol abusers. Again, no evidence for genetic transmission was found among females (Murray & Stabenau, 1982). Smaller sample adoption studies in the U.S. have replicated the support for genetic transmission of primary alcoholism in males though not for secondary alcoholism (Cadoret, Cain & Grove, 1980; Cadoret & Gath, 1978).

In order to understand how genetic influences might be transmitted, researchers in the alcoholism field have studied differences in genetically mediated biological responses to alcohol among children of alcoholics ("high risk" children) and non-alcoholics ("low risk" children). Pollack et al. (1983) reported more slow wave activity on the EEG for children of alcoholics compared with children of non-alcoholics. Schuckit, Parker and Rossman (1983) found differences in high and low risk children in serum prolactin response to administration of alcohol. Schuckit (1980) reported greater muscle relaxation in response to ethanol, and Schuckit and Rayes (1979) found increased levels of acetaldehyde after administration of alcohol in sons of alcoholics when compared with sons of non-alcoholics, suggesting the possible existence of pharmacogenetic transmission mechanisms.

Convergent evidence from twin, adoption, and biological response studies suggest that genetic factors may play a role in the etiology of some male alcoholism. However, there is not a unitary relationship here. The adoption studies which suggest a genetic factor in male alcoholism also reveal that less than 20% of the sons of alcoholics themselves become alcoholic. Factors other than genetic prediposition must be considered to explain why over 80% of the sons of alcoholics do not themselves develop alcoholism. Conversely, about half of the hospitalized alcoholics do not have a family history of alcoholism (Goodwin, 1985), suggesting that a large proportion of alcoholism is not linked to genetic factors.

Little research has been conducted on genetic predisposition and the abuse of drugs other than alcohol. The possible contribution of genetic factors to the abuse of other drugs remains to be investigated.

The evidence supporting a genetic factor in some male alcoholism is paralleled by evidence supporting the role of family environmental and interactional variables in drug and alcohol abuse. To the extent that adolescent drug abuse is part of a constellation of deviant behaviors, including delinquency, the literature on the prediction of delinquency is salient. Among the most important childhood predictors of delinquency are composite measures of family functioning (Loeber & Dishion, 1983), parental family management techniques (West & Farrington, 1973; Baumrind, 1983), and parental criminality or antisocial behavior (Langner, Gersten, Wills & Simcha-Fagan, 1983; Loeber & Dishion, 1983; Osborn & West, 1979). Disruptions in family management are a major mediating variable for antisocial behavior in children (Patterson, 1982). Variables associated with antisocial problems include households that are disorganized and have poorly defined rules and inconsistent, ineffective family management techniques. In a sample of 195 boys, Loeber and Schmaling (in press) found that boys who engaged in both overt antisocial behaviors (fighting) and covert antisocial behaviors (e.g., stealing and drug use) came from families with the greatest disturbance in child-rearing practices.

Looking more specifically at adolescent drug use, positive family relationships, involvement, and attachment appear to discourage youths' initiation into drug use (Adler & Lutecka, 1973; Wechsler & Thum, 1973; Shibuya, 1974; R. Jessor & S. L. Jessor, 1977; Kim, 1979; Norem-Hebeisen, Johnson, Anderson & Johnson, 1984). Kandel (1982) found that parental influence varies with the stages of drug use she identified. Parental role modeling of alcohol use is positively associated with adolescent use of alcohol, while the quality of the family relationship is inversely related to the use of illicit drugs other than marijuana. According to Kandel, three parental factors help to predict initiation into drug use: parent drug using behaviors (see also Kim, 1979); parental attitudes about drugs; and parent-child interactions. The latter factor is characterized by lack of closeness (see also Mercer, Hundleby & Carpenter, 1976; Kandel, Kessler & Margulies, 1978; Kim, 1979; Brooks, Luknoff & Whiteman, 1980), lack of maternal involvement in activities with children, lack of, or inconsistent, parental discipline (see also Braucht, Brakarsh, Follingstand & Berry, 1973; Blum, Henry & Sanford, 1972; Baumrind, 1983; Penning & Barnes, 1982), and low parental educational aspirations for their children. Stanton and Todd (1979) and Ziegler-Driscoll (1979) suggest that familial risk factors include a pattern of overinvolvement by one parent and distance or permissiveness by the other. Similarly, families with drug abusing children are described by Kaufman and Kaufman (1979) as ones in which fathers are "disengaged" and mothers are "enmeshed."

Baumrind (1983) classified parenting styles as authoritative, authoritarian, or permissive, and found that children who are highly prosocial and assertive generally come from authoritative families. She suggests that family antecedents which discriminate types of drug users include conventionality, family disruption, and parent non-directiveness. Reilly (1979) found that common characteristics of families with adolescent drug abusers include negative communication patterns (criticism, blaming, lack of praise), inconsistent and unclear behavioral limits, denial of the child's drug use, unrealistic parental expectations, family-self medication, and miscarried expressions of anger. Gantman (1978) reported significantly fewer positive communications and more frequent interpersonal misperceptions in families with a drug-abusing child compared with families without drug-abusing children. Norem-Hebeisen et al. (1984) also found that the quality of adolescents' relationships with their parents is related to patterns of drug use. Generally, drug users perceived their fathers as more hostile and adversarial than non-users. Ninth-grade drug users also perceived their parents as less caring and more rejecting than did non-users.

There is also evidence which suggests the independent contribution of family interactions in determining adolescent drug use apart from parent drug use. Tec (1974) found that parental drug use in a rewarding family structure only slightly promotes extensive marijuana use, while in an unrewarding context, there is a clear association between drug use by parents and their children. Research by McDermott (1984) indicates that while parental drug use and adolescent drug use are related, permissive parental attitudes toward drug use as perceived by youths may be of equal or greater importance than actual parental drug use in determining adolescent drug use.

Little research has been conducted on other forms of parental behavior and adolescent drug use and abuse. Several studies have suggested a relationship between child abuse and delinquency (Timberlake, 1981; Steele, 1976; Phouts, Schopler & Henley, 1981; Garbarino, 1981). When case records of abused and neglected children were reviewed over 12 years later, 30% were discovered to be delinquent or in need of supervision (Alfaro, 1976). Excessively severe, physically threatening, and physically violent parental discipline have been associated with aggressive and destructive acts of delinquency (Deykin, 1971; Shore, 1971; Haskell & Yablonsky, 1974). We are aware of no longitudinal studies, however, assessing the impact of child abuse on subsequent drug use and abuse.

While some researchers have reported that non-intact families predict subsequent drug use (Robins, 1980; Baumrind, 1983; Penning & Barnes, 1982; Stern, Northman & Van Slyck, 1984), there is disagreement on this point. Family structure appears to be less important as a predictor of delinquency than attachment to parents (Glynn, 1984; Long & Scherl, 1984; Nye, 1958; Sederstrom, 1978; Wilkinson, 1974; Weis et al., 1980).

The findings are consistent regarding the effects of the quality and consistency of family management, family communication, and parent role modeling on children's substance use (Baumrind, 1983; Patterson, 1982; Stanton & Todd, 1982; Mercer, Hundleby & Carpetner, 1976; Kandel et al., 1978; Pennings & Barnes, 1982). Given the consistency of these findings, family management, communication, and role modeling represent risk factors to be included in theories of the etiology of adolescent drug initiation and abuse.

EARLY ANTISOCIAL BEHAVIOR

A number of studies have shown that problematic conduct early in life continues for certain groups of children (Alterman & Tarter, 1983; Gersten et al., 1976; Ghodsian, Fogelman, Lambert & Tibbenham, 1980; Langner et al. 1983; McGee, Williams, & Silva, 1984; Patterson, 1982; Robins, 1966; Weiss, Hechtman, Milroy, & Perlman, 1985; Werner & Smith, 1977; West & Farrington, 1973). As part of a constellation of antisocial behavior problems, drug abuse is predicted by previous patterns of antisocial behavior.

Robins (1978) found that the greater the variety, frequency, and seriousness of childhood antisocial behavior, the more likely antisocial behavior is to persist into adulthood. Proneness to problem behavior and a deviance syndrome have been posited to explain drug use (R. Jessor & S. L. Jessor, 1978). The Jessors found that one could predict transitions of school aged children into drinking, loss of virginity, marijuana use, and delinquency about equally well from whichever behavior appears first, and concluded that similar antecedents foster a wide range of problem behaviors.

Early antisocial behavior has been found to predict adolescent substance use (Robins, 1978; Johnston et al., 1978; Kandel et al., 1978; Wechsler & Thum 1973). In their sample of 1,242 urban, black first-grade students, Kellam and Brown (1982) found a positive correlation between first-grade male aggressiveness, especially when coupled with shyness, and the frequency of substance use 10 years later. Rebelliousness in children also is correlated with initiation of drug use (Smith & Fogg, 1978). Early aggressiveness and irritability is associated with later substance abuse (Lewis, Robins & Rice, 1985; Nylander, 1979).

A longitudinal study of five year olds followed into adulthood (Lerner & Vicary, 1984) found that a "difficult" temperament including frequent negative mood states and withdrawal contributes to drug problems. Children characterized by withdrawal responses to new stimuli, biological irregularity, slow adaptability to change, frequent negative mood expressions, and high intensity of positive and negative expressions of affect more often become regular users of alcohol, tobacco, and marijuana in adulthood than "easy" children who evidence greater adaptability and positive affect early in life. The authors suggest that the negative mood and withdrawal responses of the "difficult" child may be analogous to the depression and social alienation frequently reported for drug abusers (Knight, Sheposh & Bryson, 1974; Paton, Kessler & Kandel, 1977; Paton & Kandel, 1978; Smith & Fogg, 1978).

While not focused specifically on drug use, Spivack's (1983) longitudinal study of high risk, early signs of delinquency, similarly revealed that conduct disturbances in adolescence could be predicted from kindergarten and first grade signs of acting out, overinvolvement in socially disturbing behaviors, impatience, impulsivity, and acting defiant and negative.

Illicit drug use is related positively to other illegal behaviors (Bell & Champion, 1979; Johnston et al., 1978; Jessor, Chase

& Donovan, 1980). Delinquency has generally been found to occur prior to drug use (Holmberg, 1985; Elliott et al., 1982; Johnston et al., 1978). Frequent drug use is associated with lower personal controls against involvement in problem behavior, greater involvement in other forms of problem behavior, and lesser involvement in conventional behaviors (Jessor et al., 1980). Clausen has summarized the evidence: "One surmises that the identification of those who will be precocious in drug behavior might well be possible in terms of early signs of rebelliousness or precocity" (1978, p. 247).

The results of Loeber's (1985) review of patterns and development of antisocial behavior are consistent with the earlier suggestion that different etiological paths may be associated with early versus late initiation of drug use and with drug use as contrasted with drug abuse. For example, antisocial behavior is associated with early initiation of drinking (Cadoret et al., 1984; Hesselbrock et al., 1984; Hesselbrock, Hesselbrock & Stabenau, 1985; Lewis, Clininger & Pais, 1983; Lewis, Rice & Helzer, 1983). Youths who begin drinking late in adolescence are less likely to engage in antisocial behavior. During adolescence, far more youths use psychoactive substances than engage in antisocial acts. Thus, initiation of substance use in late adolescence is probably not connected with antisocial behavior for a large majority of youths. In contrast, substance use in early adolescence is more frequently associated with antisocial acts (Wechsler & Thum, 1973). Early initiation of substance use is linked with a higher risk for substance abuse (Bloom & Greenwald, 1984; Robins & Przybeck, 1985).

In summary, the evidence of a positive relationship between childhood antisocial behavior and subsequent drug abuse is relatively consistent. There are several caveats, however, which should be noted. First, the earliest age at which childhood antisocial behavior can be reliably identified as predictive of drug use or abuse is not clear. Stable predictions of behavior have been found from the age of school entry, but not before (Robins, 1979; Rutter & Giller, 1983). It also should be noted that conduct disorders in the preschool years do not appear predictive of adolescent antisocial behaviors in a normal population sample (Kagan & Moss, 1962). This may reflect the normal developmental aspects of behaviors such as temper outbursts during the preschool years (Loeber, 1985; MacFarlane, Allen & Hoznik, 1962; Rutter & Giller, 1983).

Second, childhood antisocial behavior appears to be less powerful as a predictor of either adult alcoholism (McCord, 1981) or self-reported delinquency at age 18 (Farrington, 1982) than is antisocial behavior in early adolescence (Loeber, 1985). While serious antisocial behaviors in childhood appear to be virtually a prerequisite for serious antisocial behaviors (including drug abuse) in later life, less than one-half of the children with serious behavior problems will manifest these problems later (Robins, 1978). Loeber and Dishion (1983) report that 30 to 40% of children engaging in maladaptive behavior at ages 4 through 11 continue the same behavior four to nine years later (Farrington, 1978, 1979; Ghodian et al., 1980; Glavin, 1972; Janes, Hesselbrock, Myers & Penniman, 1979; Werner & Smith, 1977). Similarly, Weiss, Hechtman, Milroy and Perlman (1985) reported that 23% of the 63 hyperactive children they studied were diagnosed as having an antisocial personality disorder as adults. Thus, there is a considerable risk of false positives in identifying future drug abusers based on early behavior problems. Finally, it should be emphasized that these childhood antisocial behaviors appear most strongly related to serious behavior problems (including drug *abuse*) later in life. They are not strongly related to the occasional use of drugs or alcohol in late adolescence.

If the goal is to prevent serious maladaptive behavior associated with drug abuse in adolescence, then it may be desirable to focus prevention efforts on those youth who manifest behavior problems, including aggressive and other antisocial behaviors, during the elementary grades. On the other hand, if the goal is to prevent the occasional use of drugs, or to delay the age of initiation in the general population, such highly focused efforts may be inappropriate.

The finding that serious antisocial behavior in elementary school children predicts subsequent drug abuse hardly seems to trace the problem to its ultimate etiological roots. What are the origins of the antisocial behavior? Several possible sources appear to have been ruled out. Though ecological relationships may exist, socioeconomic status and ethnicity do not appear to be major sources of *severe* antisocial behavior (Kandel, 1978; Robins, 1978). The literature on the effects of race/ethnicity, SES, and family structure on substance use is generally unsupportive, contradictory, or inconclusive (Gersick et al., 1981; Penning & Barnes 1982; Loeber & Dishion, 1983; Kandel, 1982). Studies of alcoholism linking conduct disorders and hyperactivity with later alcoholism have suggested neuropsychological dysfunction as an underlying mechanism linking antisocial behavior and substance abuse (Grande et al., 1984). Gersick and associates (1981) suggest that the evidence supports a focus on social contexts and interpersonal transactions in understanding substance abuse.

There is disagreement as to the relative strength of the early childhood predictors discussed above. Loeber and Dishion (1983) assert that, on the whole, composite measures of family management techniques appear to be stronger early age predictors of subsequent delinquency, while Robins (1980) asserts that prior misconduct is a stronger predictor of antisocial behavior than family disorders. It should be noted, however, that Robins did not have access to independent prospective measures of families' functioning and management. Langner and associates (1983) argue that prior antisocial behavior is a better predictor of later *behavior*, but that family environment variables are better predictors of later adverse *outcomes* in school or with the police. These differences in emphasis across studies may reflect different measurement approaches. Alternately, it is possible that early behavior is a more proximate variable to later behavior which mediates between genetic predisposition, family characteristics and the later behavior. Regardless, it would appear that interventions seeking to prevent either substance abuse by adolescents or the early onset of substance use should focus on family alcohol and drug use, on family attitudes toward alcohol and other drug use, on family interaction/management factors as well as on child behavior during preadolescence.

SCHOOL FACTORS

The research on the relationship between school experiences in childhood and adolescent drug use has produced mixed results. Several researchers have attributed an independent effect to school failure as a predictor of drug abuse (Robins, 1980; Anhalt & Klein, 1976; R. Jessor, 1976; Brooks et al., 1977; Galli & Stone, 1975). Poor school performance is a common antecedent of initiation into drugs (R. Jessor & S. L. Jessor, 1977; Kandel et al., 1978; Johnston, 1973), and has been found to predict subsequent use and levels of use of illicit drugs (Smith & Fogg, 1978). Holmberg (1985) reported that truancy, placement in a special class, and early dropout from school were prognostic factors for drug abuse in a longitudinal study of 15-year-olds. Drug users and delinquents appear to perform more poorly in junior and senior high schools than do nonusers and nondelinquents (Kelly & Balch, 1971; Polk, Frease & Richmond, 1974; Frease, 1973; Senna, Rathas & Siegel, 1974; Simon, 1974; Anhalt & Klein, 1976; R. Jessor, 1976), although this relationship has not been found among college students (Miranne, 1979). Robins (1980) characterizes drug users as having average or better IQ's but being underachievers.

What is not clear from the existing research is when, developmentally, school achievement becomes salient as a possible predictor of drug use. While underachievement and school failure have been linked to adolescent substance use and delinquency, Fleming, Kellman and Brown (1982) found that children who scored high on first-grade readiness and IQ tests exhibited *earlier* and more frequent use of alcohol and marijuana. These students were more than twice as likely to become frequent users. Teacher-rated learning problems for first-grade students were not related to future substance use when shyness and aggressiveness were controlled. Aggressiveness in the Woodlawn sample of first graders was invariably accompanied by learning problems, but learning problems frequently occurred without aggressiveness and, alone, did not predict subsequent drug use (Kellam & Brown, 1982). Similarly, Spivack (1983), Spivack, Rapsher, Cohen and Gross (1978) determined that initial signs of academic achievement in the first grade were not predictive of subsequent conduct or delinquent disturbances. Other studies indicate that by the *end* of elementary school, low achievement, low vocabulary, and poor verbal reasoning are predictors of delinquency (Farrington, 1979; Rutter, Maughan, Mortimore & Ouston, 1979). Kandel (1982) suggests that low school performance does not itself lead to drug use, but that the factors leading to poor school performance are related to drug involvement. We have already noted that first-grade teacher ratings of antisocial behaviors are predictive of later drug abuse and delinquency. These findings suggest that social, not academic, adjustment is more important in the early elementary grades as a predictor of later drug abuse. Academic performance appears to emerge in importance as a predictor sometime later in elementary school. It is possible that early antisocial behavior in school predicts both academic underachievement in later grades and later drug abuse.

This suggestion is consistent with Spivack's (1983) results regarding the role of school failure in the prediction of delinquency. While academic readiness in first grade did not predict delinquency in Spivack's study, academic failure beginning in grade five did predict subsequent community delinquency among males. Spivack found that antisocial and maladaptive coping behaviors in earlier school grades contributed to academic failure in late elementary grades, which, in turn, contributed to subsequent misconduct and delinquency. Spivack (1983) concluded that academic failure in the late elementary grades exacerbates the effects of early antisocial behavior.

A second school factor related to drug use is a low degree of commitment to education. Students who are not committed to educational pursuits are more likely to engage in drug use and delinquent behavior (Hirshi, 1969; Elliott & Voss, 1974; Kim, 1979; Friedman, 1983; Galli & Stone, 1975; Robins, 1980; Brooks et al., 1977; Holmberg, 1985). The annual surveys of high school seniors by Johnston et al. (1985) show that the use of hallucinogens, cocaine, heroin, stimulants, sedatives, or nonmedically prescribed tranquilizers is significantly lower among students who expect to attend college than among those who do not plan to go on to college. Drug users are more likely to be absent from school, to cut classes, and to perform poorly than nonusers (Brooks et al., 1977; Kandel, 1982; Kim, 1979). Greater drug use has been demonstrated among dropouts (Annis & Watson, 1975). Factors such as how much students like school (Kelly & Balch, 1971), time spent on homework, and perception of the relevance of coursework also are related to levels of drug use (Friedman, 1983), confirming a negative relationship between commitment to education and drug use among junior and senior high school students.

PEER FACTORS

Association with drug using peers during adolescence is among the strongest predictors of adolescent drug use (Akers, 1977; Akers, Krohn, Lanza-Kaduce & Radosevich, 1979; Elliott et al., 1982; Hirschi, 1969; Jensen, 1972; Jessor et al., 1980; Kandel & Adler, 1982; O'Donnell & Clayton, 1979; Kandel, 1982; Catalano, 1982; Huba, Wingard & Bentler, 1979; Winfree, Theis, & Griffith, 1981; Meier & Johnson, 1977; Ginsberg & Greenley, 1978; Orcutt, 1978; Smart, Gray & Bennett, 1978; R. Jessor & S. L. Jessor, 1977; Goldstein, 1975; O'Donnell, Voss, Clayton & Room, 1976; Kaplan et al., 1982; Norem-Hebeinsen et al., 1984; Forster, 1984). Drug behavior and drug-related attitudes of peers are among the most potent predictors of drug involvement (Kandel, 1978). Peer influences are particularly important for initiation into the use of marijuana (Kandel et al., 1978). Perceived use of substances by others is also a strong predictor of use (R. Jessor & S. L. Jessor, 1978; Robins & Ratcliff, 1979; Kandel et al., 1978). It has been reported that frequent users of marijuana have a greater orientation toward friends than parents, and greater perceived support and models for use (R. Jessor & S. L. Jessor, 1978). Use of marijuana is strongly associated with use by closest friends and perceived support for use (Penning & Barnes, 1982). Social settings favorable to substance use reinforce and increase any predisposition to use (Kandel, 1978). Jessor et al. (1980) found that perceived environmental predictors (such as friends as models for use) accounted for twice the variance in drug use as compared to personality factors.

In their longitudinal study of the National Youth Panel, Elliott et al. (1982) found that social bonds to family and school influenced drug use indirectly through peer associations. Strong bonds to family and school decrease the likelihood of involvement with drug using and delinquent peers. They found only indirect effects of family and school bonding on drug use, and suggest that this reflects the time ordering of youths' experiences in the social contexts they encounter. The strength of bonding to family and school is determined before exposure to drug using peers in adolescence. However, the extent to which youths have become bonded to family and school is likely to be a factor in the selection of prosocial or drug using companions in early adolescence (Kandel et al., 1976, 1978; Elliott el al., 1982).

This suggestion raises an important question regarding the role of peers in the etiology of adolescent drug abuse which has not been adequately addressed in existing studies. At what point do peers become important in predicting adolescent substance use? Researchers have begun to study childhood peer associations longitudinally into adolescence (Coie & Dodge, 1983). Little research has focused, however, on preadolescent peer associations as possible predictors of subsequent drug initiation or abuse. There is little empirical data to assess the potential for peer focused interventions prior to the junior high school years, although the strength of the relationship between peer factors and adolescent drug use clearly supports the need for further research on the nature and etiology of peer influences prior to adolescence as these relate to drug initiation, use, and abuse.

Questions regarding the possible role of childhood peers in predicting adolescent drug use also relate to the issue of the outcome to be considered. Adolescent drug experimentation can be seen as a peer-supported phenomenon reflecting the increasing importance of peers during adolescence. On the othe hand, adolescent drug abuse appears to be embedded in a history of family conflict, school failure, and antisocial behavior. How childhood associations with antisocial peers or, conversely, childhood isolation, may be possible predictors of drug abuse is not clear. Further research is needed on the relationship between peer associations prior to adolescence and subsequent drug use and abuse.

ATTITUDES, BELIEFS, AND PERSONALITY TRAITS

Individual personality traits, attitudes, and beliefs are related to substance use. Generally, a constellation of attitudes and beliefs indicating a 'social bond' between the individual and conventional society has been shown to inhibit both delinquency and drug use (Hirschi, 1969; Hindelang, 1973). The elements of this affective bond which have been shown most consistently to be inversely related to drug use are: attachment to parents (Wohlford & Giammona, 1979; Chassin et al., 1981; Krohn et al., 1983; Adler & Lutecka, 1973; Wechsler & Thum, 1973; Shibuya, 1974; R. Jessor & S. L. Jessor, 1977; Kim, 1979); commitment to school and education (Krohn et al., 1983; Hirschi, 1969; Elliott & Voss, 1974; Kim, 1979; Friedman, 1983); regular involvement in church activities (Schlegel & Sanborn, 1979; Weschler & McFadden, 1979); and belief in the generalized expectations, norms and values of society (Hindelang, 1973; Akers et al., 1979; Krohn et al., 1983). Conversely, alienation from the dominant values of society (R. Jessor & S. L. Jessor, 1978; Smith & Fogg, 1978; Kandel et al., 1978; Kandel, 1982; Penning & Barnes, 1982) and low religiosity (Kandel, 1982: Jessor et al., 1980; Gersick et al., 1981; Robins, 1980) have been shown to be positively related to drug use.

Research also has shown a relationship between specific attitudes and beliefs regarding drugs and drug use initiation. Initiation into use of any substance is preceded by values favorable to its use (Kandel et al., 1978; Smith & Fogg, 1978; Krosnick & Judd, 1982).

A wide array of personality factors have been linked with early or frequent substance use. These include rebelliousness (Block, Keyes, & Block, 1984; Kandel, 1982; Bachman, Johnston & O'Malley, 1981; Goldstein & Sappington, 1977; Smith & Fogg, 1978; Green, 1979) and nonconformity to traditional values (Gorsuch & Butler, 1976; R. Jessor & S. L. Jessor, 1977). Similarly, high tolerance of deviance (Brooks et al., 1977; R. Jessor & S. L. Jessor, 1977), resistance to traditional authority (Goldstein & Sappington, 1977), a strong need for independence (R. Jessor, 1976; Segal, 1977); and normlessness (Paton & Kandel, 1978) have all been linked with substance use. All these qualities would appear to characterize youths who are not socially bonded to society.

Smith and Fogg (1978) reported that nonusers scored highest and early users lowest, on personal competence and social responsibility measures, such as obedience, diligence, and achievement orientation. The authors argue that personality characteristics discriminated between nonusers, early users, and later users of marijuana.

Contradictory findings or weak correlations have been found for self-esteem (Ferguson, Freedman & Ferguson, 1977; Ahlgren & Norem-Hebeisen, 1979; Paton & Kandel, 1978; R. Jessor & S. L. Jessor, 1978; Smith & Fogg, 1978; Kaplan, 1978) and locus of control (Brooks, Luckoff, & Whiteman, 1977; R. Jessor & S. L. Jessor, 1977). Wexler (1975) indicates that frequent users score lower on well-being, responsibility, socialization, self-control, tolerance, achievement, and intellectual efficacy.

There is evidence that a sensation seeking orientation may be a determinant of initiation and variety of drug use. Penning and Barnes (1982) suggest an association between marijuana use and alienation, lower motivation, and sensation seeking. Zuckerman's (1979) review concluded that heightened sensation seeking levels are characteristic of diverse drug using populations. Satinder and Black (1984) found that marijuana users scored higher than nonusers on a general sensation seeking scale and a subscale measuring need to disinhibit behavior in social situations, and suggested that sensation seeking may be a precursor to drug use. Spotts and Shoutz (1984) found measures of sensation seeking to be related to the number of drugs used by chronic drug users. The authors view their results as "consistent with the proposition that a need for stimulation or change underlies experimentation with a large number of substances" (p. 427). In a related finding, Ahmed et al. (1984) discovered that two measures of risk-taking, willingness to risk injury and willingness to risk illness, predicted expectations to use and actual use of alcohol and cigarettes. Willingness to risk illness was also associated with intentions to use and actual use of marijuana. Further research exploring the sensation seeking-drug use relationship in children is needed, since most research except the Ahmed et al. (1984) study has been conducted with young adults.

No evidence of psychopathology has been found for users as opposed to nonusers, except when users are very young (Anhalt & Klein, 1976). Gersick et al. (1981) suggest that the personality characteristics of those with an early onset of use may differ from those who initiate use later, since use becomes normative with increasing age. For example, Hesselbrock et al. (1985) found that attention deficit disorder, hyperactivity, and conduct disorders before age 12 predicted the onset of drinking. This once again emphasizes the importance of clarifying the outcome of concern. Generally, with the exception of rebelliousness, alienation, and sensation seeking, personality factors have been found to be less predictive of substance use than behavioral or interpersonal factors (Gersick et al., 1981; Kandel, 1978; Jessor et al., 1980; Long & Scherl, 1984).

EARLY INITIATION

Early onset of drug use predicts subsequent misuse of drugs. Rachal et al. (1982) report that "misusers" of alcohol appear to begin drinking at an earlier age than do "users." The earlier the onset of any drug use, the greater the involvement in other drug use (Kandel, 1982) and the greater the frequency of use (Fleming, Kellman & Brown, 1982). Further, earlier initiation into drug use increases the probability of extensive and persistent involvement in the use of more dangerous drugs (Kandel, 1982), and the probability of involvement in deviant activities such as crime and selling drugs (Brunswick & Boyle, 1979; Kleinman, 1978; O'Donnell & Clayton, 1979). In their analysis of the Epidemiological Catchment Area Study data, Robins and Przybeck (1985) found that the onset of drug use prior to the age of 15 was a consistent predictor of later drug abuse in the samples they studied. A later age of onset of drug use is usually associated with lesser drug involvement and a greater probability of discontinuation of use (Kandel et al., 1976).

THEORETICAL INTEGRATION
OF THE ETIOLOGICAL RESEARCH

To effectively use the etiological research on risk factors for adolescent substance use and abuse, existing knowledge should be integrated into a theory with explicit assumptions and hypotheses.

A number of theories have been advanced to explain adolescent substance use (Lettieri, Sayers & Pearson, 1980). Kandel's (1982) developmental perspective suggests three stages of drug involvement, with different antecedents and influences associated with each stage. The key factors associated with drug use are *parental influences, peer influences, beliefs and values,* and *involvement in certain activities.* Interaction between individual characteristics and the matrix of social influences is emphasized, with responses to social influences viewed as functions of personal characteristics and situational factors.

Robins (1980) proposes that drug misuse can be viewed as a manifestation of a deviance syndrome. Closely related is R. Jessor and S. L. Jessor's (1977) notion of problem-behavior proneness. The Jessors associate attributes within each of three systems (personality, perceived environment, and behavior systems) with the occurrence and levels of problem behavior. Similar antecedents foster a wide range of problem behaviors. According to their model, the greater the degree of problem-behavior proneness, the greater the likelihood of drug use.

Kaplan, Martin and Robbins (1982) regard deviant responses, including drug abuse, as motivated by the development of self-rejecting attitudes in the course of normative interactions. Deviant patterns are seen as alternatives to conventional means of achieving self-esteem and avoiding self-devaluing experiences. The adoption of particular deviant patterns is viewed as a function of the individual's history of experience, exposure, availability, and opportunity.

It appears reasonable from the evidence reviewed on childhood predictors of early initiation and abuse that adolescent drug abuse should be viewed from a developmental perspective. Early initiation as well as patterns of abuse can be considered results of experiences from birth through adolescence. Parental alcoholism, early antisocial behaviors, early experiences in the family, later experiences in school, and finally, interaction with peers all appear to be implicated in the etiology of drug use and abuse. From a developmental perspective, it can be argued that early experiences in the family are likely to influence social bonding to the family (Hirschi, 1969), social and self-control (Reckless, 1961), and subsequent experiences in school, as well as the likelihood that social bonds of attachment to school and commitment to education will develop (Bahr, 1979). Similarly experiences at school are likely to influence the extent to which a youth will develop social bonds of attachment and commitment to prosocial activities and prosocial others (Schafer & Polk, 1967; Hirschi, 1969). The social influence of peers clearly is salient during adolescence itself. If the process of developing a social bond to prosocial others and prosocial activities has been interrupted by uncaring or inconsistent parents, by poor school performance, or by inconsistent teachers, youths are more likely to be influenced by peers who are in the same situation and are also more likely to be influenced by such peers to engage in drug use (Elliott et al., 1982; Weis & Hawkins, 1981; Kaplan et al., 1982).

This developmental perspective has been integrated into a theory of antisocial behavior, the social development model (Hawkins & Weis, in press). The theory integrates social control theory (Nye, 1958; Reiss, 1951; Briar & Piliavin, 1965; Matza, 1964; Hirschi, 1969) and social learning theory (Bandura, 1973, 1977; Burgess & Akers, 1966; Akers, 1977; Akers et al., 1979; Krohn et al., 1981) and is similar in this regard to the work of others (Meade & Marsden, 1981; Braukman et al., 1980; Johnstone, 1981; Conger, 1976, 1980; Linden & Hackler, 1973; Johnson, 1979; Elliott et al., 1982). In contrast to other models, this social development model seeks explicitly to serve as a basis for prevention interventions. The theory describes stages of development and identifies intervention approaches which would appear appropriate at each stage. Propositions from control theory are used to identify elements in the etiology of drug use and delinquency as well as in the etiology of conforming behavior. Propositions from social learning theory are used to identify processes by which these patterns of behavior are extinguished or maintained.

In the theoretical synthesis of the social development model, a social bond to conventional society is viewed as necessary to prevent drug abuse (as opposed to experimentation). According to control theory, deviance is produced by a weak, broken, or absent bond to the conventional order. As operationalized by Hirschi (1969), the bond consists of attachment to conventional individuals, commitment to conventional lines of action, involvement in conventional activities, and belief in the legitimacy of the moral order. The stronger the components of the bond, the less likely it is that an individual will be free to engage in deviant behavior such as drug use. The studies reviewed earlier show that the elements of this social bond are negatively related to drug use.

The social developmental model extends control theory by suggesting that behavior patterns will be more or less deviant depending on the types of opportunities and social influences to which one is exposed, the skillfulness with which one performs in various activities and interactions, and the relative balance of rewards one receives from participation in these activities. The rewards one experiences for behavior directly affect the likelihood that one will continue that behavior (Bandura, 1973; 1977). These rewards are themselves a function of the opportunities available for participation in groups and activities as well as the skills an individual applies in his/her activities and interactions. Prosocial behavior is predicted when youngsters perform skillfully in conventional settings and skillfully avoid unconventional settings. We hypothesize that prevention interventions will be most successful in inhibiting early initiation and subsequent abuse of drugs and alcohol when they increase youths' opportunities for involvement in prosocial activities, youths' skills for participation in positive activities and social interactions, youths' skills to avoid participating in illicit interactions and activities, the skills of parents to effectively communicate with and set limits for their children, and parents' consistent support during their child's development.

Based on the etiological research reviewed earlier, the social development approach identifies three general contexts in which the formation of the social bond occurs (family, school, and peer group). When youths develop *opportunities* for involvement in the family, when they develop the requisite *social, cognitive, and behavior skills* to perform as expected in family interactions, and when they are *rewarded* consistently for adequate performance in the family, they will develop a bond of attachment, commitment and belief in the family. When parental family management practices are *inconsistent, punitive, or ineffective,* and when parents are inconsistent in their involvement and interactions with their children, favorable conditions are not likely to be present and a family bond is not likely to develop.

Bonding to school is conditioned by the extent to which social bonds to the family have developed by the time the child enters school as well as by the extent to which the child experiences opportunities for involvement, develops skills, and is rewarded for skillful performance at school. Thus both social and academic success at school appear to be prerequisites for bonding to school.

Similarly, social bonds to peers, whether prosocial or delinquent, will develop to the extent that youths have opportunities for involvement with those peers, the skills to perform as expected by those peers and the rewards that are forthcoming from interaction with those peers. We do not suggest that strong bonds of attachment to family and school will preclude the development of strong bonds of attachment to peers as long as the norms of family members, school personnel, and peers regarding appropriate behavior do not conflict. However, like Kandel et al. (1978) and Elliott et al. (1982), we suggest that the formation of strong bonds to family and school will decrease the likelihood that youths will develop early attachments to drug abusing peers in early adolescence, since we postulate that the behaviors rewarded in family and school and those likely to be rewarded by drug abusing youths are not compatible.

This theoretical synthesis would be incomplete if it ignored the fact that experimentation with tobacco, alcohol, and marijuana has become widespread among older adolescents. We have seen that drug experimentation is supported by attitudes and beliefs about the acceptability of alcohol and marijuana use under a variety of circumstances. Jalali and his colleagues (1981) note that many adolescents who use these gateway drugs are experimental or situational users influenced by their peers. It is apparent that adolescent peer influences can exert strong independent influences on use of the gateway drugs in spite of earlier family and school experiences related to social bonding (Elliott et al., 1982). In Hirschi's (1969) study of junior and senior high school students, even those with strong bonds to the social order were more likely to commit delinquent acts if they had delinquent friends. There appears to be an independent influence of peers of behavior during adolescence.

At this point, reconsideration of the original question regarding the behavior of concern is important. An hypothesis consistent with the etiological data is that experimentation with alcohol and drugs may be a form of adolescent individuation that is a separate phenomenon from drug abuse. Thus, relatively widespread experimentation among adolescents may be expected, within the existing broad cultural boundaries of the larger society (Baumrind, 1985). The social development perspective accounts for the occasional drug use typical of otherwise conventional high school students. These students have strong attachments to other conventional students. However, when drug use is statistically normative (in late adolescence), the risk of loss of affection or approval from these peers because of drug use is low. While parents may disapprove of drug using behavior, the peer group is the major mediator of rewards for high school aged youth. Occasional drug use appears as a likely outcome when low perceived risks or costs are coupled with the rewards for associating with drug using but otherwise conforming peers, with the perceived rewards of use, and with a lack of skills to resist peer pressure to use while still maintaining peer approval. While strong bonds to family and school may prevent experimentation in some youth, for others they may delay the age at which this experimentation takes place, thereby reducing the risk that the experimentation will escalate to drug abuse. Further, the bonds may themselves limit the use of drugs in amounts, frequencies or situations in which the social bond would be compromised by use. In other words, these bonds may inhibit the development of drug *abuse*. These speculations on the dynamics of social bonding and peer influence suggest that even socially bonded youths may come under some peer pressure to use drugs during adolescence. Thus, strategies that teach youngsters to deal successfully with these social pressures should prevent or delay initiation and reduce the likelihood that these youths will proceed beyond occasional use.

On the other hand, it is likely that youths who have not become socially bonded to family and school as a result of family conflict, school failure, and aggressive behaviors, will be easily influenced by drug prone peers and will find little reason to resist pressures to initiate drug use early in adolescence. Nor will these youths have much reason to resist using drugs more frequently when encouraged to do so by peers. These are the youths who will likely use drugs to cope with stress, loneliness, boredom, school failure or other personal or social problems. In this group, drug use itself is likely to compound previous personal and social problems with problems related to chemical dependency, legal difficulties, and drug-related deterioration in performance in school, work and family roles. Prevention interventions that focus on creating conditions for social bonding would appear beneficial in the case of these youths at highest risk of drug abuse. Enhancing opportunities, skills, and rewards for prosocial involvement should increase the likelihood that such youths become socially bonded to prosocial others and to prosocial lines of action. It is hypothesized that such social bonds should provide a stake in involvements which would reduce the likelihood of drug abuse.

As a foundation for prevention activities, the social developmental model implies that families, schools, and peer groups are appropriate objects for intervention, depending on the developmental stage of the child. Interventions that seek to increase the likelihood of social bonding to the family through alterations in the opportunity and reward structures available to children within families are appropriate from early childhood through early adolescence. Interventions that seek to increase the likelihood of social bonding to school through alterations in the opportunity and reward structures of classrooms and schools, and by directly impacting the development of both cognitive and interpersonal skills, are appropriate from the point of school entry. Interventions that seek to increase social bonding to prosocial peers by increasing opportunities and rewards for positive peer interaction and by insuring the development of interpersonal skills are appropriate when youths approach and enter adolescence. The promise of peer focused strategies delivered earlier in development is less clear.

This developmentally focused prevention model is consistent with the existing empirical evidence reviewed in this chapter regarding the etiology of adolescent drug use and abuse. Most alcohol and drug abuse prevention work has not been grounded in a clear and consistent theoretical base (Schaps et al., 1981). The social development model provides a framework for proposing and assessing interventions that seek to delay the onset of drug use, to prevent regular drug use, and to prevent drug abuse among adolescents.

REFERENCES

Adler, P. T., & Lutecka, L. (1973). Drug use among high school students: Patterns and correlates. *International Journal of the Addictions, 8,* 537–548.

Ahlgren, A., & Norem-Hebeisen, A. (1979). Self-esteem patterns distinctive of groups of drug abusing and other dysfunctional adolescents. *International Journal of the Addictions, 14*(6), 759–777.

Ahmed, S.W., Bush, P.J., Davidson, F.R., & Iannotti, R.J. (1984). *Predicting chilren's use and intentions to use abusable substances.* Paper presented at the Annual Meeting of the American Public Health Association, Anaheim, California.

Akers, R.L. (1977). *Deviant Behavior: A Social Learning Approach* (2nd ed.). Belmont: Wadsworth Press.

Akers, R.L., Krohn, M.D., Lanza-Kaduce, L. & Radosevich, M. (1979). Social learning and deviant behavior: A specific test of a general theory. *American Sociological Review, 44*(4), 636–655.

Alfaro, J. (1976). Report of the New York State Assembly Select Committee on Child Abuse. *Child Protection, 2*(1).

Alterman, A.I., & Tarter, R.E. (1983). The transmission of psychological vulnerability. Implications for alcoholism etiology. *The Journal of Nervous and Mental Disease, 3,* 147–154.

American Psychiatric Association (1980). *Diagnostic and statistical manual of mental disorders* (3rd ed.). Washington, D.C.

Anhalt, H., & Klein, M. (1976). Drug abuse in junior high school populations. *American Journal of Drug and Alcohol Abuse, 3,* 589–603.

Annis, H.M., & Watson, C. (1975). Drug use and school dropouts: A longitudinal study. *Canadian Journal of Counseling and Guidance,* (3/4), 155–162.

Bachman, J.G., Johnston, J.D., & O'Malley, P.M. (1981). *Monitoring the future. Questionnaire responses from the nation's high school seniors.* Ann Arbor: Survey Research Center.

Bahr, S.J. (1979). Family determinants and effects of deviance. In W.R. Burr, R. Hill, F.I. Nue, & I.L. Reiss (Eds.), *Contemporary theories about the family* (vol. 1). New York: The Free Press.

Bandura, A. (1973). *Aggression: A social learning analysis.* New York: Prentice Hall.

Bandura, A. (1977). Self-efficacy: Toward a unifying theory of behavioral change. *Psychological Review,* (84), 191–215.

Baumrind, D. (1985). *Familial antecedents of adolescent drug use: A developmental perspective.* (NIDA Research Monograph No. 56, U.S. Department of Health and Human Services Publication No. 1415). Washington, DC: U.S. Government Printing Office.

Baumrind, D. (1983, October). Why adolescents take chances—and why they don't. Paper presented at the National Institute for Child Health and Human Development, Bethesda, MD.

Bell, D.S., & Champion, R.A. (1979). Deviancy, delinquency and drug use. *British Journal of Psychiatry, 134,* 269–276.

Block, J., Keyes, S., & Block, J.H. (1984). *Childhood personality and environmental antecedents of drug use: A prospective longitudinal study.* Unpublished manuscript, University of California, Berkeley.

Bloom, M.D., & Greenwald, M.A. (1984). Alcohol and cigarette use among adolescents. *Journal of Drug Education, 14*(3), 195–205.

Blum, R.H., Henry, W.E., & Sanford, N. (Eds.) (1972). *The dream sellers.* San Francisco: Jossey-Bass.

Boham, M. (1978). Genetic aspects of alcoholism and criminality. *Archives of General Psychiatry, 35,* 269–276.

Braucht, G.N., Brakarsh, D., Follingstad, D., & Berry, K.L. (1973). Deviant drug use in adolescence: A review of psychosocial correlates. *Psychological Bulletin, 79*(2), 92–106.

Braukman, C.J., Kirigin, K.A., & Wolf, M.M. (1980). Group home treatment research: Social learning and social control perspectives. In T. Hirschi, & M. Gottfredson (Eds.), *Understanding crime.* Beverly Hills: Sage.

Briar, S., & Piliavin, I. (1965). Delinquency, situational inducements and commitment to conformity. *Social Problems, 13,* 25–45.

Brooks, L.S., Lunkoff, I.F., & Whiteman, M. (1977). Peer, family, and personality domains as related to adolescents' drug behavior. *Psychological Reports, 41,* 1095–1102.

Brooks, J.S., Lunkoff, I.F., & Whiteman, M. (1980). Initiation into adolescent marijuana use. *Journal of General Psychology, 137,* 133–142.

Brunswick, A.F., & Boyle, J.M. (1979). Patterns of drug involvement: Developmental and secular influences on age at initiation. *Youth and Society, 2,* 139–162.

Burgess, R.L., & Akers, R.L. (1966). A differential association-reinforcement theory of criminal behavior. *Social Problems, 4,* 128–147.

Bush, P.J. (1981). Children's perceptions of vulnerability and medicine use. Paper presented at the Annual Meeting of the American Public Health Association, Los Angeles, California.

Bush, P.J., & Davidson, F.R. (1982). Medicines and "drugs": What do children think? *Health Education Quarterly, 9,* 209–224.

Bush, P.J., & Iannotti, R.J. (1984). *The development of children's health orientations and behaviors: Lessons for substance use prevention.* Paper presented at the 1984 National Institute on Drug Abuse Review Meeting: Etiology of drug abuse: Implications for prevention. Rockville, Maryland.

Bush, P.J., Iannotti, R.J., & Davidson, F.R. (1983a). *A children's health behavior model and expectations to take medicines.* Unpublished manuscript, Georgetown University School of Medicine, Washington, D.C.

Bush, P.J., Iannotti, R.J., & Davidson, F.R. (1983b). Taking medicines: What children know and expect. Presented at the Annual Meeting Ambulatory Pediatrics Association, Washington, D.C.

Bushing, B.C., & Bromley, D.G. (1975). Sources of nonmedicinal drug use: A test of the drug-oriented society explanation. *Journal of Health and Social Behavior, 16,* 50–62.

Cadoret, R.J., Cain, C., & Grove, W.M. (1980). Development of alcoholism in adoptees raised apart from alcoholic biologic relatives. *Archives of General Psychiatry, 37,* 561–563.

Cadoret, R.J., & Gath, A. (1978). Inheritance of alcoholism in adoptees. *British Journal of Addiction, 132,* 252–258.

Cadoret, R., Troughton, E., & Widmer, R. (1984). Clinical differences between antisocial and primary alcoholics. *Comprehensive Psychiatry, 25,* 1–8.

Cannon, S.R. (1976). *Social functioning patterns in families of offspring receiving treatment for drug abuse.* Roslyn Heights: Libra.

Catalano, R.F. (1982). *Relative reward deprivation and delinquency causation.* Unpublished doctoral dissertation, University of Washington.

Chassin, L., Presson, C.C., Bensenberg, M., Corty, E., Olshavsky, R.W., & Sherman, S.J. (1981). Predicting adolescents' intentions to smoke cigarettes. *Journal of Health and Social Behavior, 22,* 445–455.

Clausen, J.A. (1978). Longitudinal studies of drug use in the high school: Substantive and theoretical issues. In D.B. Kandel (Ed.), *Longitudinal research on drug use: Empirical findings and methodological issues.* Washington, D.C.: Hemisphere-Wiley.

Coie, J.D., & Dodge, K.A. (1983). Continuities and changes in children's social status: A five-year longitudinal study. *Merrill-Palmer Quarterly, 29*(3), 261–282.

Conger, R.D. (1976). Social control and social learning models of delinquent behavior: A synthesis. *Criminology, 14,* 17–40, *15,* 117–126.

Conger, R.D. (1980). Juvenile delinquency: Behavior restraint or behavior facilitation? In T. Hirschi & M. Gottfredson (Eds.), *Understanding crime.* Beverly Hills: Sage Publications.

Cotton, N.S. (1979). The familial incidence of alcoholism. *Journal of Studies on Alcohol, 40*(1), 89–116.

Deykin, E.V. (1971). Life functioning in families of delinquent boys: An assessment model. *Social Services Review, 46*(1), 90–91.

Ellinwood, E.G., Smith, W.G., & Vaillant, G.E. (1966). Narcotic addiction in males and females: A comparison. *International Journal of Addictions, 1,* 33–45.

Elliott, D.S., & Voss, H.L. (1974). *Delinquency and dropout.* Lexington: Heath and Company.

Elliott, D.S., Huizinga, D., & Ageton, S.S. (1982). *Explaining delinquency and drug use* (Report No. 21). Boulder, CO: Behavioral Research Institute.

Farrington, D.P. (1978). The family background of aggressive youths. In L.A. Hensor, M. Berger, & D. Shaffer (Eds.), *Aggression and anti-social behavior in childhood and adolescence.* Oxford: Pergammon Press.

Farrington, D.P. (1979). Longitudinal research on crime and delinquency. In N. Morris, & M. Tonry (Eds.), *Crime and justice: An annual review of research* (vol. 1). Chicago: University of Chicago Press.

Farrington, D.P. (1982). *Stepping stones to adult criminal careers.* Paper presented at the Conference on the Development of Antisocial and Prosocial Behavior, Voss, Norway.

Ferguson, L., Freedman, M., & Ferguson, D. (1977). Developmental self-concept and (self-reported) drug use. *Psychological Reports, 41,* 531–541.

Fleming, J.P., Kellam, S.G., & Brown, C.H. (1982). Early predictors of age at first use of alcohol, marijuana and cigarettes. *Drug and Alcohol Dependence, 9,* 285–303.

Forster, B. (1984). Upper middle class adolescents drug use: Patterns and factors. *Advances in Alcohol and Substance Abuse, 4*(2), 27–36.

Frease, D.E. (1973). Schools and delinquency: Some intervening processes. *Pacific Sociological Review, 16,* 426–448.

Friedman, A.S. (1983). High school drug abuse clients. *Treatment research notes.* Rockville, MD: Division of Clinical Research, National Institute on Drug Abuse.

Galli, N., & Stone, D.B. (1975). Psychological status of student drug users. *Journal of Drug Education, 5*(4), 327–333.

Gantman, C.A. (1978). Family interaction patterns among families with normal, disturbed, and drug-abusing adolescents. *Journal of Youth and Adolescence, 7,* 429–440.

Garbarino, J. (1981). Child abuse and juvenile delinquency: The developmental impact of social isolation. In R. Hunner, & Y. Walker (Eds.), *Exploring the relationship between child abuse and delinquency.* Montclaire: Allanheld Publishers.

Gersick, K.E., Grady, K., Sexton, E., & Lyons, M. (1981). Personality and socio-demographic factors in adolescent drug use. In D.J. Lettieri, & J.P. Ludford

(Eds.), *Drug Abuse and the American Adolescent* (National Institute on Drug Abuse Research Monograph 38, DHEW Pub No. ADM 81-1166). Washington, DC: U.S. Government Printing Office.

Gersten, J.C., Langner, T.S., Eisenberg, J.S., Simcha-Fagan, D.J., & McCarth, E.D. (1976). Stability and change in types of behavioral disturbance of children and adolescents. *Journal of Abnormal Child Psychology, 4,* 111-127.

Ghodsian, M., Fogelman, K., Lambert, L., & Tibbenham, A. (1980). Changes in behavior ratings of a national sample of children. *British Journal of Social and Clinical Psychology. 19,* 247-256.

Ginsberg, I.J., & Greenley, J.R. (1978). Competing theories of marijuana use: A longitudinal study. *Journal of Health and Social Behavior, 19,* 22-34.

Glavin, J.P. (1972). Persistence of behavior disorders in children. *Exceptional Children, 38,* 367-376.

Glynn, T.J. (1984). Adolescent drug use and the family environment: A review. *Journal of Drug Issues, 4*(2), 271-295.

Goldstein, J.W. (1975). Assessing the interpersonal determinants of adolescent drug use. In D.J. Lettieri (Ed.), *Predicting adolescent drug abuse: A review of the issues, methods, and correlates.* Rockville, MD: National Institute on Drug Abuse.

Goldstein, J.W., & Sappington, J. (1977). Personality characteristics of students who become heavy drug users: An MM11 study of an avant-garde. *American Journal of Drug and Alcohol Abuse, 4,* 401-412.

Goodwin, D.W. (1971). Is alcoholism hereditary? *Archives of General Psychiatry, 25,* 545-549.

Goodwin, D.W. (1985). Alcoholism and genetics. *Archives of General Psychiatry. 42,* 171-174.

Goodwin, D.W., Schulsinger, F., & Hermansen, L. (1975). Alcoholism and the hyperactive child syndrome. *Journal of Nervous and Mental Disease, 160,* 349-353.

Goodwin, D.W., Schulsinger, F., Knop, J., Mednick, S., & Guze, S.B. (1977a). Alcoholism and depression in adopted-out daughters of alcoholics. *Archives of General Psychiatry, 34,* 751-755.

Goodwin, D.W., Schulsinger, F., Moller, N., Hermansen, L., Winokur, G., & Guze, S.B. (1974). Drinking problems in adopted and nonadopted sons of alcoholics. *Archives of General Psychiatry, 31,* 164-169.

Goodwin, D.W., Schulsinger, F., Moller, N., Mednick, S., & Guze, S. (1977b). Psychopathology in adopted and nonadopted daughters of aloholics. *Archives of General Psychiatry, 34,* 1005-1007.

Gorsuch, R.L., & Butler, M.C. (1976). Initial drug abuse: A review of predisposing social psychological factors. *Psychological Bulletin, 83,* 120-137.

Grande, T.P., Abraham, W.W., Schubert, D., Patterson, M.B., & Brocco, K. (1984). Association among alcoholism, drug abuse, and antisocial personality: A review of the literature. *Psychological Reports, 55,* 455-474.

Green, D.E. (1979). *Teenage smoking: Immediate and long-term patterns.* U.S. Department of Health, Education and Welfare. Washington, DC: U.S. Government Printing Office.

Gurling, H.M.D., Clifford, L.A., & Murray, R.M. (1981). Genetic contribution to alcohol dependence and its effects on brain function. In L. Gedder, P. Pirisi, & W.A. Nance (Eds.), *Twin research.* New York: Alan Liss.

Haskell, M.R., & Yablonsky, L. (1974). *Crime and delinquency* (2nd ed.). Chicago: Rand-McNally College Publishing Co.

Hawkins, J.D., & Weis, J.G. (in press). The social development model: An intergrated approach to delinquency prevention. *Journal of Primary Prevention.*

Hesselbrock, M.N., Hesselbrock, V.M., Babor, T.F., Stabenau, J.R., Meyer, R.E.,

& Weidenman, M. (1984). Antisocial behavior, psychopathology, and problem drinking in the natural history of alcoholism. In D.W. Goodwin, K.T. Van Dusen, & S.A. Mednice (Eds.), *Longitudinal research in alcoholism*. Boston: Nijhoff.

Hesselbrock, V.M., Hesselbrock, M.N., & Stabenau, J.R. (1985). Alcoholism in men patients subtyped by family history and antisocial personality. *Journal of Studies on Alcohol, 46*(1), 59–64.

Hesselbrock, V.M., Stabenau, J.R., & Hesselbrock, M.N. (1985). Minimal brain dysfunction and neuropsychological test performance in offspring of alcoholics. In M. Galanter (Ed.), *Recent developments in alcoholism*. New York: Plenum Press.

Hindelang, M. (1973). Causes of delinquency: A partial replication and extension. *Social Problems, 20*, 471–487.

Hindelang, M.J., & Weis, J.G. (1972). The bc-try cluster and factor analysis system: Personality and self-reported delinquency. *Criminology, 10*, 268–294.

Hirschi, T. (1969). *Causes of Delinquency*. Berkeley: University of California Press.

Holmberg, M.B. (1985). Longitudinal studies of drug abuse in a fifteen-year-old population. *Acta Psychiatrica Scandinavica, 71*, 207–210.

Hrubec, Z., & Omenn, G.S. (1981). Evidence of genetic predisposition to alcoholic cirrhosis and psychosis: Twin concordance for alcoholism and biological endpoints by zygosity among male veterans. *Alcoholism: Clinical and Experimental Research, 5*, 207–215.

Huba, G.J., Wingard, J.A., & Bentler, P.M. (1979). Beginning adolescent drug use and peer and adult interactions. *Journal of Consulting and Clinical Psychology, 47*, 265–276.

Jalali, B., Jalali, M., Crocetti, G., & Turner, F. (1981). Adolescent and drug use: Toward a more comprehensive approach. *American Journal of Orthopsychiatry, 51*(1), 120–129.

Janes, C.L., Hesselbrock, V.M., Myers, D.G., & Penniman, J.G. (1979). Problem boys in young adulthood: Teacher ratings and 12-year follow-up. *Journal of Youth and Adolescence, 8*, 453–472.

Jensen, G.F. (1972). Parents, peers, and delinquent action: A test of the differential association perspective. *American Journal of Sociology, 78*, 562–575.

Jessor, R. (1976). Predicting time of onset of marijuana use: A developmental study of high school youth. *Journal of Consulting and Clinical Psychology, 44*, 125–134.

Jessor, R., & Jessor, S.L. (1977). *Problem behavior and psychosocial development: A longitudinal study of youth*. New York: Academic Press.

Jessor, R., & Jessor, S.L. (1978). Theory testing in longitudinal research on marijuana use: In D. Kandel (Ed.), *Longitudinal Research on Drug Use*. Washington, D.C.: Hemisphere Publishing Corporation.

Jessor, R., Chase, J.A., & Donovan, J.E. (1980). Psychosocial correlates of marijuana use and problem drinking in a national sample of adolescents. *American Journal of Public Health, 70*, 604–613.

Johnson, R.E. (1979). *Juvenile delinquency and its origins: An integrated theoretical approach*. New York: Cambridge University Press.

Johnson, G.M., Schoutz, F.C., & Locke, T.P. (1984). Relationships between adolescent drug use and parental drug behaviors. *Adolescence, 19*(74), 295–299.

Johnston, L.D. (1973). *Drugs and American Youth*. Ann Arbor: Institute for Social Research.

Johnston, L.D., O'Malley, P.M., & Bachman, J.G. (1985). *Use of licit and illicit drugs by America's high school students, 1975–84*. Rockville: National Institute on Drug Abuse.

Johnston, L.D., O'Malley, P., & Evelard, L. (1978). Drugs and delinquency: A search for causal connections. In D.B. Kandel (Ed.). *Longitudinal research on drug use*. Washington, DC: Hemisphere Publishing Co.

Johnstone, J.W.C. (1981). The family and delinquency: A reappraisal. In A.C. Meade (Ed.), *Youth and society: Studies of adolescent deviance*. Chicago: Institute for Juvenile Research.

Kagan, J., & Moss, M.A. (1962). *Birth to maturity*. New York: Wiley.

Kaij, L. (1960). *Alcoholism in twins*. Stockholm: Almquist & Wiksell.

Kandel, D.B. (1978). Covergences in prospective longitudinal surveys of drug use in normal populations. In D. Kandel (Ed.), *Longitudinal research in drug use: Empirical findings and methodological issues*. Washington, DC: Hemisphere-John Witen.

Kandel, D.B. (1982). Drug use by youth: An overview. In D. Lettieri, & J.P. Ludford (Eds.), *Drug abuse and the American adolescent* (NIDA Research Monograph 38). Rockville, MD: National Institute on Drug Abuse.

Kandel, D.B. (1982). Epidemiological and psychosocial perspectives on adolescent drug use. *Journal of American Academic Clinical Psychiatry, 21*(4), 328–347.

Kandel, D.B., & Adler, D. (1982). Socialization into marijuana use among French adolescents: A cross-cultural comparison with the United States. *Journal of Health and Social Behavior, 23*, 295–302.

Kandel, D.B., Single, E., & Kessler, R. (1976). The epidemiology of drug use among New York State high school students: Distribution, trends, and change in rates of use. *American Journal of Public Health, 66*, 43–53.

Kandel, D.B., Kessler, R., & Margulies, R. (1978). Antecedents of adolescents initiation into stages of drug use: A developmental analysis. In D.B. Kandel (Ed.), *Longitudinal research in drug use: Empirical findings and methodological issues*. Washington, DC: Hemisphere-Wiley.

Kaplan, H.B. (1978). Social class, self-derogation theory of drug abuse. *Social Psychiatry, 13*, 19–28.

Kaplan, H.B., Martin, S.S., & Robbins, C. (1982). Applications of a general theory of deviant behavior: Self-derogation and adolescent drug use. *Journal of Health and Social Behavior, 23*(4), 274–294.

Kaufman, E., & Kaufman, P.N. (1979). *Family therapy of drug and alcohol abuse*. New York: Gardner Press.

Kellam, S.G., & Brown, H. (1982). *Social adaptational and psychological antecedents of adolescent psychopathology ten years later*. Baltimore: Johns Hopkins University.

Kelly, D.H., & Balch, R.W. (1971). Social origins and school failure: A re-examination of Cohen's theory of working-class delinquency. *Pacific Sociological Review, 14*, 413–430.

Kim, S. (1979). *An evaluation of ombudsman primary prevention program on student drug abuse*. Charlotte: Charlotte Drug Education Center, Inc.

Kleinman, P. (1978). Onset of addiction: A first attempt at prediction. *International Journal of Addictions, 13*, 1217–1235.

Knight, R., Sheposh, J., & Bryson, J. (1974). College student marijuana and alienation. *Journal of Health and Social Behavior, 15*, 28–35.

Krohn, M.S., Lanza-Radine, L., Radosevich, M., & Akers, R.L. (1981). *Cessation of alcohol and drug use among adolescents: A social learning model*. Paper presented at the Society of Social Problems Annual Meeting, New York.

Krohn, M.D., Massey, J.L., Laner, R.M., & Skinner, W.F. (1983). Social bonding theory and adolescent cigarette smoking: A longitudinal analysis. *Journal of Health and Social Behavior, 24*, 337–349.

Krosnick, J.A., & Judd, C.M. (1982). *Developmental Psychology, 18*, 359–68.

Langner, T.S., Gersten, J.D., Wills, T.A., & Simcha-Fagan, O. (1983). The relative roles of early environment and early behavior as predictors of later child behavior. In D.F. Richs, & B.S. Dohrenwend (Eds.), *Origins of psychopathology*. New York: Cambridge University Press.

Lawrence, T.S., & Vellerman, J.D. (1974). Correlates of student drug use in a suburban high school. *Psychiatry, 35,* 129–136.

Lerner, J.V., & Vicary, J.R. (1984). Difficult temperament and drug use: Analyses from the New York longitudinal study. *Journal of Drug Education, 14*(1), 1–8.

Lettieri, D.J., Sayers, M., & Pearson, H.W. (1980). *Theories on drug abuse: Selected contemporary perspectives* (Research Monograph No. 30). Rockville MD: National Institute on Drug Abuse.

Lewis, C.E., Clininger, C.R., & Pais, J. (1983). Alcoholism, antisocial personality, and drug use in a criminal population. *Alcohol and Alcoholism, 18,* 53–60.

Lewis, C.E., Rice, J., & Helzer, J.E. (1983). Diagnostic interactions: Alcoholism and antisocial personality. *Journal of Nervous and Mental Disease. 171,* 105–113.

Lewis, C.E., Robins, L., & Rice, J. (1985). Association of alcoholism with antisocial personality in urban men. *Journal of Nervous and Mental Disease, 173*(3), 166–174.

Linden, R., & Hackler, J.C. (1973). Affective ties and delinquency. *Pacific Sociological Review, 16*(1), 27–46.

Loeber, R. (1982). The stability of antisocial and delinquent child behavior: A review. *Child Development, 53,* 1431–1446.

Loeber, R., & Dishion, T. (1983). Early predictors of male delinquency: A review. *Psychological Bulletin, 93,* 68–99.

Loeber, R. (1985). Patterns of development of antisocial child behavior. *Annals of Child Development, 2,* 77–115.

Loeber, R.T., & Schmaling, K.B. (in press). The utility of differentiating between mixed and pure forms of antisocial child behavior. *Journal of Abnormal Child Psychology.*

Long, J., & Scherl, D.J. (1984). Developmental antecedents of compulsive drug use: A report on the literature. *Journal of Psychoactive Drugs, 16*(2), 169–182.

MacFarlane, J.W., Allen, L., & Honzik, M.V. (1962). *A developmental study of the behavior problems of normal children between 21 months and 14 years.* Berkeley: University of California Press.

Matza, D. (1964). *Delinquency and drift.* New York: Wiley and Sons, Inc.

McCord, J. (1981). Alcoholism and criminality. *Journal of Studies on Alcohol, 42,* 739–748.

McDermott, D. (1984). The relationship of parental drug use and parents' attitude concerning adolescent drug use to adolescent drug use. *Adolesence, 19*(73), 89–97.

McGee, R., Williams, S., & Silva, P. (1984). Behavioral and developmental characteristics of aggressive, hyperactive and aggressive-hyperactive boys. *Journal of the American Academy of Child Psychiatry, 23*(3), 270–279.

McGlothlin, W.H. (1975). Drug use and abuse. *Annual Review of Psychology, 26,* 45–64.

Meade, A.C., & Marsden, M.E. (1981). An integration of classic theories of delinquency. In A.C. Meade (Ed.), *Youth and society: Studies of adolescent deviance.* Chicago: Institute for Juvenile Research.

Mercer, G.W., Hundleby, J.D., & Carpenter, R.A. (1976). *Adolescent evaluations of the family as a unit and their relationships to the use of tobacco, alcohol and marijuana.* Paper presented at the 11th Annual Conference of the Canadian Foundation of Alcohol and Drug Dependencies, Toronto, Ontario.

Meier, R.F., & Johnson, W.T. (1977). Deterrence as social control: The legal and extra-legal production of conformity. *American Sociological Review, 42*(2), 292–304.

Miranne, A. (1979). Marijuana use and achievement orientation of college students. *Journal of Health and Social Behavior, 20,* 149–199.

Murray, R.M., & Stabenau, J.R. (1982). Genetic factors in alcoholism predisposition. *Encyclopedic handbook of alcoholism* (pp. 135–144). New York: Gardner Press.

Norem-Hebeisen, A., Johnson, D.W., Anderson, D., & Johnson, R. (1984). Predictors and concomitants of changes in drug use patterns among teenagers. *The Journal of Social Psychology, 124,* 43–50.

Nye, F.I. (1958). *Family relationships and delinquent behavior.* New York: Wiley and Sons.

Nylander, I. (1979). A 20-year perspective follow-up study of 2164 cases at the Child Guidance Clinics in Stockholm. *Acta Paediatricia Scandinavia, 276,* 8–45.

O'Donnell, J.A., & Clayton, R.R. (1979). Determinants of early marijuana use. In G.M. Beschner, & A.S. Friedman (Eds.), *Youth drug abuse: Problems, issues, and treatment.* Lexington: Lexington Books.

O'Donnell, J.A., Voss, H.L., Clayton, R.R., & Room R. (1976). *Young men and drugs: A nationwide survey.* NIDA Monograph 5. Washington, DC: U.S. Government Printing Office.

Orcutt, J. (1978). Normative definitions of intoxicated state: A test of several sociological theories. *Social Problems, 4,* 385–396.

Osborn, S.G., & West, D.J. (1979). Conviction records of fathers and sons compared. *British Journal of Criminology, 19,* 120–133.

Paton, S., & Kandel, D.B. (1978). Psychological factors and adolescent illicit drug use: Ethnicity and sex differences. *Adolescence, 13,* 187–200.

Paton, S., Kessler, R., & Kandel, D. (1977). Depressive mood and adolescent illicit drug use: A longitudinal analysis. *Journal of Genetic Psychology, 131,* 267–289.

Patterson, G.R. (1982). *A social learning approach, Vol. 3: Coercive family process.* Eugene: Castalia Publishing Co.

Penning, M., & Barnes, G.E. (1982). Adolescent marijuana use: A review. *International Journal of Addictions, 17,* 749–791.

Phouts, J.H., Schopler, J.H., & Henley, H.C., Jr. (1981). Deviant behavior of child victims and bystanders in violent families. In J. Hunner, & Y.E. Walker (Eds.), *Exploring the relationship between child abuse and delinquency.* Montclair: Allanheld, Osmun & Co.

Polk, K., Frease, D., & Richmond, F.L. (1974). Social class, school experience, and delinquency. *Criminology, 12,* 84–96.

Pollack, V.E., Volavks, J., Goodwin, D.W., Mednick, S.A., Gabrielli, W.F., & Knop, J. (1983). The EEG after alcohol in men at risk for alcoholism. *Archives of General Psychiatry, 40,* 857–861.

Rachel, J.V., Guess, L.L., Hubbard, R.L., Maisto, S.A., Cavanaugh, E.R., Waddell, R., & Benrud, C.H. (1980). *Adolescent drinking behavior, Vol. 1: The extent and nature of adolescent alcohol and drug use: The 1974 and 1978 national sample studies.* Research Triangle Park: Research Triangle Institute.

Rachel, J.V., Guess, L.L., Hubbard, R.L., Maisto, S.A., Cavanaugh, E.R., Waddell, R., & Benrud, C.H. (1982). Facts for planning No.4: Alcohol misuse by adolescents. *Alcohol Health and Research World,* pp. 61–68.

Reckless, W. (1961). *The crime problem.* New York: Appleton-Century-Crofts.

Reilly, D.M. (1979). Family factors in the etiology and treatment of youthful drug abuse. *Family Therapy, 11,* 149–171.

Reiss, A.J. (1951). Delinquency as the failure of personal and social controls. *American Sociological Review, 16,* 196–207.

Robins, L.N. (1966). *Deviant children grown up: A sociological and psychiatric study of sociopathic personality.* Baltimore: Williams and Wilkins.

Robins, L.N. (1978). Study childhood predictors of adult anti-social behavior: Replications from longitudinal studies. *Psychological Medicine, 8,* 611–622.

Robins, L.N. (1979). Longitudinal methods in the study of normal and pathological development. der Gegenwart vol. 1 Grundlagen und Methoden der Psychiatrie (2nd ed.). Heildeberg: Springer-Verlag, 627–684.

Robins, L.N. (1980). The natural history of drug abuse. In D.J. Lettieri, M. Sayers & H.W. Pearson (eds.), *Evaluation of treatment of drug abusers*, ACTA Psychiatra Scandinavia, *62* (Supple, 284).

Robins, L.N., & Przybeck, T.R. (1985). *Age of onset of drug use as a factor in drug use and other disorders* (NIDA Research Monograph No. 56, U.S. Department of Health and Human Services Publication No. 1415). Washington, DC: U.S. Government Printing Office, p. 178–193.

Robins, L.N., & Ratcliff, K.S. (1979). Risk factors in the continuation of childhood antisocial behavior into adulthood. *International Journal of Mental Health, 7*, 76–116.

Rutter, M., & Giller, H. (1983). *Juvenile delinquency: Trends and perspectives.* New York: Penguin Books.

Rutter, M., Maughan, B., Mortimore, P., & Ouston, J. (1979). *Fifteen Thousand Hours: Secondary schools and their effects on children.* Cambridge: Harvard University Press.

Rutter, M., Tizard, J., & Whitmore, K. (1970). *Education, Health and Behavior.* New York: Wiley.

Satinder, K.P., & Black, A. (1984). Cannabis use and sensation seeking orientation. *The Journal of Psychology, 16*, 101–105.

Schafer, W.E., & Polk, K. (1967). Delinquency and the schools. In President's Commission on Law Enforcement and Administration of Justice, Juvenile Delinquency and Youth Crime. Washington, DC: U.S. Government Printing Office.

Schaps, E., Moskowitz, J., Condon, J., & Malvin, J. (1981). *An evaluation of an innovative drug education program: First year results.* Napa: Pacific Institute for Research and Evaluation.

Schlegel, R., & Sanborn, M. (1979). Religious affiliation and adolescent drinking. *Journal of Studies on Alcohol, 40*, 693–703.

Schuckit, M. (1981). Twin studies on substance abuse: An overview. In L. Gedder, P. Pivisi, & W. Nance (Eds.), *Twin research*, New York: Alan Liss.

Schuckit, M.A. (1980). Biological markers: Metabolism and acute reactions to alcohol in sons of alcoholics. *Pharmacology, Biochemistry, and Behavior, 13*, 9–16.

Schuckit, M.A., Parker, D.C., & Rossman, L.R. (1983). Ethanol-related prolaction responses and risk for alcoholism. *Biological Psychiatry, 18*(10), 120–126.

Schuckit, M.A., & Rayes, V. (1979). Ethanol ingestion: Differences in acetaldhyde concentrations in relatives of alcoholics and controls. *Science, 203*, 54.

Sederstrom, J. (1978). *Family structure and juvenile delinquency.* Unpublished master's thesis, University of Washington, Department of Sociology.

Segal, B. (1977). Reasons for marijuana use and personality: A catrionical analysis. *Journal of Alcohol and Drug Education, 22*, 64–67.

Segal, B., Huba, G.J., & Singer, J.L. (1980). Reasons for drug and alcohol use by college students. *International Journal of Addictions, 15*(4), 489–498.

Segal, B., Singer, J.L., & Huba, G.J. (1979). *Drugs, daydreaming and personality: A study of college youths.* Hilldale: Lawrence Erlbaum Associates.

Senna, J., Rathus, S.A., & Siegel, L. (1974). Delinquent behavior and academic investment among suburban youth. *Adolescence, 9*, 481–494.

Shibuya, R.R. (1974). Categorizing drug users and nonusers in selected social and personality variables. *Journal of School Health, 44*, 442–444.

Shore, M.F. (1971). Psychological theories of the causes of antisocial behavior. *Crime and Delinquency, 17*(4), 456–468.

Simon, W. (1974). Psychological needs, academic achievement, and marijuana consumption. *Journal of Clinical Psychology, 30*, 496–498.

Smart, R.G., & Fejer, D. (1972). Drug use among adolescents and their parents: Using the generation gap in mood modification. *Journal of Abnormal Psychology, 70,* 153–166.

Smart, R.G., Gray, G., & Bennett, C. (1978). Predictors of drinking and signs of heavy drinking among high school students. *International Journal of Addictions, 13,* 1079–1094.

Smith, G.M., & Fogg, C.P. (1978). Psychological predictors of early use, late use and non-use of marijuana among teenage students. In D.B. Kandel (Ed.), *Longitudinal research on drug use: Empirical findings and methodological issues.* Washington, DC: Hemisphere-Wiley.

Spivack, G., Rapsher, L., Cohen, A., & Gross, R. (1979). *High risk early signs for delinquency and related behavioral difficulties: The first nine years of a longitudinal study.* National Institute for Juvenile Justice and Delinquency Prevention, Office of Juvenile Justice and Delinquency Prevention, Law Enforcement Assistance Administration, U.S. Department of Justice.

Spivack, G. (1983). *High risk early behaviors indicating vulnerability to delinquency in the community and school.* National Institute of Juvenile Justice and Delinquency Prevention, Office of Juvenile Justice and Delinquency Prevention, Law Enforcement Assistance Administration. Washington, DC: U.S. Government Printing Office.

Spotts, J.W., & Shoutz, F.C. (1984). Correlates of sensation seeking by heavy, chronic drug users. *Perceptional and Motor Skills, 58,* 427–435.

Stanton, M.D. (1979). The client as family member: Aspects of continuing treatment. In B.S. Brown, (Ed.), *Addicts and aftercare.* Beverly Hills: Sage Publications.

Stanton, M.D., & Todd, T.C. (1979). Structural family therapy with drug addicts. In E. Kaufman & P. Kaufman (Eds.), *Family therapy of drug and alcohol abuse.* New York: Gardner Press, Inc.

Stanton, M.D., Todd, T.C., & Associates (1982). *The family therapy of drug abuse and addiction.* New York: Guilford Press.

Steele, B. (1976). Violence in the family. In R. Helfer, & C.H. Kempe (Eds.), *Child abuse and neglect: The family and the community.* Cambridge: Ballinger.

Stern, S., Northman, J.E., & Van Slyck, M.R. (1984). Father absence and adolescent "problem behaviors": Alcohol comsumption, drug use and sexual activity. *Adolescence, 19*(74), 301–312.

Tec, N. (1974). Parent-child drug abuse: Generational continuity or adolescent deviancy. *Adolescence, 9*(35), 351–364.

Timberlake, E.M. (1981). Child abuse and externalized aggression: Preventing a delinquent lifestyle. In R.J. Hunner, & Y.E. Walker (Eds.), *Exploring the relationship between child abuse and delinquency.* Montclair: Allanheld, Osmun.

Wechsler, H., & McFadden, T. (1979). Patterns of alcohol consumption among the young: High school, college and general population studies. In H.J. Blane, & M.E. Chafez (Eds.), *Youth, alcohol and social policy.* New York: Plenum Press.

Wechsler, H., & Thum D. (1973). Teenage drinking, drug use, and social correlates. *Journal of Studies on Alcohol, 34,* 1220–1227.

Weis, J.G., & Hawkins, J.D. (1981). *Preventing delinquency: The social development approach.* National Institute for Juvenile Justice and Delinquency Prevention, Office of Juvenile Justice and Delinquency Prevention, Law Enforcement Assistance Administration, U.S. Department of Justice. Washington, D.C.: U.S. Government Printing Office.

Weis, J.G., Hall, J.B., Henney, J.S., Sederstrom, J., Worsley, K., & Zeiss, C. (1980). *Peer influence and delinquency: An evaluation of theory and practices, Part I and Part II.* National Institute for Juvenile Justice and Delinquency Prevention, Law Enforcement Assistance Administration, U.S. Department of Justice.

Weiss, G., Hechtman, L., Milroy, T., & Perlman, T. (1985). Psychiatric status of hyperactives as adults: A controlled prospective 15-year follow-up of 63 hyperactive children. *Journal of the American Academy of Child Psychiatry, 24*(2), 211–220.

Werner, E.E., & Smith, R.S. (1977). *Kauai's children comes of age.* Honolulu: University Press of Hawaii.

West, D.J., & Farrington, D.P. (1973). *Who becomes delinquent?* London: Heinemann.

Wexler, M. (1975). Personality characteristics of marijuana users and nonusers in a suburban high school. *Cornell Journal of Social Relations, 10*(2), 267–282.

Wilkinson, R. (1974). *The prevention of drinking problems: Alcohol control and cultural influences.* New York: Oxford University Press.

Winfree, L.T., Theis, H.E., & Griffith, C.T. (1981). Drug use in rural America: A cross-cultural examination of complementary social deviance theories. *Youth and Society, 12*(4), 465–489.

Wohlford, P., & Giammona, S.T. (1969). Personality and social variables related to the initiation of smoking cigarettes. *Journal of School Health, 39,* 544–552.

Ziegler-Driscoll, G. (1979). The similarities in families of drug dependents and alcoholics. In E. Kaufman, & P. Kaufman (Eds.), *Family therapy of drug and alcohol abuse.* New York: Gardner Press, Inc.

Zucker, R.A. (1979). Developmental aspects of drinking through the young adult years. In H.T. Blane, & M.E. Chafetz (Eds.), *Youth, Alcohol and Social Policy.* New York: Plenum Press.

Zuckerman, M. (1979). *Sensation seeking: Beyond the optimal level of arousal.* Hillsdale, NJ: Erlbaum.

Family Environmental and Genetic Influences on Children's Future Chemical Dependency

Karol L. Kumpfer, PhD
Joseph DeMarsh, PhD

ABSTRACT. This article reviews possible genetic and environmental factors which contribute to future chemical dependency in children of alcohol and drug abusing parents. Studies on genetic vulnerability and biological markers of alcoholism and drug abuse are reviewed. Recent studies by the authors on characteristics of families with chemically dependent parents and the affective, cognitive, and behavioral impacts on the children are discussed. The conclusion includes recommendations concerning the need for more family-focused prevention interventions for children of chemically dependent parents.

INTRODUCTION

Children of chemically dependent parents (COCDPs) are at very high risk for alcohol and drug abuse. Goodwin (1985) estimates that an adopted child of an alcoholic parent is four to five times more likely to become an alcoholic than other children. Children of chemically dependent parents are probably even more vulnerable to alcohol and drug abuse because of the added impact of living with a chemically dependent parent. COCDPs currently make up the majority of clients

Karol L. Kumpfer and Joseph DeMarsh are Research Associates, Social Research Institute, Graduate School of Social Work, University of Utah, Salt Lake City, UT 84112.

Preparation of this article was supported in part by National Institute on Drug Abuse grant DA02758-01/02 and DA03888-01 (Dr. Karol Kumpfer, Principal Investigator). The authors wish to acknowledge Bonnie Anderson, Simone Hennig and Jeffrey Bartlome for their assistance in the data collection and preparation of this article. Special thanks to Dr. Dean Hepworth for review and editing assistance.

49

in substance abuse treatment centers across the nation, and as such, they consume the majority of public and private funds for treatment. In fiscal year (FY) 1984, approximately 663 million dollars of federal, state, and local funds were spent on the treatment of children of chemically dependent persons, or approximately 65% of the total 1.02 billion dollars allocated for chemical dependency treatment nationally (Butynski, Record & Yates, 1985). By this estimate, in FY 84 as many as 650,000 of the admissions for alcohol treatment were likely children of alcoholics, and about 178,000 of the admissions for drug treatment were likely children of drug abusers.

PREVALENCE

Approximately one out of eight Americans alive today was raised by a parent or parents who were handicapped in their parental role because of chemical dependency or abuse. According to the Children of Alcoholics Foundation (1984), there are an estimated 28.6 million Americans alive today who had at least one alcoholic parent. About 6.6 million children under the age of 18 years currently live with an alcoholic parent. These figures were derived from the 1979 National Drinking Practices Survey by Clark and Midanik (1982), in which 15% of males and 6% of females reported problem drinking as calculated by scores on a loss of control scale and an alcohol dependency scale. These percentages are not necessarily equivalent to alcoholism, but they may underestimate the prevalence rates because they do not. include alcoholics in the military or in institutions or those who are homeless or refused to participate. Less is known about the numbers of children who have drug abusing parents or the number of Americans who were raised by drug abusing parents.

Relationship of Parents'
and Children's Chemical Dependency

Despite the fact that actual and perceived parental or significant adult drug use is consistently and positively correlated with adolescent drug use (Huba, Wingard & Bentler, 1980;

R. Jessor & S. L. Jessor, 1977; Kandel, Kessler & Margulies, 1978), relatively few studies have been conducted on the specific impacts of parents' chemical dependency on their children. In an exploratory correlational investigation, Huba et al. (1980) found a 53% bivariate correlation between adolescent drug use and adult use. Kandel and her associates (1978) found that 40% of the explained variance in initiation to use of illicit drugs other than marijuana was due to parental influence. Alcohol abuse by parents has also been shown to correlate with adolescent alcohol and drug abuse (Bushing & Bromley, 1975; Lawrence & Vellerman, 1974).

Most of these studies report correlations between parents' and children's alcohol and drug use rather than abuse patterns. Higher correlations may exist between chemically dependent parents and children, and even higher correlations may exist between chemically dependent mothers and children. In a study of several thousand Canadian families, Smart and Fejer (1972) found a high correlation between parents' and children's drug usage. If the mother was a regular user of prescription medications such as tranquilizers, her children were particularly vulnerable to a broad range of drugs (i.e., 71% of the children drank alcohol, 31% abused tranquilizers, 29% used marijuana, and 11% used heroin).

Involvement of Chemical Dependency in Other Social Problems

The social and economic costs of chemical dependency will equal about $850 per person in America in 1986. This is one hundred dollars more than the $754 per capita cost ($499 for alcohol abuse and $255 for drug abuse) in 1983 (Harwood, 1984). The total drain on our economy due to alcoholism and drug abuse is staggering and is estimated to be over 200 billion dollars in 1986 (Harwood, Napolitano, Kristiansen & Collins, 1984) because of accidents, crime, health care costs, fires, and lost productivity. The lifetime cost of a single drug abuser is estimated at 85 thousand dollars in lost productivity and direct economic burden on the welfare system. These costs do not include the intangible emotional suffering and negative impact on the health, welfare, and productivity of family and friends caused by substance abusers.

As discussed earlier, chemically dependent parents are more likely to have offspring who also abuse alcohol and drugs or manifest a broad range of social and mental health problems. Increased research is needed on the percentages of children of alcoholics and particularly drug abusers (since less empirical data exists for children of drug abusers) in social services programs. Preliminary clinical or research data suggest that children of chemically dependent persons are over-represented in the following special services: intensive care services for birth defects and fetal alcohol syndrome (Abel, 1981, 1982a, b); adolescent psychiatric inpatient programs (Kearney & Taylor, 1969); child psychiatric outpatient programs, (Nylander, 1960—Note: COAs were more emotionally disturbed, but used inpatient psychiatric services less often); hospital treatment for somatic complaints (Nylander, 1960); children's attention deficit disorder (ADD) or hyperactivity treatment programs, particularly those with aggressive conduct disorders (Morrison & Stewart, 1971; Cantwell, 1972, 1975); classes for the emotionally disturbed or handicapped children in the public schools (May, 1985, personal communication); teenage mother pregnancy programs (Kumpfer, Hopps, & Alister, in preparation); juvenile court case loads (MacKay, 1961, 1963); and child abuse counseling programs (Behling, 1979).

Clinicians have also reported high rates of parental chemical dependency in clients of adolescent and adult substance abuse treatment programs (Reese, 1985; Ziegler-Driscoll, 1977), but more data is needed. Additionally, clinicians have remarked on the number of perpetrators of incest who are chemically dependent on alcohol, but more research is needed to study this linkage. Child protective agency personnel also report that a large number of children in their case loads are children of alcoholics or drug abusers, but the nature and extent of the relationship is unclear because of difficulties in theoretical models, definition, methodology, and comparison groups (Liepman, 1980; Russell, Henderson & Blume, 1985).

Whether chemical dependency is a major etiological factor in these multiple problems associated with children of chemically dependent parents has been questioned, and further exploration with controlled studies is needed. As El-Guebaly and Offord (1977) have reported, the nature of the causal links is unclear. Possibly, these high correlations merely reflect a multiple problem family syndrome in which chemical dependency is but another symptom. Researchers have demonstrated, however, that many problem behaviors in chemically dependent persons disappear when the chemical dependency stops.

Cost-effective, family-based prevention interventions must be developed to prevent substance abuse. Because children of chemically dependent parents appear to be at substantially higher risk for substance abuse, this article will explore ways in which family heredity as well as the environment created by these parents may place their children at increased risk. This article will also focus on the characteristics of alcohol and drug-abusing families and their children. Finally, existing family-focused prevention programs for children and adult children of chemically dependent parents and implications for the most effective prevention strategies will be discussed.

IMPORTANCE OF FAMILIES
IN SUBSTANCE ABUSE ETIOLOGY

Recently, prevention research specialists have shown increasing interest in the family's contribution to chemical dependency in youth. There is expanding evidence that substance abuse is a multigenerational phenomenon with substantial familial (genetic and environmental) correlates (Goodwin, 1985). Coleman (1980) portrays the family as "heavily implicated in the initiation, maintenance, cessation and prevention of drug use" (Harbin & Mazier, 1975; Klagsbrun & Davis, 1977; Seldin, 1972; Stanton, 1979). Glynn (1981) argues that research has only begun to reflect the importance of the family's influence in drug abuse. In a review of the adolescent substance abuse correlates, Young and West (1985) conclude that the family has the greatest influence on substance use and abuse. Family influences were cited as correlated with alcohol abuse in 52% of the articles reviewed, 46% of the time in marijuana use, 80% of the time in illicit drug abuse, and in 59% of the studies in general substance abuse. Obviously, correlational studies do not prove cause and effect relationships; however, many family variables have strong, positive correlations with youthful substance abuse.

Prevention Based on Etiology

Who are the children most at risk for substance abuse? This question must be addressed in targeting local prevention efforts. Answers to the question may be different for alcohol, marijuana, other illigal drugs, and prescription drugs. Very little research has been done concerning children of drug abusers. More empirical data exist on children of alcoholics. Although genetic and biomedical studies are becoming increasingly sophisticated, El-Guebaly and Offord (1977) stated in their review of the literature, "the nature versus nurture controversy in the etiology of alcoholism remains unresolved. On the environmental side, it is not yet possible to know what kinds of stresses within the family heighten the risk for the development of alcoholism."

Need for Theoretical Foundations

Research on family influences on children's drug use has suffered from a lack of theoretical foundations underlying the studies. Prevention programs must be based on etiological information that specifies the likely causes and correlates of drug abuse. Because childhood prevention programs, lacking longitudinal findings, are rarely able to test ultimate outcomes, it is important to develop theoretical models against which to assess theory-predicted changes. Prevention program designers must be careful not to base intervention decisions on personal assumptions that certain family variables cause substance abuse or that substance-abusing families have certain deficits they can correct.

One striking example of prevention programming poorly grounded in etiological research involved the use by delinquency specialists in the 1970s of family communications training for prevention of delinquency. The results were disappointing. Based on his research, Parsons (1972), for example, observed that families of delinquents behaved as if they had already taken family communication courses (e.g., they didn't interrupt, and they took turns), whereas the communication patterns of normal families looked more dysfunctional (they talked over each other, and expressed more emotional affect). Designers of substance abuse prevention programs, therefore, must understand the real and essential differences between abusing and nonabusing families, and also which factors are most predictive of adolescent substance abuse. Intuition and educated guesses are undependable guides.

Methodological Problems of Prior Studies

Because of the dearth of cross-sectional and longitudinal studies of children of chemically dependent persons, additional research is needed to elucidate which risk factors contribute most to subsequent problems and how knowledge of those risk factors can be used to improve prevention programming. Prior research on children of chemically dependent persons has been flawed by an emphasis on clinical-intuitive data, lack of comparable control groups, unrepresentative client samples or experimental samples, nonstandardized data collection techniques or lack of triangulation of data sources (Olson, 1983), and foremost, lack of any theoretical foundation guiding the selection of dependent variables (Nardi, 1981). Given these constraints, this article will review the existing literature on children of chemically dependent parents, present new findings of a recent study by the authors, and make recommendations for prevention programs for children living with alcohol or drug abusers.

HEREDITY AND CHEMICAL DEPENDENCY

In this section, the authors will first review research on the genetic transmission of alcohol and recently discovered biological markers, which may be risk factors for chemical dependency. Next, the same topics will be discussed for drug dependency. This section concludes with an analysis of the interactions between environmental and hereditary risk factors.

Alcoholism—Genetic Transmission

Since biblical time, people have believed that, "The sins of the fathers are visited upon the children," and, as concluded by Plutchard, the early Greek philosopher, "Drunkards beget drunkards." For many centuries people have believed that alcoholism runs in families and is inherited in a Lamarckian manner (i.e., if the mother studied art, the children might inherit artistic talents; if the father drank, the children might be drunkards).

Most alcoholics seen clinically do indeed have alcoholic relatives. Reviews of the literature (Cotton, 1979; Goodwin, 1971) reveal that the rates of alcoholism are substantially higher in relatives of alcoholics than in relatives of nonalcoholics, even when the nonalcoholics are psychiatric patients. Approximately 50% to 75% of all clients at alcoholism treatment centers report at least one relative in the preceding two generations who had "problems with alcohol" (Cotton, 1979; Templer, Russ & Ayers, 1974). Alcoholism treatment clients who began drinking heavily as teenagers have the highest incidence of alcoholism in near relatives. In addition, women and Indian alcoholic clients report the highest incidences of alcoholic relatives (Lisansky, 1957; Rathod & Thompson, 1971; Reese, 1985; Hoffman & Noem, 1975).

The actual risk factor for offspring of alcoholic parents is unknown because of the lack of empirical longitudinal studies of children of alcoholics. Also, alcoholics from treatment populations are likely different from alcoholics in the general population.

Adoption Studies

A number of researchers in this field are convinced that alcoholism is genetically influenced (see Goodwin, 1985, for a recent review of the literature). This conclusion is drawn from studies that demonstrate concordance rates of about 60% for alcoholism in one-egg (monozygotic) twins, but less than 30% for same-sex dizygotic or fraternal twins (Kaij, 1960). The nature/nurture contribution of parents to offspring's alcoholism is difficult to assess. The clearest way to investigate the contribution of heredity vs. family environment is through the use of adoption studies. Studies in Sweden, Denmark and the United States show a twofold to ninefold increased risk for alcoholism in adopted children of alcoholics. The type of alcoholism inherited (severe, early onset, familial alcoholism or milder, late onset, familial alcoholism) and sex of youth and alcoholic parent appear to influence the magnitude of this risk factor, which suggests sex-linked, genetic transmission.

Sex Differences in Heritability

Young males or sons of alcoholics are always at greater risk than young women or daughters of alcoholics. According to the 1979 U. S. National Drinking Practices Survey (Clark & Midanik, 1982), the estimates of problem drinking as reported in a probability sample of U. S. adults (18 years and over) is considerably higher for men than for women (15% vs. 6%). In a large Swedish study of adopted sons and daughters of alcoholics and nonalcoholics (Bohman, Sigvardsson & Cloninger, 1981), only 2.8% of the adopted daughters of nonalcoholic parents became alcoholics, whereas 9.8% of the adopted daughters of alcoholic parents became alcoholics. If the mother was alcoholic, the risk factor increased to 10.3%. Sons of alcoholic mothers had a higher likelihood of becoming alcoholic than sons of alcoholic fathers (28% compared to 23%), which is twice the 14.7% risk factor observed for adopted sons with no biological parent who is alcoholic. In general, it is interesting to note that alcoholic mothers had more alcoholic sons (28% vs. 23%) and daughters (10% vs. 4%) than alcoholic fathers. Women alcoholics may have more biological markers for alcoholism than male alcoholics, because of the increased societal and biological protective factors that prevent women from abusing alcohol. These biological markers, if inherited, could increase the offspring's risk of alcoholism.

Early or Late Onset Familial Alcoholism Differences

Major correlates that distinguish the two major types of familial alcoholism are age of onset, association with criminality, and severity of alcoholism. Early onset familial alcoholism is often more severe and considered highly heritable. Adopted sons of biological fathers characterized by adolescent onset of alcohol abuse, extensive treatment, and serious criminality are at nine times the risk of alcohol abuse (Bohman et al., 1981; Cloninger, Bohman & Sigvardsson, 1981). The primary risk factors for alcoholism appear to be the number or percentage of alcoholic relatives a person has, and whether they are from Northern European ancestry (Vaillant & Milofsky, 1982). Because these genetic factors are nonresponsive to prevention, it is important to analyze psychosocial correlates that could be modified or prevented within the family context.

Increasing evidence suggests that living with alcoholics or in a pro-alcohol environment can increase a child's likelihood of becoming an alcoholic (Cadoret, O'Gorman, Throughton & Heywood, 1985). Unfortunately, extant studies have not involved sufficient numbers of children born to biological alcoholic parents and subsequently adopted by alcoholic parents to estimate this familial environment risk factor.

According to Cloninger et al. (1981), children without biological alcoholic parents raised in alcoholic adoptive families manifest no increase in likelihood of alcohol abuse; in fact, nonsignificant reduction in alcohol abuse occurs among adopted sons reared by alcoholic parents (13%) versus nonalcoholic parents (18%). A child with an inherited predisposition towards alcoholism, however, may be more vulnerable. The alcoholic family environment may interact with the genetic predisposition to magnify the likelihood of alcoholism. A susceptible child who grows up with an alcoholic parent could have a risk factor as high as nine or tenfold for early onset alcoholism.

Biological Indicators

What is inherited that increases alcohol transmission? Biomedical research in this area is still in its infancy, and the few existing studies need additional replication; but once the neuropsychological and physiological precursors of alcoholism are understood, children of alcoholics could be educated in prevention programs about these biological signs of risk, and risk assessments could be developed. Preliminary prospective studies on biological markers have been conducted primarily on sons of alcoholics and nonalcoholics, and suggest some possible biological differences, including:

a. Higher level of blood acetaldehyde, but decreased subjective feelings of intoxication (similar to an innate tolerance) at equivalent blood alcohol levels (Schuckit & Rayses, 1979; Schuckit, 1980a);

b. decreased impairment on psychomotor tests, including studies that measured reaction time to the same amount of alcohol (Alpert & Schuckit, unpublished data);

c. increased relaxation or decreased resting skeletal muscle tension as measured by electromyogram (EMG) scores in response to ethanol (Schuckit, & Bernstein, 1981);

d. decreased plasma and cerebrospinal dopamine betahydroxylase (DBH) (Schuckit, 1983);

e. increased high frequency brain waves measured by electroencephalogram (EEG) activity and an increased slow alpha response to alcohol (Vogel, Schalt, Kruger, Propping & Lehnert, 1979; Propping, Kreuger & Janah, 1980; Propping, Kruger & Mark, 1981; Pollock et al., 1983);

f. reduced P3 amplitude of visual evoked potentials in sons of alcoholic fathers (Bloom, Neville, Woods, Schuckit & Bloom, 1982), and sons (ages 6 to 13 years) who have never been exposed to alcohol in utero or postnatally and without alcohol administration (Begleiter, Porjesa, Binari & Kissin, 1984);

g. decreased memory associated with decreased P3 event-related potentials (ERP) and decreased capacity to assess significance and sufficient encoding (Hegedus, Alterman & Tarter, in press);

h. decreased sleep time (Schuckit & Bernstein, 1981);

i. decreased ability to shift cognitive set on the Minnesota Card Sort Test (Goodwin, personal communication); and

j. decreased platelet monoamine oxidase (MAO) activity (related to increased bipolar affective disorder) in alcoholic clients and their first-degree relatives (Alexopoulos, Lieberman & Frances, 1983).

Interaction of Biological Markers With Vulnerability to Alcoholism

Individual differences in level of intoxication to equal amounts of alcohol might be explained by some biological difference, such as children of alcoholics absorbing less alcohol in their brain cells. Taraschi and Rubin (1985) recently found in rat studies that the increased tolerance effects of the alcoholic may be due to a decreasing solubility of cell membranes to alcohol. A cross tolerance to sedatives, tranquilizers and general anesthetics was also noted in chronically alcoholic rats.

Alcohol also appears to increase serotonin, but subsequently to reduce it to subnormal levels in withdrawal (Kent, Campbell & Goodwin, in press); hence, it is possible that children of alcoholics may be deficient in serotonin or have an exaggerated increase in serotonin to alcohol. Goodwin (1985) suggests that this might explain the "addictive cycle" in which a person initially drinks to feel good and then later drinks to stop feeling bad. Research is continuing on the possible role of endogenous opioids, tetrahydroisoquinole (THQs), and other morphinelike compounds (salsolinol and salsoline) which have been found in greater quantities after alcohol ingestion in the spinal fluid of alcoholics (Borg, Kvande, Magnusson & Sjoquist, 1980).

Others (Harada, Agarwal, Goedde, Tagaki & Ishikawa, 1982) suggest that inherited vulnerability to alcohol is caused more by a lack of inheritance of physiological protective factors which make ingestion of alcohol unpleasant (i.e., the "oriental flush" reaction—flushing of skin, elevated heart rate, dizziness, headache, dysphoria) related to an allergic histamine reaction caused by increased blood acetaldehyde from absence of one ALDH isoenzyme. This allergic reaction may make alcohol unpleasant and decrease alcohol risk. Women's reduced abuse of alcohol may be partially caused by an increased flush response in women, though this hypothesis remains to be verified (Goodwin, 1985, personal communication).

Drug Abuse—Genetic Transmission

Considerably fewer studies focusing on genetic precursors for drug abuse have been conducted. Schuckit's (1980b) review of this literature includes no well-controlled adoption or twin studies such as are available for alcoholism. The few family studies available show a high correlation between parent's and offspring's use of drugs (Tennant, 1976; Smart &

Fejer, 1972; Annis, 1974). Whether alcoholism and drug abuse are part of the same inherited predisposition or have overlapping distributions is unknown. A few studies have tentatively linked alcohol and drug abuse in the same families (Tennant, 1976), but unfortunately these studies almost never control for related diagnoses such as antisocial personality (Schuckit, 1973). Hence, Schuckit (1980b) concludes that "there are not sufficient data to indicate that the same constellation of genetic and/or biological factors underlie the abuse of alcohol and other substances" (p. 299). With increasing polydrug use, it is becoming more difficult to differentiate individuals or families that are alcohol or drug abusers.

Antisocial Personality and Chemical Dependency

Some psychiatric research suggests that both alcoholism and drug abuse (mostly in men), antisocial personality, and Briquet's Syndrome (mostly in women) all run in the same families and are part of the St. Louisian Triad (Goodwin & Guze, 1979). These psychiatric syndromes may be somehow genetically linked through polygenetic transmission with each receiving a different mix of genetic markers or biological precursors as mentioned for alcoholism. It is also possible that drug abuse is more connected to genetic factors predictive of antisocial behavior than is alcoholism. In a recent study of alcoholism and antisocial personality, Cadoret and his associates (1985) conclude that there may be specificity of inheritance for antisocial and alcoholic conditions. Using adoption records in Des Moines, Iowa, these researchers found that having antisocial parents did not increase alcohol abuse in offspring, nor was there an increase in antisocial personality in adoptees with biological relatives with problem drinking.

Conversely, as discussed in the Hawkins' article on etiology of chemical dependency (in this issue), there appears to be a strong correlation between antisocial behavior and adolescent drug abuse, particularly *early antisocial behavior* (Robins, 1978; Johnston, O'Malley & Evelard, 1978; Kandel et al., 1978; Wechsler & Thum, 1973). In fact, the Jessors have theorized that drug use can be explained by a deviance syndrome or proneness to problem behaviors (R. Jessor & S. L. Jessor, 1977, 1978). Longitudinal studies have found that antisocial behaviors generally precede drug use (Elliott, Huizinga & Ageton, 1982; Johnston et al., 1978). Studies in the area of delinquency (Spivak, 1983) also demonstrate that such antisocial behavior may be detected as early as entry into kindergarten (which is useful for early childhood prevention programs). Earlier detection in preschool years is somewhat hampered by problem behaviors that are normal for this stage of development, such as temper tantrums and self-centered behavior (Rutter & Giller, 1983; Loeber, 1985). One study (Kellam & Brown, 1982) has found a significant positive correlation between aggressiveness and shyness in black first-grade students and frequency of substance abuse in the tenth grade. According to Hawkins et al. (1985), although "serious conduct disorders in childhood appear to be virtually a prerequisite for serious antisocial personality problems including drug abuse in later life, less than half those with serious behavior problems in childhood will manifest these problems later" (Robins, 1978, p. 80). According to this information, interventions aimed at prevention of drug abuse should consider targeting children in the elementary school grades who have both severe conduct disorders and drug-abusing parents, since at least one-half of these children are likely to become drug abusers.

Drug Abuse Biological Markers

Less research has been conducted on biomedical correlates of offspring of drug abusers than of offspring of alcoholics. Increased sensitivity to physical and psychological pain and certain medical syndromes (yet to be identified) could predispose some families to use drugs. Decreases in brain serotonin (5-HT) result in an increased sensitivity to pain (Harvey & Yunger, 1973). Clinicians working with heroin clients report a hypersensitivity to pain in these clients (Brown & Millard, 1985, personal communication), though this could be due to decreased endogenous peptide-production from prolonged heroin use. In her CNS reactance theory, Petrie (1978), proposes that people intolerant to pain are "CNS augmenters," while those tolerant to pain are "CNS reducers." She found that augmenters had a larger decrease in pain sensitivity associated with alcohol, aspirin and chlorpromazine (Petrie, 1978).

Buchsbaum (1978) linked CNS augmentation to substance abuse in studies of sensory-evoked potentials. Recent studies (Hennecke, 1984) with 10- to 12-year-old children of alcoholic fathers find that more of these children are CNS augmenters. Youth who enjoy stimulant drugs such as cocaine, amphetamines, nicotine, and caffeine may be CNS reducers.

The research needed to discover biomedical risk factors for drug abuse is likely to be more complex than for alcoholism because of the many different drugs involved. In a number of countries, however, biomedical precursors or correlates of familial drug abuse are currently attracting more attention.

Genetic vs Environmental Transmission of Familial Chemical Dependency

A Theoretical Model of Substance Abuse

Multigenerational substance abuse is likely caused by a large number of environmental and genetic factors. The authors in their attempt to organize all of the known correlates of substance abuse developed the vast array of multiple determinants shown in Figure 1. Using the Public Health Services Host/Agent/Environment model adopted by the Alcohol, Drug Abuse and Mental Health Administration as the official prevention model, Kumpfer and DeMarsh (1984) organized these multiple correlates into a three by four matrix of variables. They theorized that the four primary influences on substance abuse are the child, the family, friends/peers, and the community. Similar to the Jessors' (1980) notion of proximal and distal influences, the child's temperament and character has the most influence, the family second, peers and friends third, and the community the least. In addition, substance abuse correlates are organized into three categories of those related to cognitive factors (values and attitudes), environmental factors (stressors), and behavioral factors (skills). Use of this model makes clearer the multitude of potential risk factors for substance abuse, and helps the reader understand that: (a) prevention interventions must be powerful and pervasive to be effective, and (b) interventions influencing the child's family are likely to be the most effective in preventing substance abuse.

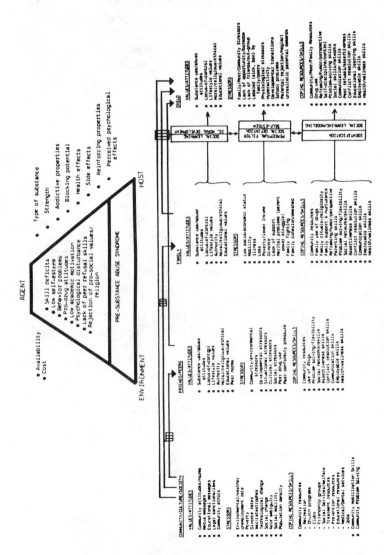

Figure 1. VASC theory of drug abuse.

64

Environmental Influences in Adoption Studies

The prior mentioned studies of the heritability of substance abuse do not rule out the possibility that almost all of the variance in transmission of substance abuse may be caused by the family environment. Adoption studies do not uniformly exclude mothers who were using alcohol, tobacco or other drugs during pregnancy which could effect the fetus. Offspring of mothers who drink during pregnancy and breast feeding have a heavy in utero and infancy exposure to the toxic effects of alcohol. They may manifest fetal alcohol syndrome (FAS) including physical anomalies, hyperactivity, attention deficit disorders, mental retardation, learning disability, and EEG abnormalities (Abel, 1981, 1982a, b) which could increase their risk of alcoholism. Additionally, adopted infants in the adoption studies spent most of their first year with the alcoholic parents. In the Swedish adoption studies (Bohman et al., 1981; Cloninger et al., 1981), the mean age of placement was eight months of age and those adoptees (239) "who stayed with their biological mothers beyond age 6 months had 1.5 times greater risk for later alcohol abuse than others (23% vs 16%, $p < .001$)."

Infant Attachment and Chemical Dependency

If alcoholic mothers are not nurturant and do not involve the child in bonding experiences (i.e., touching, holding, talking to, carrying, responding to needs), the children may experience somatosensory, effectional deprivation, which has been correlated with increased drinking and physical violence in primitive cultures (Barry, 1976; Prescott, 1980). According to Prescott (1980), children denied affectional bonds because of social isolation compensate to reduce tension, discomfort and "anomie" through thrill-seeking behaviors such as alcohol and drug abuse and physical violence (towards others and oneself). High sensation seeking found in Type T, thrill-seeking individuals (and stimulus augmenters) is considered an important precursor of drug abuse (Zuckerman, Murtaugh & Siegel, 1970, 1974). The importance of early infancy maternal bonding in the development of self-regulatory mechanisms are also discussed by Greenspan (1985), Ainsworth (1972) and Bowlby (1969).

Even in the alcohol adoption studies, genetics actually account for a relatively small part of the total variance. Prospective alcohol studies like those of Vaillant and Milofsky (1982) found that familial factors accounted for the majority of the total variance in the development of alcoholism, but still this was only 15%. Genetic factors like number of alcoholic relatives and ethnicity accounted for about one-half of the family variance, or 8%, and a range of psychosocial family environmental variables accounted for the other 7%. The authors contend that parental and familial factors are both strong genetic and environmental precursors of substance abuse because of the intensive and lengthy influence which parents have in shaping the child's environment and personality. Hence, prevention interventions aimed at motivating parents to improve the child's environment can be very powerful.

FAMILY ENVIRONMENT AND CHEMICAL DEPENDENCY

What factors in the environment of the child of a chemically dependent parent could enhance the transmission of substance abuse? Do children of drug abusers have characteristic differences from children of nondrug-abusing parents and do these differences show up in childhood so they can be addressed early in prevention programs? Because of the paucity of longitudinal family studies, prevention specialists and researchers can only speculate.

Most studies of familial factors affecting adolescent drug abuse define their study sample as drug-abusing youth and their families, rather than selecting the population on the basis of drug-abusing parents. Studies of families of youthful abusers report an abundance of disturbed and emotionally dislocated families (Rosenberg, 1969), inappropriate or dysfunctional interaction patterns (Blum & Associates, 1972; Braucht et al., 1973) and an increased incidence of other deviant behaviors by chidren (Adams et al., 1983). The interested reader is referred to review articles by Harbin and Maziar (1975), Hawkins et al. (1985), Klagsbrun and Davis (1977), Seldin (1972), and Stanton (1979) for more thorough discussions.

The few empirical studies that have focused upon the char-

acteristics of substance-abusing parents and unique characteristics of their children will be summarized briefly, and the
results will be organized later into domains of influence: environmental, affective, cognitive and behavioral.

Major Studies Reviewed

The Booz-Allen and Hamilton Study (1974)

Under contract with the National Institute on Alcohol
Abuse and Alcoholism (NIAAA), this study included 50
young adult "children" of alcoholics. The sample was composed primarily of white, highly educated, volunteers from
Northern European ancestry. Participants were interviewed
concerning a number of characteristics of their families. The
researchers discovered a high degree of emotional neglect of
children in families where one or both parents are alcoholic.

The Sowder and Burt Study (1978)

One large national epidemiological study of primarily black
heroin abusers and their children (Sowder & Burt, 1978a, b)
funded by the National Institute on Drug Abuse (NIDA) was
conducted in five sites in the USA in 1977. Comparing her-
oin-abusing parents and their children (ages 3 to 18 years) to
nondrug-abusing, multiple problem families in the same
neighborhoods, they documented negative effects of parental
neglect and conflict on the children. This study concluded
these children (particularly the youngest children) are at
greater risk for a number of academic, behavioral, and social
problems, as well as drug abuse.

The Kumpfer and DeMarsh Study (1985)

Recently, the authors (Kumpfer & DeMarsh, in press)
completed preliminary analyses of the pretests of a sample of
60 drug-dependent parents and their children who participated in a family-based prevention program compared to
those of 60 control families randomly selected from a strati-
fied cluster sample in one urban county in Utah. The survey
methodology involved an extensive self-administered test bat-

tery including the following tests: Moos (1974) Family Environment Scale, FACES-II (Olson, Portner & Bell, 1982),
Spanier (1976) Marital Adjustment Scale, Cowan (1970) Parent Attitude Test, General Well-Being Scale (National Center
for Health Statistics, 1977), Beck (1978) Depression Inventory, Family Inventory of Life Events (FILE) (McCubbin,
Patterson & Wilson, 1980), the Achenbach (1981) Child Behavior Checklist, and a child and parent questionnaire. The
results of this study will be included in the summary below. In
general, the children appear to be more affected if the mother
is the drug user, possibly because mothers are traditionally
the caretakers of the children.

Major Family Dynamic Variables
Influencing the Child's Risk Status

Review of these empirical and other clinical descriptions of
drug and alcohol abusing families suggest considerable similarities in family dynamics. Although children of substance
abusers have the same needs as all other children, these needs
may not be met, depending on the severity of the family
dysfunction due to the parent(s)' chemical dependency. Longitudinal research is needed to specify family variables that
are most predictive of future substance abuse, but preliminary
studies suggest that the major factors likely to increase the
risk status of the child are the following:

1. Age of the child when the family becomes significantly
   involved in the substance abuse of the parent or parents;
2. Degree of involvement in substance abuse of the primary caretaker and nonfulfillment of parental responsibilities;
3. Severity of emotional, physical, educational, and spir-
   tual neglect or abuse;
4. Temperament of the child and role the child assumes in
   the family;
5. Social isolation of the child and family;
6. Degree of family stress due to inconsistency in rules,
   rituals, discipline, etc.;
7. Degree of family conflict and lack of cooperative, supportive behavior; and

8. Degree of open modeling of drug or alcohol abuse by parents and siblings.

Characteristics of Chemically Dependent Families

Because many clinicians and researchers believe that the "family illness" is the same regardless of the chemical dependency (Wegscheider, 1981), the following section will combine the results from both alcohol and drug studies of substance-abusing parents. The unique characteristics of the families and impact on the children are organized by domain of influence— environmental, affective, cognitive, and behavioral.

Environmental Family Characteristics

These families are often multiproblem families that have considerable *stress* in their lives. Kumpfer and DeMarsh (in press) found that drug-abusing families had high stress as measured by the Family Inventory of Life Events (McCubbin, Patterson & Wilson, 1980). This outcome seems understandable as the test measures work strains, illness strains, losses, transitions, family and marital strain, and financial strain. These strains are exacerbated by the drain on the family's time, finances and emotional/social resources by the substance abuser.

However, increased strains could also derive from *poor life skills,* including *poor family management techniques* (e.g., disorganized households, few rules, inconsistent discipline, unpredictable schedules, decreased child supervision) (Vaillant & Miloufsky, 1982; Kumpfer & DeMarsh, in press). Children need consistency and predictability in their lives to develop stable and functional patterns of behavior. To the degree that both parents are involved in chemical dependency (as the addicted member or a co-alcoholic or co-drug abuser), the children are deprived of responsible, consistent parenting (Black, 1982). Lack of family stability is also influenced by frequent family moves (Vaillant & Miloufsky, 1982), increased separation, divorce, death, jail and prison terms (Booz-Allen & Hamilton, 1974), and decreased family rituals (Wolin, Bennett, Noonan & Teitelbaum, 1979, 1980).

Chemically dependent families are often socially isolated

from the community, partly because of their need to maintain protective boundaries (Ames, in press) and partly because of community rejection. As a result of *social isolation* and decreased social networks (Fraser & Hawkins, 1984a), these families receive less help and support from others with their problems, which could increase their family stress. Similar to the insular families described by Wahler, Leske and Rogers (1979), these families either do not try to make friends in the community or feel that they cannot have traditional friends. Kumpfer and DeMarsh (in press) found that parents in drug-abusing families had fewer friends, and were less involved in recreational, social, religious and cultural activities. Fraser and Hawkins (1984a) found street drug abusers have social networks which are about half those of other families and that the members of their social networks were significantly less involved in conventional activities. Decreased involvement with community and religious institutions has been found as one of the psychosocial precursors of drug abuse (Tennant, Detels & Clark, 1975).

Impact of Social Isolation on the Child

Due to the family's social isolation, the children in chemically dependent homes are unusually isolated and lonely. The Kumpfer and DeMarsh (in press) study found they have fewer opportunities to interact with other children ($p = .001$), have fewer friends they can tell secrets to ($p = .000$), and bring friends home less often ($p = .01$). These children report that they desire more friends, but believe that they lack the abilities to make friends ($p = .05$). The children complain about being lonely, while the parents complain that the children are too dependent on them. Moreover, the children appear to lack social skills and behaviors appropriate to their age. Sometimes they are rejected in school because of their lack of reciprocity, poor language, and inappropriate behavior. Occasionally, if the use of drugs or alcohol by the parents is well-known in the community, other parents will forbid their children to play with "those children." Ames (in press) observed in alcoholic families that the parents, in an effort to maintain protective boundaries, guarded and controlled the children's social contacts and friends "with a seemingly paranoid and unnatural intensity." Children had to play in their own yard and even fenced backyards; they were never allowed to have playmates in their own homes. In addition, children of substance abusers receive little help from their parents in activities promoting their social lives (i.e., planning parties and outings, transportation, invitations to come to their homes for dinner, slumber parties, etc., and appropriate dress and toys).

These children are hampered in social development by the constraints on sharing "family secrets" without betraying the family. Since sharing secrets is a major act of developing intimacy and friendship, this constraint further isolates the children. Lack of friends often contributes to low self-esteem, which is predictive of drug abuse in adolescents (Kaplan, 1977).

Affective/Emotional Characteristics

One factor distinguishing substance-abusing families from other families is *family cohesion and attachment*. This appears to be a significant predictor of future alcohol abuse in prospective studies (Vaillant & Miloufsky, 1982). One interesting result of the Kumpfer and DeMarsh (in press) study was that although the abusing family was significantly less cohesive on both the Moos (1974) Family Environment Scale and the Olson et al. (1982) FACES-II standardized tests, the marital dyads were significantly more cohesive or enmeshed than other randomly selected families as measured by the Spanier (1976) Marital Adjustment Scale for cohesion ($p = .009$). Why these parents tend to disengage from their children needs further research. Possibly these parents are cohesive because they are able to satisfy each other's personal needs and support each others drug procurement, whereas children tend to take more than they give to the parent. The parents may not be capable of meeting the children's needs for a number of reasons: chemical dependency, lack of parenting skills, feelings of being a failure as a parent, rejection by the child, increased narcissism, and/or lack of ability to empathize with the child and decenter from their own needs and feelings.

Emotional neglect has often been reported in substance-abusing families. The Booz-Allen and Hamilton (1974) study reported that emotional neglect most frequently discriminated alcohol-abusing and nonabusing families (reported in 65% of the substance-abusing families). Substance-abusing parents appear to be limited in their ability to involve themselves meaningfully and emotionally with their children. A number of studies have documented that substance-involved parents spend significantly less time with their children than matched families. Sowder and Burt (1978a, b) found that 68% of the heroin abusing parents spend less than 12 hours a week with their children. More recently, Kumpfer and DeMarsh (in press) found that even in a family-oriented community (Salt Lake City), drug-abusing parents averaged between 5 and 10 hours per week in the presence of (not necessarily interacting with) their children, whereas the nonabusing families spend twice as much time with their children.

One of the most significant differences between the normal and drug-abusing families in the Kumpfer and DeMarsh (in press) study was the number of family activities in which the parents were involved with the children. Drug-abusing parents spend less time in planned and structured activities with their children, such as scouts, league sports, clubs ($F = 8.7$; $p < .008$); planned but unstructured activities, such as parties, picnics, hikes and activities ($F = 32.5$; $p < .000$); unplanned but structured activities such as watching television, playing cards and games ($F = 7.5$; $p < .007$); and those activities that are both unplanned and unstructured such as informal talks and visits ($F = 15.3$; $p < .003$). Lack of quality time together is indicative of poor parent-child relationships which has been found to correlate with adolescent drug abuse (Blum & Associates, 1970; Streit, 1973). In a recent study, Hendin, Pollinger, Ulman and Carr (1981) found that marijuana abuse was often preceded by estrangement from parents due to unrealistic expectations or withdrawal of love on the part of the parents.

Family conflict, between all members of the family, has been frequently sited in chemically dependent families (Booz-Allen & Hamilton, 1974; Vaillant & Miloufsky, 1982; Black, 1982; Wegscheider, 1981; Ackerman, 1983; Moos, Bromet, Tsu & Moos, 1979). On both the child and parent interviews and the Moos Family Environment Scale, the drug-abusing families in the Kumpfer and DeMarsh (in press) study reported very high levels of family conflict (even beyond Moos' distressed families). This conflict is manifested primarily in verbal abuse and negative communication patterns—threatening, chastising, belittling, criticizing (Reilly, 1979; Booz-Allen & Hamilton, 1974), but occasionally involves physical abuse and sexual abuse. Most evidence for the latter comes primarily from clinical reports of adult children of substance-abusers and protective services reports when removing a child from a substance-abusing home.

In addition to the affective problems reported above, significantly more depression ($F = 25$; $p < .0001$) was detected in drug-abusing parents than nondrug-abusing parents (Kumpfer and DeMarsh, in press), as measured by the Beck (1978) Depression Inventory.

Emotional Impact on the Children

Clinicians have often reported that children from chemically dependent homes appear to have more of difficulty than other children in identifying and expressing feelings (Black, 1982; Wegscheider, 1981). Their feelings, which are rarely validated by their parents, are painful and ambivalent. Characteristic feelings often reported in comparative studies include: resentment (50%); embarrassment (48%); anger, fear, loneliness, depression, and insecurity (Booz-Allen & Hamilton, 1974; Sowder & Burt, 1978a, b). Emotional disturbances such as depression are found to precede adolescent drug abuse (Paton, Kessler & Kandel, 1977).

COCDPs often have difficulty in forming intimate relationships and believe they have survived primarily by relying only on themselves. Black (1982), who has worked clinically with adult children of alcoholics, found that these children have a pervasive sense of fear and guilt and "suffer their losses and indignities alone, because they don't perceive help and support as being available from their parents or anyone" (p. 5). Failure to meet their parents' exaggerated expectations, combined with difficulties in school and social situations, can leave children with a low self-concept. In her clinical studies, Brown reports an intense fear of separation and abandonment in the adult children of alcoholics (Brown & Beletsis, in press). Also, when they do form attachments, children of substance abusers often marry persons who are substance abusers or come from substance-abusing homes; hence, they recreate in their own family environment that which they experienced and were familiar with as a child.

Lack of attachment to others and society, possibly because of poor parent-child attachments, is predictive of future alcohol abuse and delinquency (Hirschi, 1969). Lack of parent-child bonding can leave children vulnerable to peer and situational inducements to use drugs or engage in delinquent behaviors (Briar & Piliavin, 1965). Parent-oriented youth have been found to use marijuana less than peer-oriented youth (Stone, Miranne & Ellis, 1979). Youth who regularly use alcohol and drugs report feeling isolated in their families and less involved in family activities (Brennan, Elliott & Knowles, 1981). One of Vaillant and Miloufsky's (1982) findings was that lack of paternal attachment was indicative of future alcoholism.

COCDPs also tend to learn the same inappropriate conflict resolution skills and lack of anger management as modeled in their homes. These children report more fighting at school and getting even (Sowder & Burt, 1978a, b). Controlling others through force also paves the way toward delinquent behaviors and crime.

Cognitive Family Characteristics

Values and attitudes of parents are difficult to define because they can differ radically from their behavior. Parents, who find that because of their addiction they must limit some of their parental responsibilities to survive, may have no less belief in the importance of good parenting. In their situation, they simply do not have the skills or resources to do so. As mentioned in Sowder and Burt (1978a, b), drug dependent parents want to be better parents, but find that their addiction and life-style interferes with that ability.

Beyond this life-style constraint, these families differ in values and attitudes from mainstream Americans. In general, they appear to place less stress on prosocial values and respect for authority or tradition. Included in this is condonation of antisocial values, such as the "ends justify the means." A number of alcoholic family studies have documented an external locus-of-control orientation (Morrison & Schuckit, 1983; Prewett, Spencer & Chaknis, 1981; Kern, Hassett & Collipp, 1981). Possibly the decreased stress on social responsibility could be caused in part by this belief that they have limited control over their lives. Decreased bonding or attachment to society is demonstrated in their decreased stress on education and academic achievement (Sowder & Burt, 1978a, b) and religious, social or cultural community involvement (Kumpfer & DeMarsh, in press). These parents tend to put less stress on cooperative involvement in the family and with groups or institutions in society. One overall theme may be increased emphasis on looking out for individual interests versus the good of the whole, which is a characteristic of a lower level of moral development and of the narcissistic personality. This self-centeredness may also be related to the unrealistic expectations for self-sufficiency which these parents have for their children (Kumpfer & DeMarsh, in press; Reilly, 1979). The parents appear to expect children after infancy to behave at levels far beyond the age-appropriate developmental level of the child. Finally, the parents model pro-drug, alcohol and criminal values (Mercer, Hundleby & Carpenter, 1976; Kandel, Kessler & Margulies, 1978; Kim, 1979; Brooks, Luckoff & Whiteman, 1980).

Impact on Children of Chemically Dependent Parents

Cognitive Deficits

COCDPs have decreased cognitive and verbal abilities, particularly as preschool children (Sowder & Burt, 1978a, b). Associated problems include increased academic problems and behavioral problems in school (Kumpfer & DeMarsh, in press), and increased learning disabilities (Gabrielli & Mednick, 1983; deMendonca, Mator & daCosta Motta, 1980). It is difficult to say whether these cognitive difficulties are caused by the parental values, or that both are caused by other mediating variables such as biomedical syndromes or social variables. Since COCDPs attend school less and are more often late for school (Kumpfer & DeMarsh, in press), this decreased exposure to academic material and limited help from their parents with homework (Kumpfer & DeMarsh, in press) could impair their ability to succeed in school. These cognitive deficits and lack of academic motivation increase the child's risk of drug abuse (Smith & Fogg, 1978).

Behavioral Characteristics

Chemically dependent parents tend to be lax or inconsistent in their discipline practices with their children, depending on their drug state (Baumrind, 1983; Braucht, Brakarsh, Follingstad & Berry, 1973; Blum & Associates, 1972). Children of alcoholics report being able to "get away" with something one day and being severely chastised the next day for the same behavior when the parent is not intoxicated (Black, 1982). The Kumpfer and DeMarsh data (in press) showed that these children have fewer rules to follow ($F = 15.8$; $p = .01$), are more disobedient at home ($F = 15.1$; $p = .000$) and helpless with housework.

The Sowder and Burt (1978a, b) study found that parents tend to be either strict or permissive in their discipline of children. A similar result was reported by Baumrind (1983), who studied prosocial children with low risk for drug abuse and found that they generally come from authoritative families, whereas drug users come from authoritarian or permissive families—but more often families characterized by parent nondirectiveness. Drug abusers characterized their home environments as cool and hostile, with weak parent-child relationships and inconsistent parental discipline (Chein, 1966).

Little Adults

As mentioned earlier, these drug-involved parents tend to abdicate their parental responsibilities and encourage their children to take care of themselves. The concept of childhood seems to be lacking. From this point of view, these children often appear amazingly healthy and capable, particularly the oldest children. They are often forced into learning life management skills at a very early age and sometime have to perform many parental chores for the rest of the family and the parents. Becky Davis, deputy director of the Texas alcohol authority, recounts a story about a 4-year-old COCDP who would get herself up, dress herself, fix breakfast and hitchhike to preschool. Black (1982) includes in her book a story of an 11-year-old girl being asked by her alcoholic father to drive the car home alone after he stopped at a bar. In tears, she dutifully attempted to drive the car home, even though both the girl and her father knew she did not know how to drive.

Despite these early demands to perform like competent adults, studies show that these children have many areas of behavioral deficits and later pay dearly for their lack of childhood. In general, these children have fewer age appropriate social skills and have more behavioral problems at home and at school (Kumpfer & DeMarsh, in press; Fine, Yudin, Holmes & Heinemann, 1976). Problem behaviors also increase the child's risk of substance abuse (R. Jessor & S. L. Jessor, 1978; O'Donnell & Clayton, 1979).

Rigid Family Roles

Though not empirically confirmed yet, clinicians (Black, 1982; Wegscheider & Wegscheider, 1978, Wegscheider, 1981; Ackerman, 1983) repeatedly categorize children of alcoholics into four different survival roles. These characteristic response patterns to their parents' alcoholism include: control or lead (the family hero, or the responsible or caretaking child, who is often the oldest); flight (the adjuster who copes by being gone, or the lost child in terms of being withdrawn, depressed); fight (the scapegoat or problem child who is often acting out and in trouble); and cope (the family mascot or placater who tries to make others happy).

These behavioral response patterns are often inappropriate to other life situations, but COCDPs may have an increased deficience in the ability to shift roles. Hence, as adults they may find that they are not as flexible as others and are not as successful in jobs or marriages. Children of alcoholics are found to do poorly on the Minnesota Card Sort Test which measures ability to shift categorical behavior with changing reinforcement contingencies (Goodwin, 1985); hence, this behavioral rigidity may carry over into a general pattern and lack of adaptability.

Alcohol and Drug Use

For whatever reason, children of substance abusers also find that they have a hard time controlling their use of alcohol and drugs. Even with the conviction that they will "never let it happen" to them, they have no clear idea of how much is too much (Brown & Beletsis, in press). When they start having more problems as adolescents and young adults because of their lack of social networks and behavioral deficits, they find it difficult to avoid substance abuse. Their parents modeled drug use for coping with problems, and they tend to find alcohol and drugs very pleasurable.

IMPLICATIONS FOR CHILDHOOD PREVENTION

Since little can be done about hereditary factors except to educate children of chemically dependent parents about the biological markers for inherited vulnerability and to educate pregnant women about the dangers of fetal alcohol syndrome, prevention approaches for high-risk children and youth need to address the familial environmental precursors previously discussed. Hence, effective prevention programs will likely be those that improve parent's and children's social skills, decrease family isolation, involve families in normative community experience, teach parents ways to improve their child and family management skills, improve family consistency in rituals, increase time parents spend with their children, improve empathy and understanding, increase parent's knowledge of age-appropriate expectations, decrease family conflict and stress, and provide good role models for the children.

Prevention Strategies for Children
of Chemically Dependent Parents

Children of chemically dependent parents (COCDPs) often need special prevention and early intervention services to prevent what many of them believe is the inevitable becoming an active alcoholic or drug abuser like their parent(s). Whether clinical services to COCDPs are considered prevention, early intervention, or treatment depends on stage of use of the

COCDPs (Macdonald, 1984). The same program could be considered prevention if the host (youth) is not yet using drugs, early intervention if the host is a moderate user, and treatment if the host is a problem or heavy/severe user. Hence, special educational groups or skills training with COCDPs may be prevention for the nonusers in the group and treatment for the abusers. Generally it is better, however, to have separate, targeted services for each of these groups.

The following sections will review prevention services for COCDPs that include the children (or adult children) only, and not the parents. The use of parent training, family skills training, and family therapy as prevention interventions for children of chemically dependent parents or to reduce a child's risk status in any family will be discussed in the author's article on family-oriented prevention interventions.

School-Based COCDP Services

Prevention programs in schools for COCDPs are rare, but increasing. A number of schools are starting to implement special groups for them (see Ackerman [1983] for an excellent discussion of what educators can do for COCDPs, including identification, developing walk-in centers or student discussion groups, and personal support). One risk in the school setting is that other students will discover the recruitment criterion for the group and stigmatize the children. Criteria for placement in the prevention groups generally includes tardiness, truancy, poor attendance, low grades, social isolation, and other signs of living with chemically dependent parents. One naturally occurring high-risk group of children in schools is composed of students attending classes for conduct-disordered children. Klein and Malouf (1985) are currently testing the effectiveness of teaching principles of functional family therapy directly to special education classes using their Group Relations Adjustment Skills Program (GRASP).

Clinic or Community-Based COCDP Services

Older children can find some support in Alateen self-help groups, but it is estimated that only 3%–5% of COAs use

Alateen (Black, 1982). A few clinicians have developed special play therapy and support groups for young children and teenagers of alcoholics (Black, 1982) that invite use of projective drawings, puppets, dolls, etc., to help the children express their feelings. Since these children have been taught to keep the family secret and not to talk, trust or feel, prevention work with COCDPs requires special clinical skills, including patience, warmth, acceptance, and understanding of the dynamics of chemically dependent families.

As part of their NIDA-funded research on various prevention strategies for 6–12 year old COCDPs, the authors developed and evaluated the effectiveness of three types of programs: parent-only training, family training, and children-only training. Only the 34-session and a 14-session Children's Skills Training program (Kumpfer & DeMarsh, 1983) will be reviewed in this article, because the others are included in the article by DeMarsh and Kumpfer. The more intensive COCDP program was run like a summer camp and merged didactic instruction with social, cultural, and recreational opportunities in half-day sessions twice a week. The shorter version was implemented during the school year at night or on weekends. The content of this prevention curriculum appears to be very effective in addressing the primary needs of the children: social skills, problem-solving and decision-making skills, conflict-resolution skills, communication skills, life skills, and homework skills. The authors hope to make the Children's Skills Training package more effective in reaching larger numbers of children by developing TV and videotape programs, which would also involve the parents in working with the children.

Adult Children of Alcoholics

A number of clinicians have developed clinical programs appropriate as prevention for some adult children of alcoholics (ACA) (El-Guebaly & Offord, 1977, 1979; Greenleaf, 1981; Deutsch, 1982). Most of these ACAs are not alcohol abusers, and some may not even drink, but they join ACA groups because "many believe that they are already alcoholic, and if they do not intervene on their own behalf, they will be powerless to prevent the inevitable of becoming actively alcoholic like their parents" (Brown & Beletsis, in press). Major topics often dealt with in these groups are issues of control, trust, acknowledgment of personal needs, responsibility, and feelings (Cermak & Brown, 1982 for a more complete review). In addition, the participants often develop family transference and behave towards the group as if it were the family of origin (Brown & Beletsis, in press). One avenue of access to COA groups has been through employee assistance programs (EAPs), some of which are stressing the development of COA self-help groups in business or referrals to outside COA groups (Foster, 1976). Quite recently, ACA groups have been growing rapidly in popularity within Alcoholics Anonymous and many are sponsored by Al-Anon.

CONCLUSION

Chemical dependency is a multigenerational problem, and until this society begins to target high-risk children for special attention, we will never break this vicious cycle and significantly impact chemical dependency. Chemical dependency runs in families, whether for environmental or genetic reasons. Hence, more prevention efforts need to be targeted at children of chemically dependent parents. Even if the parents are not chemically dependent, there are identifiable childhood behaviors and family risk factors which make a child more vulnerable to alcohol and drugs. More research is needed on these early childhood risk factors as well as methods for identifying such children early and delivering remediation.

The numerous familial and childhood antecedents of chemical dependency suggest that prevention programs need to be comprehensive, intensive, and enduring. Whenever possible, prevention strategies need to include the family and to focus on improving the child's behavior and strengthening family relationships. Considerable data support the notion that parents are the most influential childhood factor in shaping the child's later adaptation to life, including use or abuse of drugs. Parents who model nonuse or socially appropriate use of alcohol and medications, and who are warm (but provide close supervision) appear to have fewer children who become seriously involved in drugs (Auerswald, 1980; Baumrind, 1985). In addition, parents have an obligation to raise their children to be

competent, independent individuals with survival skills necessary to succeed and contribute to our society without the use of
drugs. This means responsible parenting, by giving the needed
time, love, guidance, and attention to the child.

Unfortunately, due to permissive societal values concerning
alcohol and drug use, even many competent children will experiment with drugs and alcohol, as this is typical of risk-
taking and trying out new adult behaviors. Few youth who
have social competencies and close relationships with their
parents will become drug abusers. According to the most recent analysis of Kandel's data, only 25% of all children who
initiate drug use continue usage after age 23 years (Yamaguchi & Kandel, 1984). Parents, therefore, should not condone
the use of any drugs, except medically, but must be careful
not to overreact with harsh sanctions and withdrawal of love
to experimentation with drugs (like marijuana) that are normative for their children's age and school (Baumrind, 1985).

Parents need to make sure that their children understand
the short- and long-term consequences of alcohol and drug
use. Prevention programs such as "Talking With Your Kids
About Alcohol" (Prevention Research Institute, Inc., Lexington, Kentucky) are helpful as well as materials that parents
can order from the National Federation of Parents for Drug
Free Youth. Parents could join one of the local parents
groups for the prevention of drug abuse in their local community. "Toughlove" strategies developed for adolescents who
are already abusing and who are noncompliant can be tried as
a last resort (York, York & Wachtel, 1982).

One exciting possible prevention program for high risk children and youth, which the authors are pursuing, is an
"Adopt-A-Family" approach in which a group of nonusing
families from the community can volunteer to sponsor a
family which contains a high-risk child. Our particular emphasis currently is to use "Family Friendship Circles" developed
by the Cottage Program International or local parent groups
to engage a matched high-risk family (where the parent or
grandparent is chemically dependent) in structured prevention activities (Kumpfer, Boswell & Boswell, 1985). Since
these high-risk children and families need long-term interventions, it may be more cost effective to use local families who
care about combating drug and alcohol use by youth in their

community for delivery of the strategies. Special training and scheduled social, cultural, and recreational activities and hot-line consultation will be made available to the host families.

More etiological research needs to be conducted to better understand the psychosocial and biomedical transmitters of drug abuse from parent to child. In addition, longitudinal prospective studies of COCDPs are needed. Since maternal chemical dependency tends to have a devastating impact on children, more study is needed on chemical dependency in women. Such studies should be aimed at elucidating the variables which transmit precursors of chemical dependency to the children. Currently, there are a number of prospective studies being conducted of sons of alcoholics, but none on daughters of alcoholics.

Finally, cost-effective, intensive, and long-term strategies must be found to deal with this multigenerational problem of chemical dependency. At some point in history, citizens of this country need to invest substantially in helping to break this multigenerational cycle and decreasing the high rates of alcohol and drug abuse in our youth. It may not take a lot of money if communities are willing to get involved, but the solution will certainly require a lot of time and commitment on the part of substance abuse practitioners and community members.

REFERENCES

Abel, E.L. (Ed.), (1981). *Fetal alcohol syndrome I: An annotated and comprehensive bibliography*. Boca Raton, FL: CRC Press, Inc.

Abel, E. L. (Ed.), (1982a). *Fetal alcohol syndrome II: Human studies*. Boca Raton, FL: CRC Press, Inc.

Abel, E. L. (Ed.), (1982b). *Fetal alcohol syndrome III: Animal studies*. Boca Raton, FL: CRC Press, Inc.

Achenbach, T. M. (1981). Child behavior checklist for ages 4–16. Burlington, VT: University of Vermont.

Ackerman, R. (1983). *Children of alcoholics*. Holmes Beach: Learning Publications.

Adams, G., & Gullotta, T. (1983). *Adolescent life experiences*. Monterey, CA: Brooks/Cole Publishing Co.

Ainsworth, M. D. S. (1972). Attachment and dependency: A comparison. In J. L. Gewirtz (Ed.), *Attachment and dependency* (pp. 97–138). Washington, DC: Winston.

Alexopoulos, G. S., Lieberman, K. W., & Frances, R. J. (1983). Platelet MAO activity in alcoholic patients and their first-degree relatives. *American Journal of Psychiatry, 140*(11), 1501–1503.

Ames, G. M. (in press). Middle-class protestants: Alcohol and the family. In L. A. Bennett & G. M. Ames (Eds.), *The American experience with alcohol: Contrasting cultural perspectives.*

Annis, H. M. (1974). Patterns of intra-familial drug use. *British Journal of the Addictions, 69,* 361–369.

Auerswald, E. H. (1980). Drug use and families—in the context of twentieth century science. In B. G. Ellis (Ed.), *Drug abuse from the family perspective* (DHHS Publication No. ADM 80–910, pp. 118–126). Washington, DC: U. S. Government Printing Office.

Barry, H., III (1976). Cross cultural evidence that dependency conflict motivates drunkenness. In M. W. Everett, J. O. Waddell, & D. B. Heath (Eds.), *Crosscultural approaches to the study of alcohol.* Chicago: Aldine.

Baumrind, D. (1983, October). *Why adolescents take chances and why they don't.* Presentation at the National Institute for Child Health and Human Development.

Baumrind, D. (1985). Familial antecedents of adolescent drug use: A developmental perspective. In C. L. Jones, & R. J. Battjes (Eds.), *Etiology of drug abuse: Implications for prevention,* (National Institute on Drug Abuse Research Monograph 56, DHHS Publication No. ADM 85–1335, pp. 13–44). Washington, DC: U. S. Government Printing Office.

Beck, A. T. (1978). Beck inventory. Philadelphia, PA: Center for Cognitive Therapy.

Begleiter, H., Porjesz, B., Bihari, B., & Kissin, B. (1984). Event-related brain potentials in boys at risk for alcoholism. *Science, 225,* 1493–1496.

Behling, D. W. (1979). Alcohol abuse as encountered in instances of reported child abuse. *Clinical Pediatrics, 18*(2), 87–91.

Black, C. (1982). *It will never happen to me!* Denver, CO: MAC Printing and Publishing Division.

Bloom, F., Neville, H., Woods, D., Schuckit, J., & Bloom, F. (1982). Event-related brain potential are different in individuals at high and low risk for developing alcoholism. *Proceedings of the National Academy of Sciences USA, 79,* 7900–7903.

Blum, R. H., & Associates (1970). *Students and drugs.* San Francisco: Jossey-Bass.

Blum, R.H., & Associates (1972). *Horatio Alger's children.* San Francisco: Jossey-Bass.

Bohman, M., Sigvardsson, S., & Cloninger, R. (1981). Maternal inheritance of alcohol abuse: Cross-fostering analysis of adopted women. *Archives of General Psychiatry, 38,* 965–969.

Booz-Allen & Hamilton, Inc. (1974). *An Assessment of the needs of and resources for children of alcoholic parents.* Rockville, MD: National Institute on Alcohol Abuse and Alcoholism.

Borg, S., Kvande, H., Magnusson, E., & Sjoquist, B. (1980). Salsolinol and salsoline in cerebrospinal lumbar fluid of alcoholic patients. *Acta Psychiatr Scand Suppl, 286,* 171–177.

Bowlby, J. (1969). *Attachment and loss.* Vol. I: *Attachment.* New York: Basic Books.

Braucht, G. N., Brakarsh, D., Follingstad, D., & Berry, K. L. (1973). Deviant drug use in adolescence: A review of psychosocial correlates. *Psychological Bulletin, 79,* 92–106.

Brennan, T., Elliott, D. S., & Knowles, B. A. (1981). *Patterns of multiple drug use.* Boulder, CO: Behavioral Research Institute.

Briar, S., & Piliavin, I. (1965). Delinquency, situational inducements, and commitments to conformity. *Social Problems, 13*(1), 35–45.

Brooks, J. S., Lukoff, I. F., & Whiteman, M. (1980). Initiation into adolescent marijuana use. *Journal of General Psychology, 137,* 133–142.

Brown, S., & Beletsis, S. (in press). The development of family transference in groups for the adult children of alcoholics.

Buchsbaum, M. S. (1978). Neurophysiological studies of reduction and augmentation. In A. Petrie (Ed.), *Individuality in pain and suffering* (2nd ed.). Chicago: University of Chicago Press.

Bushing, B. C., & Bromley, D. G. (1975). Sources of nonmedicinal drug use: A test of the drug-oriented society explanation. *Journal of Health and Social Behavior, 16*, 50–62.

Butynski, W., Record, N., & Yates, J. (1985). *State resources and services related to alcohol and drug abuse problems: An analysis of state alcohol and drug abuse profile data-FY 1984* (Developed in part under contract No. ADMS 271-84-7314). Washington, DC: National Association of State Alcohol and Drug Abuse Directors, Inc.

Cadoret, R. J., O'Gorman, T. W., Troughton, E., & Heywood, E. (1985). Alcoholism and antisocial personality: Interrelationships, genetic and environmental factors. *Archives of General Psychiatry, 42*, 161–167.

Cantwell, D. P. (1972). Psychiatric illness in the families of hyperactive children. *Archives of General Psychiatry, 27*, 414–417.

Cantwell, D. P. (1975). Genetic studies of hyperactive children: Psychiatric illness in biologic and adopting parents. In R. R. Fieve, D. Rosenthal, & H. Brill (Eds.), *Genetic studies of hyperactive children: Psychiatric illness in biologic and adoptive parents*. Baltimore, MD: John Hopkins University Press.

Cermak, T. L., & Brown, S. (1982). Interactional group therapy with the adult children of alcoholics. *International Journal of Group Psychotherapy, 32*, 375–389.

Chein, I. (1966). Narcotic use among juveniles. In J. A. O'Donnell, & J. C. Ball (Eds.), *Narcotic Addiction*. New York: Harper & Row.

Children of Alcoholics Foundation. (1984, April). *Report of the conference of research needs and opportunities for children of alcoholics*. New York: Children of Alcoholics Foundation, Inc.

Clark, B., & Midanik, L. (1982). Alcohol use and alcohol problems among U.S. adults: Results of the 1979 national survey. In U.S. Department of Health and Human Services, *Alcohol and health monograph No. 1: Alcohol consumption and related problems* (DHHS Publication No. ADM 82–1190). Washington, DC: U.S. Government Printing Office.

Cloninger, R., Bohman, M., & Sigvardsson, S. (1981). Inheritance of alcohol abuse. *Archives of General Psychiatry, 38*, 861–868.

Coleman, S. B. (1980). Incomplete mourning in the family trajectory: A circular journey to drug abuse. In B. G. Ellis (Ed.), *Drug abuse from the family perspective* (DHHS Publication No. ADM 80–910, pp. 18–31). Washington, DC: U.S. Government Printing Office.

Cotton, N. S. (1979). The familial incidence of alcoholism. *Journal of Studies on Alcohol, 40*(1), 89–116.

Cowen, E. L., Huser, J., Beach, D. R., & Rappaport, J. (1970). Parental perceptions of young children and their relation to indexes of adjustment. *Journal of Consulting and Clinical Psychology, 34*(1), 97–103.

deMendonca, M. M., Mator, A. P., & daCosta Motta, A. (1980). *Contribution to the study of the academic underachievement in children of alcoholics*. Unpublished manuscript, Centrol de Medicina Pedagogica, Lisbon, Portugal.

Deutsch, C. (1982). *Broken bottles, broken dreams: Understanding and helping the children of alcoholics*. New York: Teacher College Press.

El-Guebaly, N., & Offord, D. R. (1977). The offspring of alcoholics: A clinical review. *The American Journal of Psychiatry, 134*(4), 357–365.

El-Guebaly, N., & Offord, D. R. (1979). On being the offspring of an alcoholic: An update. *Alcoholism: Clinical and Experimental Research, 3*, 148–157.

Elliott, D. S., Huizinga, D., & Ageton, S. S. (1982). *Explaining delinquency and drug use*. Boulder, CO: Behavioral Research Institute.

Fine, E. W., Yudin, L. W., Holmes, J., & Heinemann, S. (1976). Behavioral disorders in children with parental alcoholism. *Annals of the New York Academy of Sciences, 273,* 507–517.

Foster, W.O. (1976). The employed child of the alcoholic. *Labor Management Alcoholism Journal, 6*(1), 13–18.

Fraser, M., & Hawkins, J. D. (1984a). Social network analysis and drug misuse. *Social Service Review, 58,* 81–97.

Fraser, M. W., & Hawkins, J. D. (1984b). The social networks of opioid abusers. *International Journal of the Addictions, 19*(8), 903–917.

Gabrielli, W. F., & Mednick, S. A. (1983). Intellectual performance in children of alcoholics. *The Journal of Nervous and Mental Disease, 171*(7), 444–447.

Garfield, S., & Bergin, A. (1971). *Handbook of psychotherapy and behavior change.* New York: John Wiley & Sons.

Glynn, T. J. (Ed.). (1981). *Drugs and the family* (Research Issues Monograph No. 29). Rockville, MD: National Institute on Drug Abuse.

Goodwin, D. (1971). Is alcoholism hereditary? A review and critique. *Archives of General Psychiatry, 25,* 545–549.

Goodwin, D. W. (1985). Alcoholism and genetics: The sins of the fathers. *Archives of General Psychiatry, 6,* 171–174.

Goodwin, D. W., & Guze, S. B. (1979). *Psychiatric diagnosis,* 2d ed. New York: Oxford University Press.

Greenleaf, J. (1981). *Co-alcoholic, para-alcoholic.* Los Angeles, CA: Greenleaf Associates.

Greenspan, S. I. (1985). Discussion of research strategies to identify developmental vulnerabilities for drug abuse. In C. L. Jones, & R. J. Battjes (Eds.), *Etiology of drug abuse: Implications for prevention* (National Institute on Drug Abuse Research Monograph 56, DHHS Publication No. ADM 85-1335, pp. 136–154). Washington, DC: U.S. Government Printing Office.

Harada, S., Agarwal, D. P., Goedde, H. W., Tagaki, S., & Ishikawa, B. (1982). Possible protective role against alcoholism for aldehyde dehydrogenase isoenzyme deficiency in Japan. *Lancet ii,* 827.

Harbin, H. T., & Maziar, H. M. (1975). The families of drug abusers: A literature review. *Family Process, 14,* 411–431.

Harvey, J. A., & Yunger, L. M. (1973). Relationship between telencephalic centers of serotonin and pain sensitivity. In J. Barchas, & E. A. Usdin (Eds.), *Serotonin and behavior* (pp. 179–190). New York: Harcourt Brace Jovanovich.

Harwood, H. J. (1984). *Economic costs to society of alcohol and drug abuse and mental illness: 1980.* Presentation at Research Triangle Institute State Directors' Meeting. Research Triangle Park, NC: Research Triangle Institute.

Harwood, H. J., Napolitano, D. M., Kristiansen, P. L., & Collins, J. J. (1984). *Economic costs to society of alcohol and drug abuse and mental illness: 1980* (Contract No. ADM 283-83-002). Research Triangle Park, NC: Research Triangle Institute.

Hawkins, J. D., Lishner, D., & Catalano, R. F. (1985). Childhood predictors and the prevention of adolescent substance abuse. In C. L. Jones, & R. J. Battjes (Eds.), *Etiology of drug abuse: Implications for prevention,* (National Institute on Drug Abuse Research Monograph 56, DHHS Publication No. ADM 85-1335, pp. 75–126). Washington, DC: U. S. Government Printing Office.

Hegedus, A. M., Alterman, A. I., & Tarter, R. E. (in press). *Alcoholism: Clinical and Experimental Research.*

Hendin, H., Pollinger, A., Ulman, R., & Carr, A. C. (1981). *Adolescent marijuana abusers and their families* (National Institute on Drug Abuse Research Monograph 40, DHEW Publication No. ADM 81-1168). Washington, DC: U. S. Government Printing Office.

Hennecke, L. (1984). Stimulus augmenting and field dependence in children of alcoholic fathers. *Journal of Studies on Alcohol, 45*(6), 486–492.

Hirschi, T. (1969). *Causes of delinquency.* Berkeley: Unversity of California Press.

Hoffman, H. & Noem, A. A. (1975). Alcoholism and abstinence among relatives of American Indian alcoholics. *Journal of Studies on Alcohol, 36,* 165.

Huba, G. J., Wingard, J. A., & Bentler, P. M. (1980). Longitudinal analysis of the role of peer support, adult models, and peer subcultures in beginning adolescent substance use: An application of setwise canonical correlation methods. *Multivariate Behavioral Research, 15,* 259–279.

Jessor, R., & Jessor, S. L. (1977). *Problem behavior and psychosocial development: A longitudinal study.* New York: Academic Press.

Jessor, R., & Jessor, S. L. (1978). Theory testing in longitudinal research on marijuana use. In D. Kandel (Ed.), *Longitudinal research on drug use.* Washington, DC: Hemisphere Publishing Co.

Jessor, R., & Jessor, S. (1980). A social-psychological framework for studying drug use. In D. J. Lettieri, M. Sayers, & H. W. Pearson (Eds.), *Theories on drug abuse,* (National Institute on Drug Abuse Research Monograph 30, DHHS Publication No. ADM 80-067, pp. 102–109). Washington, DC: U.S. Government Printing Office.

Johnston, L. D., O'Malley, P., & Evelard, L. (1978). Drugs and delinquency: A search for casual connections. In D. B. Kandel (Ed.), *Longitudinal research on drug use.* Washington, DC: Hemisphere Publishing Co.

Kaij, L. (1960). *Studies on the etiology and sequels of abuse of alcohol.* Sweden: University of Lund, Department of Psychiatry.

Kandel, D. B. (1980). Developmental stages in adolescent drug involvement. In D. J. Lettieri, M. Sayers, & H. W. Pearson (Eds.), *Theories on drug abuse,* (National Institute on Drug Abuse Research Monograph 30, DHHS Publication No. 80-967, pp. 120–127). Washington, DC: U.S. Government Printing Office.

Kandel, D. B., Kessler, R., & Margulies, R. (1978). Antecedents of adolescents initiation into stages of drug use: A developmental analysis. In D. B. Kandel (Ed.), *Longitudinal research in drug use: Empirical findings and methodological issues* (pp. 73–99). Washington, DC: Hemisphere-Wiley.

Kaplan, H. B. (1977). Antecedents of deviant responses: Predicting from a general theory of deviant behavior. *Journal of Youth and Adolescence, 6,* 89–101.

Kearney, T. R., & Taylor, C. (1969). Emotionally disturbed adolescents of alcoholic parents. *Acta Paedopsychiatr (Basel), 36,* 215–221.

Kellam, S. G., & Brown, H. (1982). *Social adaptational and psychological antecedents of adolescent psychopathology ten years later.* Baltimore: Johns Hopkins University.

Kent, T. A., Campbell, J. R., & Goodwin, D. W. (in press). Blood platelet uptake of serotonin in chronic alcoholics. *Lancet.*

Kern, J. C., Hassett, C. A., & Collipp, P. J. (1981). Children of alcoholics: Locus of control, mental age, and zinc level. *Journal of Psychiatric Treatment and Evaluation, 3,* 169–173.

Kim, S. (1979). *An evaluation of ombudsman primary prevention program on student drug abuse.* Charlotte, NC: Charlotte Drug Education Center, Inc.

Klagsbrun, M., & Davis, D. I. (1977). Substance abuse and family interaction. *Family Process, 16,* 149–173.

Klein, N. C., & Malouf, R. E. (1985). *Final report: Group relations approach to substance problems (GRASP)-1984/85 project.* Salt Lake City, UT: Western States Family Institute.

Kumpfer, K. L., Boswell, B. N., & Boswell, R. H. (1985, July). *Cottage family friendship circles: A family prevention research project.* Concept paper submitted to the National Institute on Alcohol Abuse and Alcoholism.

Kumpfer, K. L., & DeMarsh, J. (1983). *Strengthening Families Program: Children's skills training curriculum manual* (Prevention Services to Children of Substance-abusing Parents). Social Research Institute, Graduate School of Social Work, University of Utah.

Kumpfer, K. L., & DeMarsh, J. (1984, February). *Prevention services to children of substance-abusing parents: Project rationale, description and research plan.* Technical report submitted to National Institute on Drug Abuse, Rockville, MD.

Kumpfer, K. L., & DeMarsh, J. P. (in press). Prevention strategies for children of drug-abusing parents. *Proceedings of the 34th Annual Congress on Alcoholism and Drug Dependence,* Calgary, Alberta.

Lawrence, T. S., & Vellerman, J. D. (1974). Correlates of student drug use in a suburban high school. *Psychiatry, 35,* 129–136.

Liepman, M. R. (1980). Some theoretical connections between family violence and substance abuse. *Catalyst 1*(3), 37–42.

Lisansky, E. S. (1957). Alcoholism in women; social and psychological concomitants. I. Social history data. *Quarterly Journal of Studies on Alcohol, 18,* 588–623.

Loeber, R. (1985). Patterns of development of antisocial child behavior. *Annals of Child Development, 2,* 77–115.

Macdonald, D. I. (1984). *Drugs, drinking and adolescents.* Chicago: Year Book Medical Publishers.

MacKay, J. R. (1961). Clinical observations on adolescent problem drinkers. *Quarterly Journal of Studies on Alcohol, 22,* 124–134.

MacKay, J. R. (1963). Problem drinking among juvenile delinquents. *Crime and Delinquency, 9,* 29–38.

McCubbin, H. I., Patterson, J. M., & Wilson, L. (1980). Family inventory of life events and changes (FILE), Form A. St. Paul, MN: Family Social Science.

Mercer, G. W., Hundleby, J. D., & Carpenter, R. A. (1976, June). *Adolescent evaluations of the family as a unit in their relationships to the use of tobacco, alcohol and marijuana.* Paper presented at the 11th Annual Conference of the Canadian Foundation of Alcohol and Drug Dependencies, Toronto, Ontario.

Moos, R. H. (1974). Family environment scale. Palo Alto, CA: Consulting Psychologists Press, Inc.

Moos, R. H., Bromet, E., Tsu, V., & Moos, B. (1979). Family characteristics and the outcome of treatment for alcoholism. *Journal of Studies on Alcohol, 40*(1), 78–88.

Morrison, C., & Schuckit, M. A. (1983). Locus of control in young men with alcoholic relatives and controls. *Journal of Clinical Psychiatry, 44,* 306–307.

Morrison, J. R., & Stewart, M. A. (1971). A family study of the hyperactive child syndrome. *Biol. Psychiatry, 3,* 189–195.

Nardi, P. M. (1981). Children of alcoholics: A role-theoretical perspective. *The Journal of Social Psychology, 115,* 237–245.

National Center for Health Statistics (1977, September). *A concurrent validation study of the NCHS general well-being schedule.* (Vital and health statistics series 2, No. 73: DHEW Publication No. HRA 78-1347). Washington, DC: U.S. Government Printing Office.

Nicholas, M. (1984). *Family therapy: Concepts and methods.* New York: Gardner Press.

Nylander, I. (1960). Children of alcoholic fathers. *Acta Paediatr Scan., 49,* 1–134.

O'Donnell, J. A., & Clayton, R. R. (1979). Determinants of early marijuana use. In G. M. Beschner, & A. S. Friedman (Eds.), *Youth drug abuse: Problems, issues and treatment* (pp. 63–110). Lexington, MA: Lexington Books.

Olson, D. (1983, November). *Methodological concerns with family life skills research.* A paper presented at the National Institute on Drug Abuse Technical Review: Family Life Skills Training and its Research, Rockville, MD.

Olson, D. H., Portner, J., & Bell, R. (1982). Family adaptability & cohesion evaluation scales (FACES II). St. Paul, MN: Family Social Science.

Parsons, B. V. (1972). *Family crisis intervention: Therapy outcome study.* Unpublished doctoral dissertation, University of Utah.

Paton, S., Kessler, R., & Kandel, D. (1977). Depressive mood and adolescent alcohol and drug use: A longitudinal analysis. *Journal of Genetic Psychology, 131,* 267–289.

Petrie, A. (1978). *Individuality in pain and suffering* (rev. ed.). Chicago: University of Chicago Press.

Pollock, V. E., Volavka, J., Goodwin, D. W., Mednick, S. A., Gabrielli, W. F., Knop, J., & Schulsinger, F. (1983). The EEG after alcohol administration in men at risk for alcoholism. *Archives of General Psychiatry, 40,* 857–861.

Prescott, J. W. (1980). Somatosensory affectional deprivation (SAD) theory of drug and alcohol use. In D. J. Lettieri, M. Sayers, & H. W. Pearson (Eds.), *Theories on drug abuse,* (National Institute on Drug Abuse Research Monograph 30, DHHS Publication No. ADM 80-967, pp. 286–296.) Washington, DC: U.S. Government Printing Office.

Prewett, M. J., Spencer, R., & Chaknis, M. (1981). Attribution of causality by children with alcoholic parents. *The International Journal of Addictions, 16*(2), 367–370.

Prochaska, J. (1979). *Symptoms of Psychotherapy.* Georgetown: Dorsey Press.

Propping, P., Kruger, J., & Janah, A. (1980). Genetic aspects of alcohol action on the electroencephalogram (EEG). In H. Begleiter (Ed.), *Biological effects of alcohol.* New York: Plenum Press.

Propping, P., Kruger, J., & Mark, W. (1981). Genetic disposition to alcoholism: An EEG study in alcoholics and their relatives. *Human Genetics, 59,* 51–59.

Rathod, N. H., & Thompson, I. G. (1971). Women alcoholics: A clinical study. *Quarterly Journal of Studies on Alcohol, 32,* 45–52.

Reese, D. (1985, January). *Characteristics of men and women alcoholics in inpatient treatment.* Paper presented at Social Research Institute colloquium, University of Utah.

Reilly, D. M. (1979). Family factors in the etiology and treatment of youthful drug abuse. *Family Therapy, 11,* 149–171.

Research Triangle Institute (1984). *Economic costs to society of alcohol and drug abuse and mental illness: 1980.* Research Triangle Park, North Carolina.

Robins, L. N. (1978). Sturdy childhood predictors of adult antisocial behavior: Replications from longitudinal studies. *Psychological Medicine, 8,* 611–622.

Rose, M., Battjes, R., & Leukefeld, C. (1984). *Family life skills training for drug abuse prevention* (DHHS Publication No. ADM 84-1340). Washington, DC: U.S. Government Printing Office.

Rosenberg, C. M. (1969). Young drug addicts: Background and personality. *Journal of Nervous and Mental Disease, 148,* 66–73.

Russell, M., Henderson, C., & Blume, S. (1985). *Children of alcoholics: A review of the literature.* New York: Children of Alcoholics Foundation, Inc.

Rutter, M., & Giller, H. (1983). *Juvenile delinquency: Trends and perspectives.* New York: Penguin Books.

Schuckit, M. (1973). Alcoholism and sociopathy—diagnostic confusion. *Quarterly Journal of Studies on Alcohol, 34,* 157–164.

Schuckit, M. (1983). A prospective study of genetic markers in alcoholism. In I. Hanin, & E. Usden (Eds.), *Biological markers in psychiatry and neurology.* Oxford: Pergamon Press.

Schuckit, M., & Rayses, V. (1979). Ethanol ingestion: Differences in blood acetaldehyde concentrations in relatives of alcoholics and controls. *Science, 203,* 54–55.

Schuckit, M. A. (1980a). Self-rating of alcohol intoxication by young men with and without family histories of alcoholism. *Journal of Studies on Alcohol, 41*(3), 242–249.

Schuckit, M. A. (1980b). A theory of alcohol and drug abuse: A genetic approach. In D. Lettieri, M. Sayers, & H. W. Pearson (Eds.), *Theories on drug abuse,* (National Institute on Drug Abuse Research Monograph 30, DHHS Publication No. ADM 80-967, pp. 297–302). Washington, DC: U.S. Government Printing Office.

Schuckit, M. A., & Bernstein, L. T. (1981). Sleep time and drinking history: A hypothesis. *American Journal of Psychiatry, 138*(4), 528–530.

Schuckit, M., Engstrom, D., Alpert, R., & Duby, J. (1981). Differences in muscle-tension response to ethanol in young men with and without family histories of alcoholism. *Journal of Studies on Alcohol, 42,* 918–924.

Seldin, N. E. (1972). The family of the addict: A review of the literature. *International Journal of the Addictions, 7,* 97–107.

Smart, R. G., & Fejer, D. (1972, April). Drug use among adolescents and their parents: Closing the generation gap in mood modification. *Journal of Abnormal Psychology, 79*(2) 153–160.

Smith, G. M., & Fogg, C. P. (1978). Psychological antecedents of teenage drug use. In R. G. Simmons (Ed.), *Research in community and mental health* (Vol. 1, pp. 87–102). Greenwich, CN: JAI Press.

Sowder, B., & Burt, M. (1978a). *Children of Addicts and Nonaddicts: A Comparative Investigation in Five Urban Sites.* (Report to NIDA.) Bethesda, MD.: Burt Associates, Inc.

Sowder, B., & Burt, M. (1978b, November). *Children of Addicts: A population in need of coordinated comprehensive mental health services.* Paper presented at the American Association of Psychiatric Services for Children, Atlanta, GA.

Spanier, G. B. (1976, February). Measuring dyadic adjustment: New scales for assessing the quality of marriage and similar dyads. *Journal of Marriage and the Family,* 15–28.

Spivak, G. (1983). *High risk early behaviors indicating vulnerability to delinquency in the community and school.* National Institute of Juvenile Justice and Delinquency Prevention, Office of Juvenile Justice and Delinquency Prevention, Law Enforcement Assistance Administration. Washington, DC: U.S. Government Printing Office.

Stanton, M. D. (1979). The client as family member: Aspects of continuing treatment. In B. S. Brown (Ed.), *Addicts and aftercare: Community integration of the former drug abuser.* Beverly Hills, CA: Sage Publications.

Stone, L. H., Miranne, A. C., & Ellis, G. J. (1979). Parent-peer influence as a predictor of marijuana use. *Adolescence, 14*(53), 115–122.

Streit, F. (1973). A test and procedure to identify secondary school children who have a high probability of drug abuse (Doctoral dissertation, Rutgers University). *Dissertation Abstracts International, 34,* 5177B. (University Microfilms No. 74-8875)

Taraschi, T. F., & Rubin, E. (1985). Biology of disease: Effects of ethanol on the chemical and structural properties of biologic membranes. *United States-Canadian Division of the International Academy of Pathology, 52*(2), 120–131.

Templer, D. I., Russ, C. F., & Ayers, J. (1974). Essential alcoholism and family history of alcoholism. *Quarterly Journal of Studies on Alcohol, 35,* 655–657.

Tennant, F. S. (1976). Dependency traits among parents of drug abusers. *Journal of Drug Dependence,* 6(1), 83–88.

Tennant, F. S., Jr., Detels, R., & Clark, V. (1975). Some childhood antecedents of drug and alcohol abuse. *American Journal of Epidemiology, 102,* 377–385.

Vaillant, G. E., & Milofsky, E. S. (1982). The etiology of alcoholism: A prospective viewpoint. *American Psychologist, 37*(5), 494–503.

Vogel, F., Schalt, E., Kruger, J., Propping, P., & Lehnert, K. F. (1979). The electroencephalogram (EEG) as a research tool in human behavior genetics: Psychological examinations in healthy males with various inherited EEG variants. *Human Genetics, 47,* 1–45.

Wahler, R., Leske, G., & Rogers, E. (1979). The insular family: A deviance support system for oppositional children. In L. S. Hamerlynck (Ed.), *Behavioral systems for the developmentally disabled. 1: School and family environments.* New York: Brunner/Mazel.

Wechsler, H., & Thum, D. (1973). Teenage drinking, drug use, and social correlates. *Quarterly Journal of Studies on Alcohol, 34,* 1220–1227.

Wegscheider, D., & Wegscheider, S. (1978). *Family illness: Chemical dependency.* Crystal, MN: Nurturing Networks.

Wegscheider, S. (1981). *Another chance: Hope and help for the alcoholic family.* Palo Alto, CA: Science and Behavior Books.

Wolin, S. J., Bennett, L. A., & Noonan, D. L. (1979). Family rituals and the recurrence of alcoholism over generations. *American Journal of Psychiatry, 136,* 589–593.

Wolin, S. J., Bennett, L. A., Noonan, D. L., & Teitelbaum, M. A. (1980). Disrupted family rituals. *Journal of Studies on Alcohol, 41*(3), 199–214.

Yamaguchi, K., & Kandel, D. B. (1984). Patterns of drug use from adolescence to young adulthood: III. Predictors of progression. *American Journal of Public Health, 74,* 673–681.

York, P., York, D., & Wachtel, T. (1982). *Toughlove.* New York: Bantam Books.

Young, S., & West, S. (1985, April). *Factors influencing the onset of substance abuse: a chronological review of the literature, 1973–1983.* Final report to Utah State Division of Alcoholism and Drugs.

Ziegler-Driscoll, G. (1977). Family research study at Eagleville hospital and rehabilitation center. *Family Process, 16,* 175–189.

Zuckerman, M. Neary, R. S., & Brustman, B. A. (1970). Sensation-seeking scale correlates in experience (smoking, drugs, alcohol, hallucinations and sex) and preference for complexity (designs). *Proceedings of the 78th Annual Convention of the American Psychological Association,* Vol. 5. Washington, DC: American Psychological Association.

Zuckerman, M., Murtaugh, T., & Siegel, J. (1974). Sensation seeking and cortical augmenting-reducing. *Psychophysiology, 11,* 535–542.

PART II: PREVENTION

Introduction

Prevention, as a scientifically quantified and evaluated process, has experienced much controversy since its inception during the late sixties as a method of approaching the problems of chemical abuse. This section reflects the evolution in prevention which has occurred over the last decade along with a variety of strategies which have withstood the test of scientific investigation.

Bukoski discusses research and projects in school-based initiatives and looks at a number of skill based projects which focus on developing resistance to use. DeMarsh and Kumpfer review recent family oriented prevention activities which include parent training (affective and behavioral), family skills training, family therapy, and family self-help groups. Wallack presents information on the media programs focused towards youth. He discusses television promotion programs, the advertising industry's role and a comprehensive integrated approach to the media role in chemical abuse prevention. Johnson et al. discuss the results of ongoing community prevention research projects.

School-Based Substance Abuse Prevention: A Review of Program Research

William J. Bukoski, PhD

ABSTRACT. Recent reviews of school-based substance abuse prevention research indicate that a variety of prevention activities have been inplemented in schools throughout the country. This review classifies prevention programs into one of five educational domains: cognitive, affective/interpersonal, behavioral, environmental and therapeutic. Research findings for each domain are discussed.

Over the last decade, school-based drug education programs have been viewed as one of the primary methods to prevent drug, alcohol use/abuse and cigarette smoking. Numerous and quite distinctly different preventive strategies have been developed and implemented in the form of special curriculum or as units within a school health education program. In general, the content of prevention programs has attempted to alert youth to the nature and consequences of substance abuse through information dissemination, affective education techniques, and most recently social skill training. In addition to instructional programs focused upon a child's cognitive and social development, school administrators have attempted to establish and enforce clear-cut school policies, procedures, and sanctions concerning the use and sale of

William J. Bukoski is a Psychologist with the Prevention Research Branch of the National Institute on Drug Abuse, Room 10A-20, 5600 Fishers Lane, Rockville, MD 20857.

drugs on school grounds. The purpose of this paper is to provide an overview of school-based programs designed to prevent the use and abuse of substances, such as alcohol, tobacco, marijuana, and other drugs. Since drug education frequently focuses upon multiple substances to include alcohol and cigarettes, the terms substance abuse education and drug education will be used interchangeably in this paper.

Depending upon the emphasis given, these diverse prevention activities will be classified by the author for the purpose of this paper into one of five educational domains relevant to the learning experiences of the child: cognitive, affective/interpersonal, behavioral, environmental, and therapeutic.

The *cognitive* domain focuses upon increasing students' knowledge of the pharmacologic effects and physical/social hazards of substance use, and molding of attitudes and belief structures that are not supportive of personal substance use and abuse.

The *affective* and *interpersonal* domain includes prevention activities that attempt to strengthen the child's inner emotional and psychological resources by improving self-concept and self-worth and by assisting children to become more knowledgeable about their own feelings and those of others. In many instances, these programs do not focus on the use of drugs per se, but on the general process of a child's social and psychological development and adjustment. The objectives of these programs are reached with a variety of methods to include classroom activities, the use of peer group discussions and professional consultation on an individual or group basis.

The *behavioral* domain includes approaches to prevention based upon the tenets of behavioral therapy and train youth in socially relevant and appropriate responses to resist social pressure (from peers, family and media) to use alcohol, tobacco and marijuana. These programs structure the training through six steps: instruction and coaching in resistance techniques and other social skills, modeling of the desired behavior by peers, guided practice and role playing, feedback from peers/instructor, social reinforcement through praise, and training for generalization of the new skill to the child's natural environment.

The *environmental* domain includes preventive strategies and school management activities implemented by school administrators to deal with student drug problems. These range from establishment and enforcement of tougher school drug policies to better coordination of school prevention activities with relevant student, PTA, community, and parent groups. These approaches recognize that students and parents have an important preventive role to play in changing school norms regarding drug use behavior.

Finally, the *therapeutic* domain includes preventive interventions for those children who are already experiencing a variety of adjustment problems with school, family, and community. This domain includes programs that focus upon early identification and referral or provide an alternative day school learning environment. These separate, yet state-certified educational programs, offer to problem youth the opportunity to continue their education, but within a therapeutic group environment. Youth are referred to day school programs (when these programs are available) by school officials, youth welfare agency staff, or by juvenile probation personnel for a variety of offenses, such as incorrigible behavior, truancy, or suspected drug or alcohol use/abuse. The purpose of these programs is to provide individual or group counselling, special educational programming and the required instruction in basic subjects such as math, science, reading, in a more disciplined and structured, yet non-resident setting. Student participation in these programs varies from attending the program full time for a specified period and thereafter returning to their regular schools, to attending the program several days a week in conjunction with their regular school program.

A variety of substance abuse prevention programs have been initiated by schools. Figure 1 illustrates how these educational activities can be classified by this descriptive typology. As indicated, drug education is not a unitary concept. Rather, it embraces a variety of approaches and subject content that correspond to different models of the etiology of adolescent drug use, the social and psychological development of children, and the perception of school officials and parents as to appropriate social monitoring and intervention practices by responsible adults. Numerous excellent references are available which further describe these preventive program approaches and related research. (Glynn and Leuke-

Figure 1: Prevention Education Domains and Program Focus

| Individual | | | School | |
Cognitive	Affective/ Interpersonal	Behavioral	Environmental	Therapeutic
o Pharmacologic effects of drugs on biologic systems and behavior	o Decision making o Values clarification o Problem solving o Communication processes	o Refusal skill training (Saying No)	o School Policy: -adoption/ enforcement of school drug policy	o Alternative Day School Programs -basic education -counseling -drug education -behavior management
o Health and social causes and consequences of drug abuse	o Self-concept develop. o Increasing awareness of emotions o Discussion (rap) groups	o Social Consequences o Normative Expectations o (Short-term) Health Consequences o Counter Advertising Techniques	o Detection: -Locker searches -Under cover agents	
o School/ community norms and legal sanctions	o Peer counselling o Counselling intervention	o Within Class Role Models o Personal Commitment to Refuse drugs	o School organization: -students against drunk driving -PTA programs -school teams approach	
o General health education		o Alternatives	o Community organization: -chemical people -concerned parents movement	

98

feld, 1983; Ellis, Indyke and Debevoise, 1980; Manatt, 1983; and Bell and Battjes, in press).

In addition to considerable variation in subject matter content and focus, drug education as it pertains to the individual student has been inplemented with a variety of instructional methods to include: didactic instruction by classroom teachers or health educators; reality oriented assembly programs presented by ex-addicts, law enforcement officials or physicians; small group discussions facilitated by either trained counsellors or peer leaders; the use of films, video tapes or filmstrips; information brochures, pamphlets; self-tests; monographs; and drug paraphernalia displays. Prevention instruction has been presented as discrete lessons in a regular class or has been structured into formal drug and alcohol abuse curricula to include teacher manuals, student guides, films, and posters. Prevention programs have ranged from "one-shot" activities prompted by the interests of a school principal, teacher or parent to a semester or year long formal instructional programs mandated by a school system for specified grades.

For the most part, the program audience has been elementary, junior or senior high school populations, rather than selected groups of previously identified high risk youth. In general, school prevention programs have focused prevention instruction on the individual student in the general school population. Rarely have prevention programs systematically included parents, guardians, or older siblings as an integral part of the instruction. Often drug education is focused on the middle/junior high and senior high school population though substance abuse education for elementary school students has been made available in some school systems with the adoption of a K-12 substance abuse program, such as in the New York State. When the target audience is elementary grade students, the focus of the instruction tends to be more developmental and general in nature, such as dealing with values, decisions, intrapersonal feelings, and communicating with others. Recently, however, this is beginning to change with the addition of more drug specific information into the curriculum.

Overall, the extent and quality of formal instruction devoted to drug education or health education in the schools is not actually known (Krueter, Christenson & Davis, 1983). Though forty-three States recommend health education, only twenty-four States include health education as a graduation requirement (Gilbert & Pruitt, 1984). On a more practical basis, Gilbert and Pruitt estimate that secondary school students receive on the average of 43.7 hours of health instruction over the course of four years of high school or roughly 1% of the available instructional time. In comparison, approximately 16.7% of instructional time is devoted to English and 10% to Social Studies. The amount of health instruction in grades K-8 has not been determined. There is a strong indication that with the current trend in schools to emphasize basic instruction in math, reading and the sciences, there may be a growing resistance to using class time for perceived social problems, such as drug abuse, consumer education or unsafe driving (Adler, 1983).

This observation seems to be supported by national annual survey data that in part addresses the issue. Analysis of multiple year data from the National Drug Abuse Survey of High School Seniors (Johnston, Bachman & O'Malley, 1976–1983) indicates that the percentage of seniors having received any drug education course or lectures in school declined from 79.2% in 1976 to 67.8% in 1982. For the most part, these instructional experiences were not formal courses but films, lectures or discussions that occurred within a regular class. In 1982, 75.5%* of the seniors in the Johnston survey reported receiving some (minimal) drug education activity while only 20.2%* reported receiving a special formal course about substance abuse.

Despite the relative infrequent exposure to drug education, these students reported that the information presented by their prevention sessions/courses was of value and that the drug information provided by school prevention activities made them less interested in trying drugs. Those students less interested in trying drugs because of the knowledge gained in their drug education courses increased from 50.5% in 1976 to 56.9% in 1982, and reached a high of 58.8% in 1981. From these data it appears that despite the health and social significance of substance abuse, most students have not experienced a structured course of instruction in drug abuse prevention.

---

*Note: Multiple responses to this item were possible. The other categories included were film or lecture outside of my regular courses (25.2%) and special discussion ("rap" groups) about drugs (20.7%).

As indicated, drug prevention education has not been a unitary instructional phenomenon that is implemented with uniformity across school systems. Rather, the nature and scope of drug prevention education varies from state to state, school system to school system, and from classroom to classroom. The degree of emphasis given to drug abuse within the public schools varies with the perceived social significance of the problem as viewed by society, school administrators, school boards, the instructional staff and parents.

REVIEW OF RESEARCH FINDINGS

In general, research indicates that most substance abuse prevention education has not been shown effective in preventing or delaying the onset of drug or alcohol use/abuse (Kinder, Pape & Walfish, 1980; Plant, 1980; Schaps, DiBartolo, Moskowitz, Pulley & Churgin, 1981; Goodstadt & Sheppard, 1983; Battjes, 1985). While research indicates that drug prevention programs can increase the level of drug knowledge for students participating in the program, for the most part these increases were not accompanied by changes in drug use attitudes, intentions or behaviors (Moskowitz, 1983). In many drug education courses that have been researched in the past, the programs did not include behavioral objectives regarding drug use (Braucht, Follingstad, Brakarsh & Berry, 1973; Goodstadt, 1981) which made it difficult to assess possible contributing factors to this lack of effectiveness.

The development of effective, testable drug abuse prevention programs has been hampered by the lack of prevention theories of the etiology of drug abuse that have direct relevance for prevention program design. As a result, the development and implementation of drug abuse educational curricula has tended to be atheoretical and based upon educational judgements relevant to the correlates of drug abuse which do abound in the research literature.

Cognitive Domain

Moskowitz (1983), in his review of drug education, discussed research related to the first three domains of school-based prevention. Pertinent to the cognitive domain, he indicates that the causal relationship between changing drug use knowledge, attitudes, intentions and behaviors (in that sequence) has not been demonstrated. Rather, research shows that this model fails to account for the influence of prior substance abuse and that intentions to use do not account sufficiently for the variance of use when controlling for prior use (Bentler & Speckart, 1979; Huba, Wingard & Bentler, 1980, 1981; Schlegal, Crawford & Sanborn, 1977). Situational factors tend to play an important role in adolescent drug use. Research by Schaps, Moskowitz, Marvin and Schaffer (1982) of a drug education program administered to three experimental cohorts of seventh and eighth graders indicates that even a well developed, well implemented, and rigorously evaluated drug education course failed to demonstrate a pattern of positive behavioral changes in drug use (or mediating variables) over a short (immediate posttest) or a long term (one year posttest).

Affective Domain

The second domain in drug education, *affective/interpersonal,* includes programs that attempt to improve self-concept, to develop self-understanding and acceptance, and to promote responsible decision making. These approaches usually do not focus directly on drug use/abuse, but instead are viewed as generic prevention programs. Though many school-based drug education programs include activities to improve a youth's view of self and increase his/her awareness of the decision making process, little empirical support exists for this strategy to delay the onset of drug use behavior (Huba et al., 1980; Goodstadt, 1980). For example, Goodstadt and Sheppard's (1983) research of three prevention program types (cognitive, values clarification, decision making) indicates that though the cognitive (knowledge of alcohol) approach did raise levels of knowledge for high school students, no prevention strategy (decision making, values clarification strategy, or the cognitive strategy) produced significant (and predicted differences) in attitudes toward alcohol use, reported use or intention to use alcohol in the future.
Recent large scale studies of affective strategies by Schaps et al. (1984), such as Effective Classroom Management tech-

niques for elementary and junior high school teachers (Moskowitz, 1984), Magic Circle (Moskowitz, Schaps & Malvin, 1982), or Jigsaw, a cooperative learning strategy (Moskowitz, Schaps, Schaeffer & Malving, 1984), did not result in significant predicted changes between treatment and control students on drug related variables.

It is possible that affective education strategies have failed to prevent the onset of drug or alcohol use because they may have placed too much emphasis on concepts and process and too little emphasis on the direct acquisition and mastery of those social skills necessary to increase personal and social competency, particularly those skills needed by youth to resist peer pressures to begin using drugs.

Behavioral Domain

The third domain of school-based prevention, *behavioral* training of relevant social skills, currently offers the most promise for school-based prevention programming. It will become, therefore, a major focus of this paper. This approach is based upon the theoretical and experimental research of Bandura (1977) who postulates a theory of social learning which incorporates both behavioral and cognitive components as explanatory elements for the acquisition and maintenance of behavior. In this view, health behaviors, such as cigarette smoking, exercise, and weight control are socially acquired and dependent upon the interaction of the individual within the social environment. Role modeling, reinforcement, establishment of normative expectations, and coping with social pressures are essential features of this theory of behavioral change.

Substance abuse prevention programs based upon these principles consider that the onset of cigarette smoking, alcohol use and other drug use, such as marijuana, are acquired behaviors derived from social pressures and reinforced by friends, family, the media and community norms (Johnson & Sollis, 1983). For program interventions to change health behaviors successfully, a person must be trained in the appropriate social skills, such as using assertive expressions and must be provided with a strong sense of self-belief that he or she can perform this skill successfully at the appropriate time and circumstance (Pentz, 1983). This latter program element involves a cognitive structure which Bandura labels as self-efficacy. In simplest terms, to acquire and maintain a relevant health behavior, a person must have both mastered a specific overt behavior (e.g., assertive expression of self-rights/wishes) and have the self-confidence that he or she can perform that behavior succesfully within the social setting. Both are essential and both must be addressed explicitly by the intervention program.

Most of the research on this approach to drug education has focused upon the prevention of cigarette smoking by adolescents. The prevention of cigarette smoking is important because of the addictive quality of tobacco (DHHS, 1984) and because cigarette smoking is considered as one of several risk factors to the onset in use of other drugs, such as marijuana (Kandel, 1982). A variety of independent researchers have demonstrated that prevention program interventions, based upon the concepts of social learning theory, can prevent or delay the onset of cigarette smoking by some adolescents when comparing treatment and control groups (Evans, 1976; Evans, Henderson, Hill & Raines, 1979; Perry, Killen, Slinkard & McAlister, 1980; Hurd et al., 1980; Johnson, 1982; Telch, Killen, McAlister, Perry & Maccoby, 1982; Botvin & Eng, 1982; Botvin, Eng & Williams, 1980; Botvin, 1983; Botvin, Baker, Renick, Filazzola & Botvin, 1984; Flay et al., 1985). Flay (in press) in a recent review of four generations of research of social psychological approaches to smoking prevention covering twenty-six school based studies, indicates that these programs appear to be effective in preventing smoking onset. Though individual studies have methodological weaknesses that can be criticized, the overall positive effects reported are comparable across studies. Flay indicates that, in general, students in the experimental prevention curricula have demonstrated lower rates of smoking onset than controls. Despite the promise of these findings, Flay also indicates that much has yet to be learned from research on these techniques, such as why they may work, for whom they may work best, how well they work with youth at higher risk of smoking onset than average school populations, and how long the preventive effects would be expected to be maintained.

Several research reports describe the key components of

these programs (Johnson, 1982; DHHS, 1984; Battjes, 1985). In general, these preventive interventions have ranged in length from 5 to 20 classroom sessions, administered over one semester or over one school year. The major focus of most efforts has been to provide youth social pressure resistance and assertiveness skills to counter the strong influences to smoke cigarettes emanating from peers, the media and adult role models. Short-term health consequences of smoking (rather than long-term health consequences, e.g., the risk of cancer) are depicted as well, such as indicating the immediate physiologic effect of increased respiration rate and decreased lung capacity that results from smoking just one cigarette. More recent program efforts have given primary emphasis to the social consequences of smoking, because these issues appear to be more salient for youth. Youth are guided through Socratic teaching techniques to assess the immediate, social consequences of smoking cigarettes, such as having bad breath, accidentally burning holes in one's clothing, and actually looking foolish while attempting to imitate adult smoking behaviors.

A methodological procedure common to this collection of studies is the validation of cigarette self-report data with physiological measures, such as saliva thiocyanate or expired air carbon monoxide. Through standardized procedures, a sample of saliva or expired air is taken from students in the study, analyzed and then cross-checked against self-report data. In the case of saliva thiocyanate testing, the analysis is usually completed for a sample of students in the study. In essence, physiological testing provides a quantitative measure of cigarette use and in addition, may improve the accuracy of student self-reporting of cigarette use because of student knowledge and awareness of the validity of these measures.

The social psychological prevention programs also share common or comparable instructional methods or techniques. Rather than provide the content of the course in didactic fashion, these programs employ instructional activities that are characteristic of behavioral training. Rosenthal and Bandura (1978) have delineated four key components that are basic to a behavioral approach to instruction: role modelling of the desired behavior, guided practice and rehearsal of the new behavior, feedback on skill attainment, and reinforcement of the desired behavior.

From descriptions of the prevention interventions included in the earlier research literature and from the recent reviews of research by Flay (in press) and Battjes (1985), the presence of these four behavioral components within the instruction is evident. *First,* peer models demonstrating desired behavior (e.g., saying no to cigarettes) are included within the context of the training process. In the series of studies cited above, both live role models (peers) and videotaped or filmed role models have been utilized. *Second,* the intervention provided students sufficient, guided practice and rehearsal of the new skill in the social setting. Students were provided structured opportunities (through role play) to master the appropriate verbal responses needed to say "no" to a variety of social pressures to smoke a cigarette. *Third,* positive feedback in the form of constructive criticism on skill performance was provided by the teacher and classmates. Feedback was used to pinpoint the strengths of the role playing activity, and to offer suggestions for improvement. *Fourth,* reinforcement for the desired behavior was provided through several means, such as class applause for a role play that was well done, individual words of encouragement provided by the teacher and by fellow students, and in some studies by replay of a video tape of a saying no role play or personal testimony not to use drugs as presented by students in the classroom.

In several studies, a *fifth* behavioral component has been employed, training for generalization. This has been accomplished through the use of homework assignments for students which involved parents or siblings, completion of role play dialogue checklists and the use of questions and answers on the activities covered in prior classes before starting a new session. A variation of extended practice was employed in several of the studies. Students were asked at the end of the training course, as a course assignment, to write out how and why they would resist an offer to smoke that might realistically occur after school. Then they are asked to read their responses against smoking before the class. Finally, some programs have used student administered surveys of their parents or guardian on attitudes toward cigarette smoking by adolescents. This homework activity provided students an opportunity to discuss with family members several of the issues on resisting pressure to smoke being discussed in their prevention programs and to explore with family members the social and health consequences of smoking.

Rather than focusing primarily on resistance training, a more generalized but comparable behavioral approach has been developed and tested by Botvin (1982). This program, entitled "Life Skills Training" (LST), teaches adolescents general social skills, such as expression of one's rights, praise, disagreement; initiating meaningful conversation; refusal skills; decision making; and coping with anxiety. In Botvin's model, resistance training is but one of several social skills taught to sixth and seventh graders. Research on this technique for the prevention of cigarette smoking has been positive in that over a series of controlled studies, the program has been shown to significantly reduce the onset of cigarette use when comparing treatment and control students (Botvin et al., 1980; Botvin et al., 1982).

In a recent study, Botvin et al. (1984) tesed a twenty-session LST program with seventh graders to assess changes not only in cigarette smoking but also alcohol and marijuana use. Four schools were randomly assigned to each treatment level (peer-led LST and teacher-led LST) and two schools served as controls. Peer leaders were selected from the tenth and eleventh grades. Both peer leaders and teachers were trained by the researchers to implement the program. First year results indicate that at posttest statistically significant positive effects were attributed to the peer-led treatment with those students reporting significantly less alcohol use per occasion, and significantly less monthly and weekly use of marijuana. Cigarette smoking (monthly use) was also significantly reduced for students in the peer-led LST program. This research is continuing with the addition of a booster program in the second year in the two schools and follow-up assessment of the use of alcohol, cigarettes, and marijuana.

A general life skills approach to the prevention of cigarette smoking has been studied by other researchers as well with comparable degrees of reported effects (Pentz 1983; Schinke and Blythe, 1982; Schinke, Gilchrist & Snow, 1985). In addition, other studies support the use of social skills training for deficiency remediation or for the promotion of positive behaviors in related problem areas, such as delinquency, academic failure, social inhibition, aggressive behavior and some psychiatric disorders (Goldstein, Sherman, Gershaw, Sprafkin & Glick, 1978, Quay and Quay, 1965; Brady, 1984).

Overall, the social skills approach to substance abuse prevention and for other social problem areas shows striking promise, particularly in comparison to prior approaches such as the cognitive and affective approaches to prevention which have been and continue to be characteristic of school-based drug prevention programs.

School Environment Domain

In addition to focusing upon the individual student, prevention programs have attempted to modify the school environment and enhance the capability of the school system to better meet the learning needs of students exhibiting problem behaviors with alternative instructional programs that are both educational and therapeutic in nature.

Recognizing the threat of drug use to the health and learning potential of students, schools have tried to establish drug free instructional environments. Numerous activities have been implemented to meet this goal and can be classified under one of three catagories: school policy/enforcement; drug detection; and organization development and activation.

Through the enactment and enforcement of clear and unambiguous school policy prohibiting student use and sale of alcohol and drugs, schools clearly communicate to students, faculty and parents that substance use and abuse is inconsistent with sound educational practices and will be met with appropriate corrective actions (USDOJ, 1978). This response frequently includes punitive measures, such as suspension from school; educational measures, such as referral to counselling; and, corrective measures involving parents, law enforcement officials and/or drug treatment personnel.

Model school policies on alcohol and drugs have been developed by Federal, state and local agencies. For example, the Drug Enforcement Administration (USDOJ, 1978) produced a handbook for school policy and has supported pilot community projects to develop and test school substance abuse policy. This model has been used by a variety of States (e.g., Maryland State Department of Education, 1982) to create statewide school policy on alcohol and drugs that provides guidance to school administrators and teachers relevant to planning prevention education programs; identifying teacher training needs; student referral to treatment; rights of students; the appropriate role of school staff, relevant to disciplinary actions; and the role of law enforcement agencies, parents and the community.

A second category of school action has been detection. A variety of techniques and tactics have been employed by school officials acting within their own school's policy to identify both the students using drugs and individuals dispensing drugs on school grounds. Newspaper stories and magazines (Tressler, 1985) on these efforts indicate that the tactics employed include: the search of lockers and persons suspected of drug use/possession; the deployment of law enforcement officers acting as students and operating as undercover agents; and more recently, the use of annual drug screening tests of students through urinalysis (Narvaez, 1985). In the latter case, the School Board of East Rutherford, New Jersey voted to require annual drug tests through analysis of urine samples of all high school students beginning in the Fall of 1985. The School Board's action would permit the tests to be done by a physician at the school or by a private physician and would require medical certification that the student is in healthy condition in order to attend school.

Through detection techniques such as these, schools are attempting to establish a learning environment that is not conducive to drug use or ambiguous about the unacceptability of student drug use. Schools recognize that if a school's alcohol and drug policy is to work, it needs to be enforced. Detection techniques are one mechanism for creating a drug free school environment.

The third category of school focused prevention is organization development and activation. Schools recognize that parent and community input, involvement, and cooperative effort is essential for creating a school environment free of drugs. One example, is the Department of Education's Alcohol and Drug Abuse Education Program and its School Teams Approach (U.S. Dept. of Education, 1982). Under training grants supported by the U.S. Department of Education, school team volunteers include: principals, teachers, school counselors, community representatives, school board members and parents who receive specialized training in prevention program development, group organization and action planning at one of five regional training centers. The training is designed to assist teams to organize, plan, and effectively implement substance prevention activities upon return to their respective schools. Follow-up assistance is also provided to trained teams. Since the inception of the program in 1970, it has trained over 4,500 school-community teams (U.S. Department of Education, 1982). The purpose of the program is to create a knowledgeable cadre of prevention oriented school and community leaders who develop a prevention action plan that will alert the school and community to the problem of drug abuse and provide prevention related information and educational activities. Teams are trained to select or develop programs/activities most needed by their own schools. These activities have varied from developing a public service announcement and brochure on how to give a safe (alcohol/drug free) party to workshops for students and parents on improving communication.

A variety of other examples of school organization and activation can be discussed to include: NIDA's Teens in Action (Adams & Resnick, 1985); prevention activities sponsored by Concerned Parents for Drug Free Youth (Manatt, 1983); programs that focus on creating positive peer influences (NIDA, 1984); and, the Chemical People project (Community Action Project, n.d.). Though the primary organization and specific emphasis is different for each of these prevention programs, all have attempted to involve the school and activate students and school personnel to prevent substance abuse. Most importantly, all of these programs have attempted a comprehensive approach to prevention to include not only school staff and youth but also parents, community leaders, the media, law enforcement officials and health care providers representing the treatment community.

Therapeutic Domain—Alternative Day Schools

Beyond creating a drug free school environment, school administrators have also focused upon expanding and enhancing the capacity of the school system to meet the learning needs of students exibiting problem behaviors, such as truancy, persistent disruptive behavior, and poor academic performance. In these cases, drug use/abuse may be implicated or suspected as a related problem. One attempt has been through the development of alternative day schools. These programs integrate remedial basic education with therapeutic techniques to include individual counselling, group counselling, and behavioral modification/management techniques involving a token economy or reinforcement schedules to elicit positive school behaviors (Ottenberg, Olsen & Schiller, 1985; Cohen, 1985).

In an evaluation of four alternative day school programs in Pennsylvania, Pomerantz and Clark (1983) indicate that children attending alternative day schools demonstrate behavioral patterns and psychological profiles characteristic of high risk youth. The life histories of these students indicate repeated instances of misbehavior, acting out at school, and in many cases, frequent, experimentation with a variety of substances, to include alcohol and marijuana. The alternative day offers youth at risk of substance abuse and addiction, school failure, delinquency, and continual drift toward a negative life style to regain control of their lives through a highly structured academic and therapeutically oriented alternative. The objective of an alternative day school program is to redirect students from the road to academic and social failure and return these youth (usually within a year) to the regular school program for the completion of their education with a higher probability of success.

Though drug prevention through changes in the school's environment and its capacity to better meet individual dysfunctionality appears promising, rigorous research on their preventive effects is just emerging. In general, concrete research findings gathered under controlled conditions are lacking. What does exist are positive assessments, anecdotal in nature, from students, teachers, parents and school administrators. Though these reports are encouraging, systematic assessment and controlled research is needed to better understand the needs of high risk youth and to assess the extent to which a variety of different preventive activities can delay or prevent the onset of adolescent substance abuse.

CONCLUSION

School administrators are faced with many difficult decisions concerning the selection of an appropriate programmatic response to the problem of adolescent drug use/abuse. A variety of prevention techniques have been tried and researched in the past without positive indication of effectiveness. Behavioral training in relevant social skills, particularly resistance or assertiveness training, offers promising research findings that these programs can prevent the onset of cigarette smoking and possibly the use of alcohol and marijuana by junior high students. Further research, however, is needed to determine why these strategies work, for whom they work best, the duration of the positive effect and the conditions required for effective implementation of these curriculum within operational school settings. In addition, research is needed to determine the effectiveness of prevention activities and management practices that attempt to establish a drug free school environment and that better meet the needs of high risk youth. If schools are to succeed in their educational mission, the threat of drug use and abuse must be recognized and effective preventive interventions implemented.

REFERENCES

Adams, T., & Resnik, H. (1985). *Teens in action*. National Institute on Drug Abuse (DHHS Pub. No. ADM 85-1376). Washington, DC: U.S. Government Printing Office.

Adler, M. (1983). *The paideia problems and possibilities*. New York: McMillan Publishing Co.

Bandura, A. (1977). *Social learning Theory*. Englewood Cliffs, N.J.: Prentice Hall.

Battjes, R. (1985). Prevention of adolescent drug abuse. *The International Journal of Addictions, 20* (6&7), 1113–1135.

Bell, C., & Battjes, B. (Eds.) (1985). *Prevention research: Deterring drug abuse among children and adolescents* (DHHS Publ. No. ADM 85-1334). Washington, DC: U.S. Government Printing Office.

Bentler, P., & Speckart, G. (1979). Models of attitude-behavior relations. *Psychological Review, 86,* 452–464.

Botvin, G. (1983). Prevention of adolescent substance abuse through the development of personal and social competence. In T. Glynn, & C. Leukefeld (Eds.), *Preventing adolescent drug abuse: Intervention strategies* (DHHS Pub. No. ADM 83-1280). Washington, DC: U.S. Government Printing Office.

Botvin, G. (1982). Broadening the focus of smoking prevention strategies. In T. Coates, A. Peterson, & C. Perry (Eds.), *Adolescent Health: Crossing the barriers*. New York: Academic Press.

Botvin, G., Baker, E., Renick, N., Filazzola, A., & Botvin, E. (1984). A cognitive-behavioral approach to substance abuse prevention. *Journal of Addictive Behaviors. 9*, 137–147.

Botvin, G., Eng, A. & Williams, C. (1980). Preventing the onset of smoking through life skills training. *Preventive Medicine. 9*, 135–143.

Botvin, G., & Eng, A. (1982). The efficacy of a multicomponent approach to the prevention of cigarette smoking. *Preventive Medicine. 211*, 199–21.

Brady, J. (1984). Social skills training for psychiatric patients. *American Journal of Psychiatry, 141* (3), 333–340.

Braucht, G., Follingstad, D., Brakarsh, D., & Berry, K. (1973). Drug Education. A review of goals, approaches and effectiveness and a paradigm for evaluation. *Quarterly Journal of Studies on Alcohol, 34*, 1279–1292.

Cohen, A. (1985). Drug treatment in school and alternative school settings. In A. Friedman, & G. Beschner (Eds.), *Treatment services for adolescent substance abusers.* National Institute on Drug Abuse (DHHS Pub. No. ADM 85-1342). Washington, DC: U.S. Government Printing Office, 178–194.

Community Action Project (n.d.). *The Chemical People: Project Handbook.* Harrisburg, PA: WITF (TV) Communication Center.

Department of Health and Human Services (1984). *Drug abuse and drug abuse research.* National Institute on Drug Abuse (DHHS Pub. No. ADM 85-1372). Washington, DC: U.S. Government Printing Office, 85-104; 35–53.

Ellis, B. Indyke, D., & Debevoise, N. (Eds.). (1980). *Smoking programs for youth* (DHHS Pub No. 80-2156. National Cancer Institute). Washington, DC: U.S. Government Printing Office.

Evans, R. (1976). Smoking in Children: Developing a social psychological strategy of deterrence. *Journal of Preventive Medicine. 5*, 122–127.

Evans, R., Henderson, A., Hill, P., & Raines, B. (1979). Current psychological social, and educational programs in control and prevention of smoking: A Critical Methodological Review. In A. Gotto, & R. Raoletti (Eds.). *Atherosclerosis Review, 6.* New York. Raven Press.

Flay, B. (in press). Social psychological approaches to smoking prevention. *Advances in Health Promotion and Education.*

Flay, B., Ryan, K., Best, J., Brown, K., Kersell, M., d'avernas, J., & Zanna, M. (1985). Are social-psychological prevention programs effective? The waterloo study. *Journal of Behavioral Medicine, 8*(1), 37–59.

Gilbert, G., & Pruitt, B. (1984). School health education in the United States. *Hygie III 4*, 10–15.

Glynn, T., & Leukefeld, C. (Eds.) (1983). *Preventing adolescent drug abuse: Intervention strategies* (DHHS Pub. No. ADM 83-1280). Washington, DC: U.S. Government Printing Office.

Goldstein, A., Sherman, M., Gershaw, W., Sprafkin, R., & Glick, B. (1978). Training aggressive adolescents in prosocial behavior. *Journal of Youth and Adolescence, 1*, 73–92.

Goodstadt, M. (1980). Education: A turn-on or a turn-off. *Journal of Drug Education, 10*, 89–99.

Goodstadt, M. (1981). Planning and evaluation of alcohol education programs. *Journal of Alcohol and Drug Education, 26*, 1–10.

Goodstadt, M., & Sheppard, M. (1983). Three approaches to alcohol education. *Journal of Studies on Alcohol. 44*(2), 362–380.

Huba, G., Wingard, J., & Bentler, P. (1980). Applications of a theory of drug use to prevention programs. *Journal of Drug Education, 10*, 25–38.

Huba, G., Wingard, J., & Bentler, P. (1981). Intentions to use drugs among adolescents: A longitudinal analysis. *The International Journal of the Addictions. 16*, 331–339.

Hurd, P., Johnson, C., Pechacek, T., Bast, C., Jacobs, D., & Leupker, R. (1980). Prevention of cigarette smoking in seventh grade students. *Journal of Behavioral Medicine. 3*, 15–28.

Johnson, C. (1982). Prevention in adolescence: Initiation and cessation. In *The Health Consequences of smoking, Cancer: A Report of the Surgeon General*. U.S. Department of Health and Human Services, Office of Smoking and Health. Washington, DC: U.S. Government Printing Office, 289–304.

Johnson, C., & Solis, J. (1983). Comprehensive community programs for drug abuse prevention: Implication of the community heart disease prevention programs for future research. In T. Glynn, & C. Leukefeld, (Eds.). *Preventing Adolescent Drug Abuse: Intervention Strategies*. National Institute on Drug Abuse (DHHS Pub. No. ADM 83-1280). Washington, DC: U.S. Government Printing Office.

Johnston, L., Bachman, J., & O'Malley, P. (1976–1983). *Monitoring the future. 1,7*, Ann Arbor, Michigan: The University of Michigan.

Kandel, D. (1982). Epidemiological and psychosocial perspectives on adolescent drug use. *Journal of the American Academy of Child Psychiatry. 21*(4), 328–347.

Kinder, B., Pape, N., & Walfish, J. (1980). Drug and alcohol education programs: A review of outcome studies. *The International Journal of the Addictions. 15*, 1035–1054.

Krueter, M., Christenson, G., & Davis, R. (1983, Sept. 14–16). *School health education research: Future issues and challenges*. A technical paper presented at the Working Conference on School Health Education Research, National Heart Blood Promotion, Bethesda, Maryland.

Manatt, M. (1983). *Parents, peers and pot II* (DHHS Pub. No. ADM 83-1290). Washington, DC: U.S. Government Printing Office.

Maryland State Department of Education. (1982). Division of Instruction. *School policy: Alcohol and other drugs*. Baltimore, MD: State Dept. of Education.

McAllister, A., Perry, C., Killen, J., Slinkard, L., & Maccoby, N. (1980). Pilot study of smoking, alcohol and drug abuse prevention. *American Journal of Public Health. 70*, 719–721.

Moskowitz, J. (1983). Preventing adolescent substance abuse through drug education. In T. Glynn, & C. Leukefeld, (Eds.), *Preventing adolescent drug abuse: Intervention strategies*. National Institute on Drug Abuse (DHHS Pub. No. ADM 83-1280). Washington, DC: U.S. Government Printing Office.

Moskowitz, J., Malvin, J., & Schaeffer, G. (1985). Evaluation of jigsaw. A cooperative learning technique. *Contemporary Educational Psychology, 10*(2), 104–112.

Moskowitz, J., Schaps, E., & Malvin, J. (1982). Process and outcome evaluation in primary prevention: The magic circle program. *Evaluation Review, 6*, 775–778.

Moskowitz, J., Schaps, E., Schaeffer, G., & Malvin, J. (1984). Evaluation of a substance abuse prevention program for junior high school students. *International Journal of the Addictions, 19*(4), 419–430.

Narvaez, A. (1985, August 9). Schools drug-test plan meets criticism in Jersey. *The New York Times*, 23.

National Institute on Drug Abuse. (1984). *Adosescent peer pressure* (DHHS Pub. No. ADM 84-1152). Washington, DC: U.S. Government Printing Office.

Ottenberg, D., Olsen, G., & Schiller, B. (1985). The day treatment center: An alternative for adolescent substance abusers. In A. Friedman, & G. Beschner (Eds.), *Treatment services for adolescent substance abusers*. National Institute on Drug Abuse (DHHS Pub. No. ADM 85-1342). Washington, DC: U.S. Government Printing Office, 195–203.

Pentz, M. (1983). Prevention of adolescent abuse through social skill development. In T. Glynn, & C. Leukefeld, (Eds.). *Preventing adolescent drug abuse: Intervention strategies*. National Institute on Drug Abuse (DHHS Pub. No. ADM 83-1280). Washington, DC: U.S. Government Printing Office.

Perry, C., Killen, J., Slinkard, L., & McAlister, A. (1980). Peer teaching and smoking prevention among junior high school students. *Adolescence 15,* 277–281.

Plant, M. (1980). Drugtaking and prevention: The implications of research for social policy. *The British Journal of Addiction.* 75 245–254.

Pomerantz, S., & Clark, V. (1983). *The conceptual framework and instrumentation of the early intervention project.* Technical Paper No. 2. An unpublished technical paper developed under NIDA grant #r18 DA03071 by staff of the Early Intervention Project, Eagleville Hospital, Norristown, PA.

Quay, H., & Quay, L. (1965). Behavior problems in adolescence. *Child Development. 36,* 215–220.

Rosenthal, T., & Bandura, A. (1978). Psychological modeling: Theory and practice. In S. Garfield, & A. Bergin, (Eds.), *Handbook of Psychotherapy and Behavior Change.* New York: Wiley.

Schaps, E., DiBartolo, R., Moskowitz, J., Pulley, C., & Churgin, S. (1981). Primary prevention evaluation research: A review of 127 impact studies. *Journal of Drug Issues, 11,* 17–43.

Schaps, E. Moskowitz, J., Condon, J., & Marvin, J. (1982). Process and outcome evaluation of a drug education course. *Journal of Drug Education. 12,* 353–364.

Schaps, E., Moskowitz, J., Marvin, J., & Schaeffer, G. (1984). *The NAPA drug abuse prevention project: Research findings* (DHHS Pub. No. ADM 84-1330). Washington, DC: U.S. Government Printing Office.

Schinke, S., & Blythe, B. (1982). Cognitive-behavioral prevention of children's smoking. *Child Behavior Therapy 3*(4), 25–42.

Schinke, S., Gilchrist, L., & Snow, W. (1985). Skills intervention to prevent cigarette smoking among adolescents. *Public Health Briefs.* 75(6), 665–667.

Schlegal, R., Crawford, C., & Sanborn, M. (1977). Correspondence and mediational properties of the fishbein model: An application to adolescent alcohol use. *Journal of Experimental Social Psychology, 13,* 421–430.

Telch, M., Killen, J., McAlister, A., Perry, C., & Maccoby, N. (1982). Long term follow-up of a pilot project on smoking prevention with adolescents. *Journal of Behavioral Medicine, 5,* 1–8.

Tressler, D. (1985, March 3). The case of the high school drug bust. *Women's Day,* 5–8.

U. S. Department of Education (1982). *The school team approach. Alcohol and drug abuse education program.* Washington, DC: U.S. Department of Education.

U.S. Department of Justice (1978). *School drug abuse policy guidelines.* Drug enforcement administration (Pub. No. 1978-260-993-2202). Washington, DC: U.S. Government Printing Office.

Family-Oriented Interventions for the Prevention of Chemical Dependency in Children and Adolescents

Joseph DeMarsh, PhD
Karol L. Kumpfer, PhD

ABSTRACT. Researchers and clinicians are begining to recognize the valuable resource that parents and families are for increasing the effectiveness of substance abuse prevention programs for youth and adolescents. To date, however, most prevention interventions have been developed for use in community or school-based programs. There is a growing number of family-oriented interventions which have been developed specifically as substance abuse prevention programs, or may be easily adapted for use by prevention specialists. This article will review these family-oriented interventions and discuss outcome effectiveness data when available.

INTRODUCTION

The impact of the family in the genesis, maintenance and alleviation of drug abuse is gaining recognition and credibility (Coleman, 1980). More professionals view substance abuse as a "family affair" (Huberty, 1974) and are developing their prevention strategies accordingly.

Family-oriented prevention interventions include those in-

Joseph DeMarsh and Karol L. Kumpfer are Research Associates, Social Research Institute, Graduate School of Social Work, University of Utah, Salt Lake City, UT 84112.

Preparation of this article was supported in part by National Institute on Drug Abuse grant DA02758-01/02 and DA03888-01 (Dr. Karol Kumpfer, Principal Investigator). The authors wish to acknowledge Bonnie Anderson, Simone Hennig and Jeffrey Bartlome for their assistance in the data collection and preparation of this article.

terventions that involve the parent or family and focus on strengthening the family's role in positive socialization of the child in hopes of preventing future alcohol or drug abuse in a child who is currently not an abuser. Family-oriented interventions could occur in many settings: in schools, in clinics, in homes, in community centers, and generally include parent training, family skills training, or family therapy. Because most prevention interventions in this country have been school or community-based, less information is available on the effectiveness of family-oriented approaches. Problems in developing family-oriented prevention interventions include family recruitment and the cost of such interventions. In addition, prevention specialists have been reluctant to implicate and intervene in such a private and important American institution as the family.

This article will: (a) briefly trace the historical development of family-oriented interventions in the prevention field, (b) present general evidence demonstrating the value of including families in prevention activities, (c) describe several of the various family-oriented prevention programs currently available (presented in Table 1), (d) present outcome effectiveness data when available, and (e) present serveral suggestions regarding the development and implementation of family-oriented prevention interventions.

EVOLUTION OF FAMILY-ORIENTED PREVENTION STRATEGIES

Prevention strategies have been slowly evolving to more pervasive and powerful interventions as awareness grows that many etiological factors of chemical dependency must be addressed to have significant impact. In this regard, substance abuse prevention programs utilizing the family system have finally come of age. This trend, however, has emerged only after multiple explorations in the prevention field utilizing a variety of theoretically grounded programs were implemented and evaluated.

The mid-1960s to 1970s witnessed the first widespread attempts at prevention in the alcohol and drug field, the majority of which involved educational and affective education programs. Typically, these programs presented factual information about alcohol, tobacco, and other drugs which included discussions about long-term health effects, legal ramifications, and pharmacological effects. These programs assumed that increasing youth's knowledge about these substances would act as a deterrent for subsequent abuse (Goodstadt, 1978; Department of Health & Human Services [DHHS], 1984). Frequently, these programs also included: (a) "scared straight" strategies, and (b) "affective" or "humanistic" components designed to increase self-esteem and other prosocial skill in an attempt to dissuade drug use.

The 1984 DHHS publication cites a number of outcome evaluations for these programs including Berberian, Gross, Lovejoy and Paprella (1976), Braucht, Brakarsh, Follingstad and Berry (1973), Dorn and Thompson (1976), Goodstadt (1974), Pyramid (1976), Richards (1969), Schaps, DiBartolo, Moskowitz, Palley and Churgin (1981), Swisher and Hoffman (1975). While most of the aforementioned evaluation studies bewail the fact that inadequate evaluations by the prevention programs typify the yield in general, their conclusions consistently indicate these programs to be ineffective in terms of substance abuse prevention. As the DHHS (1984) publication states:

> . . . the inescapable conclusion to be drawn from the substance abuse prevention literature is that few of these programs have demonstrated any degree of success in terms of actual prevention of substance use or abuse. Traditional educational approaches to substance abuse prevention appear to be inadequate because they are too narrow in focus. The "affective education" approaches, on the other hand, appear to have placed too little emphasis on the acquisition of skills that are likely to increase general personal competence and enable students to cope with the various interpersonal and intrapersonal pressures to begin using alcohol, tobacco, and drugs (p. 46).

Following the experiences of these early prevention efforts, substance abuse professionals seem to have reevaluated theoretical assumptions of both substance abuse prevention programs and substance abuse in general. This process resulted in a general agreement that to be effective, substance abuse prevention programs should be more broadly focused to address the numerous precursors of substance abuse that several researchers began to identify (Sowder & Burt, 1978; R. Jessor & S.L. Jessor, 1977), and to train and coach youth in several personal competency and prosocial skills that appear necessary to lead drug-free lives. Accordingly, two rather distinct approaches to prevention began to appear: (a) peer resistance "say-no" strategies, and (b) personal competency and social skills training approaches.

The "say-no" approach was initially developed to prevent adolescent cigarette smoking (Evans, 1976) and has been subsequently utilized primarily in the tobacco and alcohol fields as delay of onset and prevention strategies. Students are typically trained in identifying various social pressures they encounter that encourage smoking and drinking, and then coached by facilitators and peers in specific tactics for resisting these pressures. Numerous investigators have modified this approach and included a variety of training methods including videotaping, role plays, and other learning experiences (McAlister, Perry & Maccoby, 1979; Perry, Killen, Telch, Slinkard & Dannaher, 1980; Johnson, Graham & Hansen, 1981).

To date, a number of investigations have provided encouraging results concerning the effectiveness of these approaches for preventing onset of cigarette smoking (Perry et al., 1980; Hurd et al., 1980; Telch, Killen, McAlister, Perry & Maccoby, 1982; Botvin & Eng, 1982; Flay & Sobel, 1983). Results for alcohol and marijuana have been disappointing (Johnson, Hansen, Flay, Graham & Sobel, 1985).

The second distinct approach found in recent substance abuse prevention programs, personal competency and social skills training, is grounded primarily on a social learning and deficit model of human development. In addition to providing the aforementioned peer-resistance techniques, these programs teach skills designed to enhance personal and social competency, improve general life functioning, strengthen self-esteem and children's notions of self, as well as those necessary to minimize the effect of specifically targeted substance abuse precursors. While these programs' actual content may vary widely, they all assume that remediation of existing deficits (e.g., communication skills, dysfunctional family interactional patterns, antisocial and behavioral problems, low self-esteem) and enhancement of personal competency (including Bandura's notion of self-efficacy, 1977) will reduce the risk of future substance abuse.

While both the "say-no" and personal competency programs have been demonstrated to be effective in reaching their specified intermediary goals, there are still many unresolved issues in terms of their effectiveness as substance abuse prevention programs. The majority of these programs, however, have been implemented in 6th to 9th grades with white, middle-class students. Only recently have these strategies been applied to marijuana, and none for more serious polydrugs and narcotics or opiates. More longitudinal and outcome effectiveness studies are necessary to first, validate this approach for preventing onset of marijuana and other drug consumption, and second, to determine its effectiveness as a substance abuse prevention strategy for high-risk populations. As previously stated, it is the present author's opinion that a qualitative difference exists between delaying or preventing the onset of recreational and/or experimental use of drugs by white, middle-class students, and preventing or decreasing the incidence and prevalence of actual drug abuse by high-risk populations (e.g., children of chemically dependent parents). Also, there has been a lack of follow-up data on programs reporting delay of onset results. It is unclear how long these effects will last and whether active interventions or booster sessions are necessary to maintain their effects.

Due to these unresolved issues concerning peer resistance and personal competency programs, plus findings that document the increased effectiveness of educationally based strategies as a function of family participation (discussed more fully in the following section), interest is increasing in the development of family-oriented prevention programs. To be cost beneficial, prevention programs need to spend more dollars on fewer youth and high-risk youth. Since the family is heavily implicated in substance abuse, the authors believe prevention interventions aimed at strengthening the family's role in socializing the child to be a productive member of society will decrease adolescent substance abuse.

STRENGTHENING EDUCATION-BASED PREVENTION THROUGH FAMILY INVOLVEMENT

In a number of educational programs around the country, prevention planners are adding components aimed at involving parents in the youths' awareness of the consequences of chemical dependency and increasing family communication about alcohol and drug use. Some programs have added family homework assignments to health courses on alcohol and drugs, (i.e., generic K-12 programs similar to the "Here's Looking at You" program, and special alcohol and tobacco provention programs developed by the Department of Health in many states). Others, like the "Students Against Drunk Driving" (SADD) program, have students sign contracts with their parents that they will not drink and drive and will ask for parental help to drive them home if they are inebriated. Some programs actually train parents how to teach their own children about alcohol and drugs, as in the "Talking With Your Kids About Alcohol" program developed by the Prevention Research Institute (Lexington, Kentucky). Few of these programs have outcome evaluations. The few that do are reviewed here (see Bry, 1983, for a more complete review). These studies suggest that educational, school-based prevention programs for youth may be augmented by adding a family component.

To assess the impact media has on junior high school students' cigarette use, Flay et al. (in press) compared one group of students who, in addition to the media campaign, were given written homework assignments that were to be completed with parents to another group of students who received no family homework assignments. Flay's preliminary results indicate students with family homework assignments were only half as likely as the control group to start smoking during the two months between the pre and posttests (7% vs. 14%, respectively). In addition, 35% of the smoking parents successfully quit smoking and 69% reduced their smoking or attempted to quit.

Grady, Gersick and Boratynski's (in press) offered a parent training program (Preparing Parents for Teenagers) to parents of 6th grade children participating in a school generic skill-building program. Specifically, this six-session intervention is designed to facilitate parent's effectiveness as both decision makers (in terms of limit setting, giving advice, and communicating), and as the ones who assist their children in developing their own decision-making skills (which shifts the parents' role from authoritative to consultative).

In their first evaluation study, Grady and Boratynski (in press) report their parent program was highly successful in reaching its short-term objectives. When compared to a delayed treatment control group, participating parents showed significant increases in their ability to respond empathetically to pre-adolescents' concerns, and in their ability to help individuals consider alternatives and consequences.

In a year-long, school-based intervention directed at poor academic performance, Bein and Bry (1980) also found family involvement essential for maintaining grades and attendance. Subjects were 40 seventh graders who displayed at least two substance abuse precursors and were randomly assigned to one of four conditions: (a) no intervention control, (b) regular goal setting teacher conferences, (c) teacher conferences and weekly group award meetings for students, and (d) conferences, group award meetings, calls and letters to parents describing their child's progress and encouraging home support. A reduction in juvenile justice involvement was also noted following exposure to the family involvement condition (Bry & Witte, 1982).

No Single Family-Oriented Approach

Since the goals of family-oriented prevention strategies are to strengthen families in a number of ways, family-oriented prevention programs represent a variety of approaches and techniques rather than any one universal program. Some work on improving parent-parent interactions while others focus on improving parent-child interactions. Some target communication and affective skill building, while others focus on child management principles and parenting styles. Although there are few outcome evaluations of family-oriented substance abuse prevention programs, several programs have been found effective in reaching theoretically specified intermediary goals, such as decreasing school behavior problems, increasing academic performance, improving family communication and interactional patterns, and other psychological and behavioral correlates that may be causally linked with substance abuse.

Review and Evaluation
of Family-Oriented Prevention Programs

In order to review the different types of family-oriented programs, the authors have organized existing family-oriented substance abuse prevention programs in Table 1 according to target participants (family unit vs. parents only) and by the type of training (behavioral, affective, cognitive/communication). Very few family-oriented prevention programs are currently available, and even fewer have adequate outcome effectiveness evaluations. Hence, a number of other family-oriented training programs are included in this review that, while currently not adapted or tested as substance abuse prevention strategies, hold great potential for future use in the field because they: (a) address constellations of behavioral and psychological variables that have been identified by Bry and Pedraza (1983), Kumpfer and DeMarsh (in press) and others as risk factors or precursors to subsequent substance abuse, and (b) represent several of the new and innovative strategies for working with families. Specifically, these are programs such as Briggs (1975), B. Guerney, L. Guerney and Andronica (1966), L. Guerney (1975), B. Guerney (1977), Dinkmeyer and McKay (1976), Jenson (1980), Haley (1973, 1976) and others.

There are several other fine reviews of family-oriented strategies including Sowder, Dickey, Glynn and Burt (1980), DHHS Publication ADM 85-1372 (1984), Rose, Battjes and Leukefeld (1984), Glynn, Lukefeld and Ludford (1983).

The following review will first cover parent training programs and then family training programs, by area of primary focus (behavioral, affective or cognitive). Originally, a third category was included that described prevention programs involving children only without their parent(s), such as children's skills training, Children of Alcoholics (COA) groups, Adult Children of Alcoholics (ACA) groups, etc. (Kumpfer & DeMarsh, 1984). These strategies, however, are used primarily with identified children of chemically dependent per-

TABLE 1

FAMILY LIFE SKILLS SUBSTANCE ABUSE PREVENTION PROGRAMS

	PARENT TRAINING		FAMILY TRAINING	
	REFERENCES	TARGET SKILLS	REFERENCES	TARGET SKILLS
BEHAVIORAL	Alvy (1985) Confident Parenting Alexander & Parsons (1973) Contingency Contracting Training Guerney, L. (1980) Parenting Skills Jenson (1980) CBTU Parent Program Kumpfer & DeMarsh (1983) Parent Training Miller (1975) Systematic Parent Train. Patterson et al. (1975) Families Program	Target Problem Behaviors Goal Statements Reinforcement Limit Setting Behavioral Tracking Data Collection Differential Attention	Forehand & McMahon (1981) Family Skills Training Kumpfer & DeMarsh (1983) Family Life Skills Training	Attending Child's Game Parent's Game Goal Statements
AFFECTIVE	Ackerman (1983) Children of Alcoholics Briggs (1975) Your Child's Self-Esteem Guerney, L. (1977) Foster Parent Training	Developing Self-Concepts Communication of Feelings Empathy Skills	Guerney, G. (1964) Filial Play Therapy Guerney & Stover (1971) Filial Therapy Wegscheider (1981) Another Chance	Empathy Training Expression Family Communication
COGNITIVE/COMMUNICATION	Dinkmeyer & McKay (1976) Systematic Training for Effective Parenting (STEP) Ginnatt (1969) Parent Education Glenn (1984) Developing Capable Young People Gordon (1970) Parent Effectiveness Training (P.E.T.) York et al. (1982) "Toughlove" Parent Support Groups	Communication Skills Problem-Solving Skills Mediating Skills Disciplining Skills Interactional Skills Child Rearing Empathy Skills Family Solidarity	Alexander & Parsons (1982) Functional Fam. Therapy Carkhuff/Boswell (1973) The Cottage Program Carnes (1981) Understanding Us Guerney, G. (1977) Relationship Enhancement L'Abate (1977) Structured Enrichment Stanton & Todd (1983) Structured Fam. Therapy Streit (1978) Fam. Communica. Workshop Szapocznik (1983) Fam. Effectiveness Train.	Empathy Training Expression Decision Making Crisis Resolution Assertiveness Communication Skills Mediating Skills Interactional Skills Organization Perception of Self and Family

sons, and will not be discussed here. Interested readers are referred to the preceding Kumpfer/DeMarsh article in this issue.

PARENT TRAINING PREVENTION PROGRAMS

Introduction

The idea of educating parents to improve their children's development and welfare is not a new idea. In recent years, however, with new evidence that parenting is not an inborn skill, training parents to be more effective with their children has gained popularity. Parent training is now considered "a necessary component of any comprehensive prevention plan" (Alvy, 1985) which can impact a wide range of social and health problems, including child abuse and neglect (Helfer & Kempe, 1976), juvenile delinquency (Fraser & Hawkins, 1982), childhood mental health problems and behavior problems (Jenson, 1980), and substance abuse (Rose et al., 1984).

Many of these parenting skill building programs are adaptable to a variety of setting and are conducted in schools, homes, churches, and treatment agencies. Most of these programs were developed by professionals in the mental health field to improve the effectiveness of their therapy with children by training the parents to conduct the same therapeutic strategies in the homes. These programs are based on various psychological theories such as Rogerian psychology (Gordon's Parent Effectiveness Training [P.E.T.]), Adlerian psychology (Dinkmeyer & McKay's Systematic Training for Effective Parenting [STEP]), and behavioral psychology (Patterson, 1976). Parents are generally taught in small groups the principles of effective parenting, including attending, reinforcement, appropriate disciplines, and communication skills. Parents are then given homework assignments to try new skills with the child at home.

Parent training programs have been criticized as being primarily designed for highly functional and motivated parents and for Caucasians. Currently, adaptations are being developed and tested for minority parents and parents with known parenting problems, such as abusive parents (Bavolek, Comstock & McLaughlin 1983; Wolfe, Kaufman, Aragona & Sandler, 1981), black and Hispanic parents (Alvy, 1985; Alvy, Fuentes, Harrison & Rosen, 1980a), substance abusing parents (Kumpfer & DeMarsh, 1983a).

This section on parent training will discuss a few of the most used programs and will discuss the few that have been adapted for substance abuse prevention in high-risk youth: children of drug abusers (Kumpfer & DeMarsh, 1983a) and minorities (Alvy et al., 1980a, b). The various parent training programs are summarized under the heading of programs that primarily stress behavioral, affective, or cognitive/communication skills. The authors realize that this classification system is primarily a convenience and that many programs extend beyond the boundaries imposed and overlap in both content and objectives with other programs.

Parent Training: Behavioral Management

Behavioral parent training programs teach parents appropriate ways of dealing with their children's problem behaviors and ways of increasing positive parental interactions with their children. The parents learn to target problem behaviors, ignore inappropriate behaviors and reward appropriate behaviors. Facilitators usually implement these programs in group settings of 5 to 10 parents, and usually run from 8 to 14 weekly sessions.

These programs are based on social learning theory which posits that children's behaviors are learned, shaped, and maintained by events in the natural environment, and therefore can be altered via environmental engineering. As parents are significant and powerful figures in a child's environment, this approach is especially well suited for parent training programs.

Because of the emphasis on observable behaviors and accurate data collection, parent training programs are among the very few family-oriented prevention programs with adequate outcome evaluations. Early studies such as Alexander and Parsons (1973) and Patterson (1974) demonstrated decreases in conduct disorders of school-aged and adolescent boys by teaching parents and teachers to reprogram the boys' social environment through contingency contracting. Objective observations and parental reports indicate significant improvements in the boys' behaviors occurred following the training and were maintained in a 12-month follow-up (Patterson & Fleischman, 1979). Other evaluations of parent training programs reporting similarly positive results may be found in Einstein et al. (1971), Blum (1980), and Krasnegor (1979).

The authors have recently completed implementation and data collection of their parent training model (part of the Strengthening Families Program, Kumpfer & DeMarsh, 1983a) funded by a three-year National Institute on Drug Abuse (NIDA) grant. This parenting program, based on a modified TEACH model (Jenson, 1980), is noteworthy because it is specifically designed to be used as a substance abuse prevention strategy for children with opiate, narcotic and polydrug abusing parents. The curriculum needed to be lengthened to 14 sessions and the principles simplified for work with these dysfunctional parents. Unlike most parenting programs, in the last four sessions the parents (having completed all of the didactic material) design and implement a complete behavioral program with their child. Hence, the trainer is still available to provide feedback and support to the parents when they implement what they have learned. The structured curriculum includes a trainer's manual, parent's manual, films and videotapes, homework assignments, and evaluation forms (process, outcome, and client satisfaction).

Although data are still being analyzed, preliminary outcome effectiveness evaluation results suggest that regardless of the parents' stage of dysfunctionality in terms of their own substance abuse, the parents can be coached and assisted in developing more effective parenting styles. Following exposure to the program, parents report having less problems handling school-aged children ($t = 5.3$; $p < .001$), and demonstrated increased knowledge of child behavior management principles ($t = 3.9$; $p < .001$). This increased knowledge and improved parent discipline effectiveness had direct impact on the behavior of the children, who were reported to scream less ($t = 2.5$, $p < .02$), have fewer temper tantrums ($t = 2.2$, $p < .05$), get angry less ($t = 2.7$, $p < .001$), have improvements in their home behaviors ($t = 4.9$, $p < .001$), and display fewer problems than other children their own age ($t = 2.1$, $p < .02$). Further, the children were reported by their parents to be happier ($t = 2.6$, $p < .05$), and to like school better ($t = 11.3$, $p < .001$), and also to have shown an increase in their outside activities ($t = 3.8$, $p < .001$). The children reported a significant decrease in intention to smoke ($t = 3.1$, $p < .001$) and drink ($t = 3.3$, $p < .001$), but not for drugs.

Another attempt to modify the traditional parent training programs for use in preventing drug abuse is the behavioral child management program "Confident Parenting" developed by Alvy at the Center for the Improvement of Child Caring in Los Angeles specifically for black parents. This program has evolved from many years' experience helping black parents to learn more appropriate parenting skills. Preliminary data (Alvy, 1985) suggests that punishment and spanking or traditional black discipline techniques are used more by black parents, whereas white parents use more discussion, ordering and removal of child from situations. Also, the black parents paid less attention when the child did follow instructions. This pilot data demonstrated a need for culturally appropriate parent training. Special adaptations included lengthening the typical number of sessions to 15, using a call-and-response format similar to black minister-congregation exchanges for some teaching, motivating parents' attendance through the use of the "Pyramid of Success for Black Children," and the addition of new instructional units on topics particularly relevant to blacks (e.g., Single Parenting, Pride in Blackness, Traditional Black Discipline vs. Modern Black Self-Disciplining, Drugs and Our Children, etc.) A three-year evaluation of this program is currently underway, supported by NIDA, and the outcomes will not likely be available until the end of 1988.

Parent Training: Affective

Two examples of parent training programs that utilize affective components are Briggs' (1975) program for developing self-esteem in children, and Guerney's (1975) Foster Parent Training. While these programs are typical of the "state-of-the-art" in prevention in that only very little in the area of outcome evaluations were found, they have been included in this article due to their programmatic strengths and favorable reports from clinicians.

Briggs' program is grounded on the assumption that the

difference between fully functioning children and those who "flounder" through life lies in their attitude toward themselves, their degree of self-esteem (Briggs, 1975, p. 3). Coopersmith (1967) is referenced to support Briggs' contention that self-esteem is not related to family wealth, education, geographic location, social class, father's occupation, or whether the mother is always present in the home, but comes rather from the quality of the relationship that exists between the child and those who have a significant role in the child's life. Helping children build high self-esteem is, according to this program, the key to successful parenting and prevention.

The Briggs' program instructs parents in: (a) how self-esteem is built, (b) how a child's self-view affects behavior, (c) what price a child pays when self-esteem is low, and (d) what parents can do to foster positive self-esteem. This step-by-step program is organized in a "how to" publication written for parents. While portions of the program have been incorporated in other prevention programs (Kumpfer & DeMarsh, 1983a, b), no outcome effectiveness studies relating Briggs' program to substance abuse prevention could be found.

The L. Guerney (1975) Foster Parent Training Program addresses the need for a brief, practical training program for foster parents. While there is an overlap of this program with other behaviorally oriented parent training programs, it has been included here because of its emphasis on affective training strategies and foster children's emotional contexts. This program utilizes a highly structured curriculum consisting of 10 sessions which include lectures, films guided discussions, and homework assignments.

Special training films and manuals have been developed for the Foster Parent Training Program which simulate several parent groups and show potential leaders how best to respond to certain common situations which arise within the groups. In addition, the program includes a set of child statement sequence films called "What Do You Say Now?" to be used during training groups for practicing specific response skills.

Parent Training: Cognitive/Communication

Another type of family-oriented parent training prevention program involves training parents in techniques designed to facilitate family communication and problem solving. A noteworthy example of these problems is Gordon's (1970) *Parent Effectiveness Training* (P.E.T.) which focuses on enhancing communication skills, with training in such areas as behavioral skills to resolve parent-child problems, approaches to influence behaviors, and mediation skills. P.E.T. consists of 24 hours of group instruction (6 to 15 parents) by trained facilitators in nonclinical settings. Instruction involves lectures, discussions and role plays. Gordon's summary of 25 evaluation studies of the effectiveness of the P.E.T. program found: increased confidence and self-esteem in the parents; increased acceptance, trust, and understanding of the children; improved attitudes and child-rearing behaviors; improved moral reasoning, feelings of parental acceptance, and increased academic achievement in the children (Rose et al., 1984).

A second example of cognitive/communication parent training programs is Dinkmeyer and McKay's (1976) *Systematic Training for Effective Parenting* (STEP) program. This program is essentially a cognitive and educationally oriented one which maintains that maladaptive family interactions occur due to a lack of knowledge, experience, and information. Similar to P.E.T., STEP is usually presented in a group setting (8 to 12 parents), meets two hours weekly for 8 to 12 weeks, and consists of lectures, discussions and role plays. STEP assists parents and children to develop fundamental skills required for living together in an atmosphere of equality and democracy. Specific objectives include developing an understanding that behaviors have purpose and are goal directed, and to encourage appropriate family interactions.

Rose et al. (1984) cite several evaluation studies of the STEP program which, among other findings, report changes in parental attitudes toward child rearing practices (Shapiro, 1976; Downing, 1971), parents' self-reported changes in their children's behaviors (Fears, 1976), that mothers were less authoritarian and less controlling following STEP training (Berrett, 1975; Freeman, 1975), and that mothers felt they benefited from the knowledge, learned skills, and became more aware of their role (Cullen, 1968).

Another example of a cognitive/communication parent training program is Glenn's (1984) "Developing Capable Young People." This program sets the family in a historical context and discusses how families have changed over the last 50 years. By so doing, Glenn builds the case that strengthening family solidarity and parents' child-rearing skills will help develop more happy, mature, and capable young children, and hence reduce the risk for addictive behaviors later in life.

A unique aspect of Glenn's program is his definition of parenting. Briefly, Glenn views parenting as a process rather than a biological role that occurs "whenever a more mature, more capable individual interacts with a less mature, less capable individual in order to increase the capability and maturity of the latter." Accordingly, Glenn's parenting program is appropriate for friends, clergy, teachers, coaches, anyone who is involved and contributing to a child's socialization process.

Glenn's 10-session program is supplemented with audio cassettes, trainer and participant manuals, structured exercises and transparencies. Seven skills are discussed and practiced throughout the duration of the program and deal with developing adequate perceptions of self and others, skills for effective parenting communication, self-discipline, social interactions, and other prosocial skills. These skills are based on the following three assumptions:

1. Parent training programs should stress what needs to be done (goals) and general principles for accomplishing it *rather* than emphasizing how to do it (techniques).
2. The only type of person it takes to be a good parent is one who is concerned and willing to learn.
3. Parenting and families should be viewed as processes rather than roles so that everyone involved can feel that they are appropriate and valid in the program.

While Glenn's program has served as a model and has been adapted to a variety of educational and family-oriented programs, we could find no evaluation data concerning its effectiveness as a substance abuse prevention strategy.

Summary of Parent Training Prevention Programs

The effectiveness of parent training programs in behavioral management techniques for decreasing children's inappropriate behaviors and increasing positive interactions, school performance, self-esteem, and communication, is well documented throughout the literature (Millman, Schafer & Cohen, 1980; Garfield & Bergin, 1971). These skills training technologies hold great potential for prevention of chemical dependency because many of the behavioral clusters these programs have been effective in treating at home and in schools are the same behaviors that have been identified in the alcohol and drug fields as precursors of substance abuse. Because parent training strategies have only recently been utilized in the substance abuse field, their long-term prevention effectiveness has yet to be determined. While the present authors support future investigations with these techniques, because of their demonstrated effectiveness in other contexts, and their cost-effectiveness as prevention programs, the authors anticipate they will be found less effective than family skills training programs which involve the whole family.

FAMILY TRAINING PREVENTION PROGRAMS

Introduction

The second major group of family-oriented prevention programs to be considered deals with strategies involving the family unit, parents and children together. This section will discuss family skills training programs (behavioral, affective and cognitive/communication), family therapy, and family self-help programs.

Family Training: Behavioral

At the beginning of their NIDA research, the authors could find only one behavioral parent training program which involved the parent working directly with the child in the presence of the therapist to compare parent-only, child-only, and family skills training programs in effectiveness in substance abuse prevention. This family skills training program was developed by Forehand and McMahon (1981) and is explained in their book, *Helping the Noncompliant Child*. Experimental effectiveness data suggests that both the parents and children have positive behavioral changes as well as high levels of satisfaction with the program after participation. This program is ideal for working with dysfunctional parents, since the therapist is available to observe the interaction between the parent and child and to model appropriate behavior. Recently, Bavolek and his associates (1983) and Wolfe and his associates (1981) have applied these family skills training strategies to another category of dysfunctional parents, those who are abusing their children.

The Kumpfer/DeMarsh Family Skills Training Program

This family component of the Strengthening Families Program (Kumpfer & DeMarsh, 1983b) is based on a combination of a number of family skills training programs, mainly Forehand and McMahon's (1981) Helping the Noncompliant Child Program and Guerney's (1977) Relationship Enhancement Program. This program was designed specifically as a drug abuse prevention program for high-risk families; namely those where the parents are drug users. Because Forehand and McMahon (1981) found that the direct family skills training was enhanced by a prior session of didactic material explaining the basics of social learning and behavioral principles, the Kumpfer/DeMarsh program involves the parents in a parenting class in the first hour while the children are in a children's social skills class. In the second hour, the parents and the child meet with an individual trainer to practice the principles learned. This is a highly structured program and includes training manuals, video tapes and films, homework assignments, and evaluation forms. The curriculum contains 14 two-hour sessions that contain three major parts: Child's Game, Communication Enhancement, and Parent's Game.

In the first part, the parent is introduced to the concept of *Child's Game*. This is basically filial play therapy (similar to that of L. & B. Guerney's Filial Therapy, 1966), except that the therapist is always there to prompt and model for the parent. The parents are instructed to track and monitor their children's behaviors. They are taught to give a running verbal commentary of their child's behavior as it happens. Child's Game helps parents develop empathy and learn to enjoy their children. The nonpunitive environment also helps children to express and act out their feelings, a deficit often found in children living with chemically dependent parents.

In the second phase, the family is briefly trained in communication skills based on the Relationship Enhancement principles of Dr. Bernard Guerney. The discussion topics are selected to involve sensitive issues for the family concerning alcohol and drug use. Training in improving family relationships and communication was felt necessary before the parents are taught control techniques.

During the third phase of the Strengthening Families curriculum, the parents(s) learn to start introducing controls and restrictions ("Parent's Game") to the child's play. Typically, they start making requests for the child to comply with cleanup and certain play behaviors. The therapist is always present to provide immediate feedback in the form of correcting mistakes, rewarding successes, and cues for proper behavior.

Outcome Data

Although experimental data are still being analyzed, preliminary outcome effectiveness evaluations indicate improvements in three theoretically-specified areas that are thought to influence a child's "risk status": (a) family function, (b) children's behavior problems, and (c) children's expressiveness.

Family functioning seemed to improve on several dimensions following participation in the Family Skills Training Program, including increased family communication of problems ($t = 6.2$, $p < .001$), improved relations among siblings ($t = 2.6$, $p < .05$), improved ability to think of family-oriented activities ($t = 4.1$, $p < .001$), clarity of family rules ($t = 3.2$, $p < .001$), and more social contacts by parents ($t = 2.8$, $p < .001$).

Likewise, improvements in children's behavior problems were found. Parents reported their children behaved less impulsively ($t = 3.2$, $p < .02$), were more well-behaved at home ($t = 6.2$, $p < .001$), and had fewer problem behaviors in general ($t = 6.3$, $p < .001$). Also, children self-reported improved relations with peers ($t = 7.3$, $p < .001$).

The Family Skills Training component of the Strengthening Families Program curriculum also appears to have impacted the extent to which children are able to express themselves within the family context, both verbally and otherwise. Children were found to ask for more help with their homework ($t = 2.0$, $p < .05$), to talk to people more when they feel sad ($t = 3.4$, $p < .001$), to seek more attention from parents ($t = 9.1$, $p < .001$), and to cry more ($t = 10.1$, $p < .001$). Similar to the Parent Training Program, the children reported at posttest significant decreases in their intentions to use tobacco and alcohol, but not drugs.

Family Skills Training: Affective

The Guerney Filial Therapy Program

This program was developed as a psychotherapeutic program for assisting families to help emotionally disturbed children under 10 years of age (Guerney et al., 1966). As will be discussed later, this program is especially well suited as a substance abuse prevention strategy because of: (a) its fine track record as a preventive mental health program, and (b) recent findings that this program's objectives address the mental health and behavioral problems found in children of chemically dependent parents (Kumpfer & DeMarsh, 1984; Sowder & Burt, 1978).

In this program, parents of emotionally disturbed children are trained groups of six to eight to apply principles and techniques used in client-centered play therapy to play sessions at home with their children. The course of treatment is usually 12–18 months with two-hour weekly meetings. After approximately a 10-week training period, parents receive supervision on their home play sessions and clarification of other family problems.

Qualitative evidence of the effectiveness of this Filial Therapy Program is found in the 1971 Final Report as well as in an early 1964 pilot study. Briefly, these studies report consistent findings that parents: (a) were able to learn the roles and skills of the program to a highly satisfactory degree, (b) showed increases in empathic abilities at a significant level, and (c) showed a significant reduction in their dissatisfaction with their child. Further, children were shown to become less dependent on their mothers for direction and displayed more leadership skills. In the case of aggressive children, overt and verbal statements of aggression toward mothers are usually seen to increase (formerly, this aggression was hidden or displaced), while general aggression immediately begins to diminish (Guerney & Stover, 1971).

Family Skills Training: Cognitive/Communication

The final set of programs discussed in this section involves those prevention strategies that work with the entire family unit (parents and children) with strategies involving cognitive/communication skill building techniques. The five programs discussed are: B. Guerney's (1977) Relationship Enhancement (RE), L'Abate's (1975a) Structured Enrichment (SE), Streit's (1978) Family Communication Workshop, Szapocznik's (1983) Family Effectiveness Training, and Carnes' (1981) Understanding Us.

Guerney's Relationship Enhancement Program

The aims of this program are to restructure the manner in which family members verbally interact and respond to each other through a blend of humanistic and behaviorally oriented techniques (Guerney, 1977). Specifically, family members are trained in four modes (behavioral skills) that facilitate both understanding and communication. The first two modes (empathic and responder) deal with specific types of communication skills. The third mode (mode switching) involves training family members in the dynamic process that occurs when one moves from a speaking role to a listening one or vice versa. The fourth mode (facilitator) is one in which a family member demonstrates and trains other family members in the relationship enhancement process. The RE program focuses on the learning and acquisition of new skills as opposed to therapeutic intervention. The program (implemented by trained and certified leaders) can be delivered in single family or group settings, varies in length depending on the severity of problems of the target group, is usually implemented in nonclinical settings, and involves demonstrations, role plays and feedback.

Rose et al. (1984) report variations of Guerney's RE program have been successfully implemented with dyads, triads and other combinations of individuals other than the family unit who are interested in both easing the strain of troubled relations and enhancing already positive ones. Controlled experimental studies with premarital couples (D'Augelli, Deyss, Guerney, Heshenberg & Sporopsky, 1974), newlyweds (Collins, 1977), mothers and daughters (Guerney, Confal & Vogelson, 1981) all report positive results (Rose et al., 1984; Bry, 1983).

The L'Abate Structured Enrichment Program

More flexible than the aforementioned RE program, the final form and content of this program are a function primarily of the family's educational level and presenting problems (L'Abate, 1975a). SE programs have the latitude to cover a variety of topics relevant to individual families and instruct family members in many different life skills such as organization, communication, crisis resolution, values clarification, nonverbal expressiveness, and others. SE programs vary considerably in length (typically 4 to 12 sessions), are implemented in nonclinical settings (the majority of work to date having been completed with graduate and college students in the university setting), and are designed to impart information in a gradual and progressive fashion (information dissemination usually progresses from the least to the most complex).

While only a limited amount of evaluation data exists, L'Abate (1977) reports that of 55 clinical and nonclinical families who were distributed into experimental (receiving SE training) and control (not receiving SE) groups, experimental families demonstrated improvements in their perceived family well-being. This finding held whether the experimental families were clinical (requesting help with an identified patient) or nonclinical, though results were more positive for nonclinical families. Rose et al. (1984) comments that, "such results support the use of enrichment programs for families at a prevention level . . ." (p. 19).

Streit's Family Communication Workshop

Among many of Streit's endeavors in the alcohol, drug and delinquency fields is a Family Communication Workshop program developed for use with substance-abusing/high-risk adolescents, their families, and significant peers (Streit, 1978). The theoretical assumptions grounding this program are based on the work of Blum and Associates (1970) and Jessor (1975) who, through survey and interview techniques, developed a list of variables which seem to correlate with adolescent use/nonuse of marijuana. Among other indicators, these researchers have identified parental controls, parental affection and support, and parental traditionality in ideological outlook to be related to degree of marijuana use.

Accordingly, when applied to substance abuse prevention, Streit's workshop was presented in an attempt to increase family supportiveness, cohesion, parental control, and appropriate perceptions. Workshops are usually implemented in nonclinical community group settings for families with adolescents, and usually involve six, two-hour sessions.

Campbell (1983) utilized a pre/post quasi-experimental design to evaluate 11 families ($N = 33$ participants) who participated in the Streit Family Communication Workshop. Changes in a number of theoretically specified intermediary variables (including perceptions, control and family cohesion) were measured by the Moos (1974) Family Environment Scale. The 11 families were white, middle- and upper-class families who had at least one adolescent between the ages of 12 and 16 years. The leaders were trained couselors working with support couples who had themselves participated in a Streit workshop. The sessions explored perception, psychological and physiological growth, peers, love, sexuality, discipline, and communication, with each class including such techniques as open discussions, group problem solving and case studies.

Campbell reports significant changes on two variables from pretest to posttest. First, less conflict within the family was reported by individuals ($t = 1.96$, df $= 66$, $p < .05$). Second, considerable differences in perceptions between family members was reported on two scales: a significant increase of agreement concerning the degree of moral-religious emphasis in the family ($t = 2.41$, df $= 66$, $p < .001$), and significantly more disagreement in family members' perceptions of family conflict ($t = 1.71$, df $= 66$, $p < .05$). However, several other of Campbell's initial hypotheses, that Streit's workshop would increase supportiveness, cohesion and control, were not supported.

These results do support Streit's program as a viable substance abuse prevention effort. First, it significantly increased one aspect of family functioning that has been identified by R. Jessor (1975), Glynn (1983) and Kumpfer and DeMarsh (1984) as an important precursor of subsequent substance abuse by children—moral/religious emphasis. Second, the increased discrepancy of family members' perceptions of conflict may help dissipate the kind of family "enmeshment" Minuchin (1974) hypothesizes to also contribute to the children's risk status for future substance abuse. As Campbell (1983) discusses, "Through course work [Streit's], members could challenge this enmeshment to become individuals experiencing conflict, rather than pieces of a family unit. This individuation from this enmeshed system could leave individuals free to grow and differ" (p. 4).

Szapocznik's Family Effectiveness Training Program

One of the few prevention programs (other than the authors') written specifically for the prevention of drug abuse is that of Szapocznik's (1983) Family Effectiveness Training Program (FET). Developed for use with high-risk Hispanic families (Cuban Americans) with young children, FET is composed of two primary components: "(1) A family development component aimed at interactional/structural problems, lack of adequate parenting skills, and drug education; and (2) a cultural component which provides the content for reframing family intergenerational conflicts into cultural ones" (p. 2).

FET is implemented by a trained facilitator in a classroom setting for 13 weekly sessions. Each facilitator works with one family providing both didactic and experiential materials (e.g., lectures, role plays, discussions).

Similar to several aforementioned programs, the Szapocznik program attempts to reduce certain drug abuse precursors, including conduct disorders in children, acculturation stresses, and lack of drug information among parents, to lessen the high-risk status of 6- to 12-year-old children for developing later substance-abusing behaviors.

Rose et al. (1984) report encouraging preliminary outcome effectiveness results, "that FET families and children demonstrate a significantly greater reduction in high-risk variables (e.g., childhood conduct disorders) than families and children who did not participate in FET" (p. 22).

Carnes Understanding Us Program

The final program to be reviewed is one developed by Carnes (1981) as an outpatient program for chemically dependent families. Carnes' "Understanding Us" (UU) curriculum combines the marital enrichment program of Miller and Wackman (1968) with Olson et al.'s (1979) circumplex model of family functioning. The UU program emphasizes health and wellness within the family and is designed more to encourage an entire family's self-exploration of identity, problems, and tensions through the process of reframing, rather than teaching a special set of skills (e.g., as in Forehand & McMahon's program for helping the noncompliant child, 1981). No evaluation research is available to date. A more thorough review and discussion of the UU program may be found in Rose et al. (1984).

Family Therapy

A number of clinicians are using family therapy as a prevention or early intervention strategy for high-risk children and youth. Klein, Alexander and Parson's (1977) discovery that functional family therapy is an effective prevention strategy for younger siblings of delinquents was a major breakthrough in this area. Hence, to the degree that family therapy reduces risk factors for nonusers or nonchemically dependent members of the family (the spouse and the children), it is a preventive strategy. Unfortunately, many public and private funding sources for substance abuse prohibit payment for anyone but the abuser.

Family therapy can take many forms. Gallant, Rich, Bey and Terranova (1970) have experimented with the use of multiple-couple groups. Steinglass (1975) briefly employed the free use of alcohol (while being videotaped) in the initial assessment stages of an experimental inpatient program at NIAA's Laboratory for Alcohol Research to help the staff and couples better understand the role that alcohol played in the family dynamics. In Utah, the Teen Alcohol and Drug Schools have employed multiple family therapy principles successfully for years. One unique feature of this program is that the children and parents are switched for initial communication exercises. It appears easier for people to practice new skills with different parents or children.

To work successfully with chemically dependent families, the therapist or trainer needs to have a thorough understanding of the dynamics and typical developmental stages of these families (see Steinglass, 1980; Kaufman, 1980). The pioneering work of Wegscheider (1981) and Ackerman (1983) in family therapy with alcoholics has promoted understanding in this field. Since recruitment is often a problem, Szapocznik and his associates (1984) have experimented with one-person family therapy and found it effective. In addition, Szapocznik has developed culturally-relevant family therapy for Hispanic families of Cuban descent. Maldanado and his associates have successfully used their family therapy model as an early intervention strategy for Hispanic (Spanish and Mexican descent) first offender youth, and as a prevention strategy for siblings (Courtney, 1984; Kumpfer, Williams & Maldanado 1985).

Family Self-Help Groups

Self-help groups, such as Al-Anon for spouses of alcoholics, and Alafam for families of alcoholics, are increasing in popularity. Over 5,000 Alafam groups exist throughout the world, making them the single largest prevention program involving families of chemically dependent persons. These groups closely parallel Alcoholics Anonymous meetings. According to Ablon (1974), they teach the basic lesson that alcoholism is a disease and three basic principles: (a) loving detachment from the alcoholic, (b) reestablishment of their own self-esteem and independence, and (c) reliance on a "higher power." Through shared experiences, the groups teach that many families have the same problems, and that they are not alone. Some treatment clinics for chemical dependency also involve spouses (para-alcoholics) or families in groups. One of the authors (Kumpfer, 1975) specializes in prevention groups for wives of chemically dependent men using a specially structured curriculum. Through increased understanding, these spouses and families are not only increasing the probability that the alcoholic will achieve and maintain sobriety, but they are decreasing their own risk of becoming alcoholics. (For further information on para-alcoholics and co-alcoholics see Greenleaf, 1981).

RECRUITMENT AND ATTRITION PROBLEMS

Earlier articles reviewed (Bry, 1983, and others) supported the notion that the effectiveness of prevention programs can be enhanced through family involvement. While supporting this notion, protocol applications demonstrate that recruitment and attrition problems in family-oriented programs can threaten both cost and outcome effectiveness (Alegre-Jurado, 1976; Slipp, Ellis & Kressel, 1974; Stanton, 1979; Stanton & Todd, 1981; Ziegler-Driscoll, 1977).

Many substance abuse professionals have commented on these issues, including Seldin (1972) who has called it a "monumentally discouraging task" (p. 105), and Davis (1977–78) who maintains that addicts' families are "among the most difficult of all psychotherapy patients to get into the office" (p. 178). Stanton and Todd (1981) summarize the experience of many professionals in the field and conclude, ". . . with the possible exception of highly select samples, the difficulty of engaging addicts' families in treatment cannot be overestimated" (p. 74). Even when parent or family training programs are offered in public schools, community centers or agencies, a minority of parents choose to become involved. Though Grady and her associates (in press) found about 50% of the parents in the participating schools registered for their six-session parent training course, only about 25% of all the parents completed the program. As mentioned by Bry (1983), recruitment issues are one of the most serious problems facing family approaches.

The preceding cautionary paragraph is not intended to discourage but to identify an area of concern so preliminary steps may be taken to minimize their effect. Stanton and Todd (1981), for instance, identify nine areas to consider, and suggest some fine recruitment principles for each. Other suggestions to minimize recruitment and attrition problems, many of which target fathers, may be found in Alegre-Jurado (1976), Berg and Roseblum (1977), Coleman (1976), Davis (1977–78), L'Abate (1975b), Sager et al. (1968), and Vaglum (1973). In addition, the present authors have found reimbursing the parents for their family's involvement (either monetarily, through a significant token or coupon system, or counting hours of participation in the prevention program toward meeting counseling requirements that some methadone and residential facilities have) to be effective in maintaining their involvement. Selecting a time when most parents are free of job or family responsibilities or offering alternate times for sessions and free child care increases participation rates.

Chemically dependent parents are often anxious and mistrusting of family interventions. Their substance abusing lifestyles provide a level of suffering and pain that parents often find difficult to move beyond, and they fail to consider the effects of their behaviors upon their children. The various illegal activities in which substance abusers often find themselves engaged serves to exacerbate and generalize a sense of mistrust of professionals, agencies and other "unknown" physical and social agencies.

With problems in recruitment for family-oriented substance abuse prevention efforts mentioned repeatedly throughout the literature and attrition rates of 45% to 50% being commonplace, prevention specialists should be sensitive to the potentially serious treatment and research problems they may encounter. The need for more creative and effective strategies as well as continued professional dialogue concerning these issues seems apparent. Possibly cultural messages which repeatedly stress that responsible parenting requires skills which not all parents have, and that these skills can be acquired in parenting and family skills training courses could change parents' willingness to participate.

CONCLUSION

Theoretically based models and clinically based reports argue for the inclusion of family units in prevention activities designed to assist young, high-risk populations from developing substance-abusing behaviors. There are, however, few outcome evaluation studies to support these arguments. Those that do exist typically have small *N*s, lack the rigors of experimentally designed and controlled studies, and have yet to provide longitudinal data documenting the lasting effectiveness of family-oriented prevention programs.

The authors, however, believe the present lack of supporting data is indicative of the current "state" of prevention research and not a "trait" of family-oriented prevention programs. Given: (a) the growing consensus that chemical dependency is a "family affair", (b) the positive outcome effectiveness of family-oriented treatment for psychotherapy in general and substance abuse in particular, (c) disappointing outcomes of education and affective or alternative education prevention programs, and (d) the large number of identified substance abuse precursors addressed by these family programs, family-oriented prevention efforts appear to hold great potential in decreasing the high rates of adolescent substance abuse in this country. When targeting early childhood for prevention efforts, the importance of enlisting the family's help in decreasing risk factors becomes even more apparent since the family is the major socialization agent for children.

REFERENCES

Ablon, J. (1974). Al-Anon family groups: Impetus for change through the presentation of alternatives. *American Journal of Psychotherapy, 28*(1), 30.

Ackerman, R. (1983). *Children of alcoholics.* Holmes Beach: Learning Publications.

Alegre-Jurado, C. (1976). *A dropout study of clients in an individual drug free outpatient treatment program for drug abusers.* Unpublished Doctoral dissertation, University of Miami.

Alexander, J. F., & Parsons, B. V. (1973). Short-term behavioral intervention with delinquent families: Impact on family process and recidivism. *Journal of Abnormal Psychology, 81,* 219–225.

Alvy, K. T. (1985, June). *Parenting programs for black parents.* Paper presented at the Primary Prevention of Psychopathology Conference (Families in transition: Primary prevention programs that work), sponsored by the National Institute of Mental Health, University of Vermont, Burlington.

Alvy, K. T., Fuentes, E. G., Harrison, D. S., & Rosen, L. D. (1980a). *The culturally-adapted parent training project: Original grant proposal and first progress report.* Studio City, CA: Center for the Improvement of Child Caring.

Alvy, K. T., Rosen, L. D., Harrison, D. S., & Fuentes, E. G. (1980b, September). *Effects of parent training programs with poverty-level minority group parents.* Paper presented at the meeting of the American Psychological Association Convention, Montreal.

Arkin, R. M., Roemhild, H. J., Johnson, C. A., Luepker, R. V., & Murray, D. M. (1981). The Minnesota smoking prevention program: A seventh grade health curriculum supplement. *Journal of School Health, 51*(19), 661–616.

Bandura, A. (1977). *Social learning theory.* Englewood Cliffs, NJ: Prentice Hall.

Bavolek, S. J., Comstock, C. M., & McLaughlin, J. A. (1983). *The nurturing program: A validated approach to reducing dysfunctional family interactions.* Final report, Grant No. 1R01MH34862. Rockville, MD: National Institute of Mental Health.

Berberian, R. M., Gross, C., Lovejoy, J., & Paparella, S. (1976). The effectiveness of drug education programs: A critical review. *Health Education Monographs, 4*(4), 377–398.

Berg, B., & Rosenblum, N. (1977). Fathers in family therapy: A survey of family therapists. *Journal of Marriage and Family Counseling, 3,* 85–91.

Berrett, R. D. (1975). Adlerian mother study groups: An evaluation. *Journal of Individual Psychology, 31,* 179–182.

Bien, N. Z., & Bry, B. H. (1980). An experimentally designed comparison of four intensities of school-based prevention programs for adolescents with adjustment problems. *Journal of Community Psychology, 8,* 110–116.

Blum, R. H. (1980). An argument for family research. In B. G. Ellis (Ed.), *Drug abuse from the family perspective* (DHHS Publication No. ADM 80-110, pp. 104–116). Washington, DC: U.S. Government Printing Office.

Blum, R. H., & Associates. (1970). *Students and drugs.* San Francisco: Jossey-Bass.

Botvin, G. J., & Eng, A. (1982). The efficacy of a multicomponent approach to the prevention of cigarette smoking. *Preventative Medicine, 11,* 199–211.

Braucht, C. N., Brakarsh, D., Follingstad, D., & Berry, K. L. (1973). Deviant drug use in adolescence: A review of psychosocial correlates. *Psychological Bulletin, 79,* 92–106.

Briggs, D. (1975). *Your child's self-esteem.* New York: Dolphin Books.

Bry, B. H. (1983). Empirical foundations of family-based approaches to adolescent substance abuse. In T. J. Glynn, C. G. Leukefeld, & J. P. Ludford (Eds.), *Preventing adolescent drug abuse: Intervention strategies* (National Institute on Drug Abuse Research Monograph 47, DHHS Publication No. ADM 83-1280, pp. 154-177). Washington, D. C.: U. S. Government Printing Office.

Bry, B. H., & Pedraza, M. (1983, March). *Extent of adolescent substance abuse as a function of number of risk factors: An extension and replication.* Paper presented at the Fifteenth Banff International Conference on Behavioral Sciences, Banff, Alberta.

Bry, B. H., & Witte, G. (1982, May). *Impact of a behaviorally oriented, school-based, group intervention program upon alienation and self-esteem.* Paper presented at the Eastern Evaluation Research Society meeting, New York City.

Campbell, P. (1983). Streit family workshops: Creating change in a family environment. *Journal of Drug Education, 13*(3), 223–227.

Carnes, P. (1981). *Family development I: Understanding US.* Minneapolis: Interpersonal Communications Programs.

Coleman, H. F. (1976). How to enlist the family as an ally. *American Journal of Drug and Alcohol Abuse, 3,* 167–173.

Coleman, S. B. (1980). Incomplete mourning in the family trajectory: A circular journey to drug abuse. In B. G. Ellis (Ed.), *Drug abuse from the family perspective* (DHHS Publication No. ADM 80-910, pp. 18–31). Washington, DC: U.S. Government Printing Office.

Collins, J. (1977). Experimental evaluation of a six-month conjugal therapy relationship enhancement program. In B. Guerney (Ed.), *Relationship enhancement: Skill-training programs for therapy, problem prevention, and enrichment.* San Francisco: Jossey-Bass.

Coopersmith, S. (1967). *The antecedents of self-esteem.* San Francisco: W. H. Freeman & Co.

Courtney, R. J. (1984). *Functional family therapy intervention for Hispanic juvenile offenders and their parents.* Project consultation on the Institute for Human Resources development prevention program. Salt Lake City: Utah State Division of Alcoholism and Drugs.

Cullen, J. S. (1968). The effectiveness of parent education discussion groups: A follow-up study. *Mental Hygiene, 52,* 590–599.

D'Augelli, A., Deyss, C., Guerney, B., Heshenberg, B., & Sporopsky, S. (1974). Interpersonal skill training for dating couples: An evaluation of an educational mental health service. *Journal of Consulting Psychology, 21,* 385–389.

Davis, D. I. (1977–78). Forum—Family therapy for the drug user: Conceptual and practical considerations. *Drug Forum, 6,* 197–199.

Department of Health & Human Services. (1984). *Drug abuse and drug abuse research* (DHHS Publication No. ADM 85-1372). Washington, DC: U. S. Government Printing Office.

Dinkmeyer, D., & McKay, G. D. (1976). *Systematic training for effective parenting.* Circle Pines, MN: American Guidance Service, Inc.

Dorn, N., & Thompson, A. (1976). Evaluation of drug education in the longer term is not an optional extra. *Community Health, 7,* 154–161.

Downing, C. J. (1971). *The development and evaluation of a program for parent training in family relationship and management skills.* Unpublished doctoral dissertation, Indiana University.

Einstein, S., Lavenhar, M., Wolfson, E., Louia, D., Quinones, M., & McAteer, G. (1971). The training of teachers for drug abuse education programs. *Journal of Drug Education, 1*(4), 323–345.

Evans, R. I. (1976). Smoking in children: Developing a social psychological strategy of deterrence. *Preventative Medicine, 5,* 122–127.

Fears, S. (1976). Adlerian parent study groups. *The School Counselor, 23*(5), 320–329.

Flay, B., & Sobel, J. (1983). The role of mass media in preventing adolescent substance abuse. In T. Glynn & C. Leukefeld (Eds.), *Preventing adolescent drug abuse: Intervention strategies* (DHHS Publication No. ADM 83-1280). Washington, DC: U.S. Government Printing Office.

Flay, B. R., Ryan, K. B., Best, J. A., Brown, K. S., Kersell, M. W., D'Avernas, J. R., & Zanna, M. P. (1983). Cigarette smoking: Why people do it and ways of preventing it. In P. J. McGrath, & P. Firestone (Eds.), *Pediatric and adolescent behavioral medicine.* New York: Springer.

Flay, B. R., Johnson, C. A., Hansen, W. B., Ulene, A., Grossman, L. M., Alvarez, L., Sobel, D. F., Hochstein, G., & Sobel, J. L. (in press). Evaluation of a mass media enhanced smoking prevention and cessation program. In J. P. Baggaley & J. Sharpe (Eds.), *Experimental research in TV instruction* (Vol. 5). St. John's, Newfoundland: Memorial University.

Forehand, R. L., & McMahon, R. J. (1981). *Helping the noncompliant child. A clinician's guide to parent training.* New York: The Guilford Press.

Fraser, M. W., & Hawkins, J. D. (1982). *Parent training for delinquency prevention: A review.* Report prepared for National Institute for Juvenile Justice & Delinquency Prevention. Seattle, WA: Center for Law and Justice.

Freeman, C. W. (1975). Adlerian mother study groups: Effects on attitudes and behavior. *Journal of Individual Psychology, 31*(1), 37–50.

Gallant, D. M., Rich, A., Bey, E., & Terranova, L. (1970). Group psychotherapy with married couples: A successful technique in New Orleans alcoholism clinic patients. *Journal of Louisiana State Medical Society, 122,* 41.

Garfield, S., & Bergin, A. (1971). *Handbook of psychotherapy and behavior change.* New York: John Wiley & Sons.

Ginsberg, B. (1977). Parent-adolescent relationship development program. In B. Guerney (Ed.), *Relationship enhancement: Skill-training programs for therapy, problem prevention, and enrichment.* San Francisco: Jossey-Bass.

Glenn, H. S. (1984, June). *Developing capable young people.* Paper presented at the 33rd Annual University of Utah School on Alcoholism and Other Drug Dependencies, Salt Lake City, UT.

Glynn, T., Leukefeld, C., & Ludford, J. (1983). *Preventing adolescent drug abuse: Intervention strategies* (DHHS Publication No. ADM 83-1280). Washington, DC: U. S. Government Printing Office.

Goodstadt, M. S. (1978). Alcohol and drug education. *Health Education Monographs, 6*(3), 263–279.

Goodstadt, M. S. (1974). Myths and methodology in drug education: A critical review of the research evidence. In M. S. Goodstadt (Ed.), *Research on methods and programs of drug education.* Toronto: Addiction Research Foundation.

Gordon, T. (1970). *Parent effectiveness training.* New York: P. H. Wyden.

Grady, K., Gersick, K., & Boratynski, M. (in press). Preparing parents for teenagers: A step in the prevention of adolescent substance abuse. *Journal of Family Relations.*

Greenleaf, J. (1981). *Co-alcoholic, para-alcoholic.* Los Angeles, CA: Greenleaf Associates.

Guerney, B. G., Jr. (1964). Filial therapy: Description and rationale. *Journal of Consulting Psychology, 28*(4), 304–310.

Guerney, B. G., Jr. (Ed.). (1977). *Relationship enhancement: Skill-training programs for therapy, problem prevention, and enrichment.* San Francisco: Jossey-Bass.

Guerney, B. G., Jr., Confal, J., & Vogelsong, E. (1981). Relationship enhancement versus a traditional approach to therapeutic/preventative/enrichment parent-adolescent programs. *Journal of Consulting and Clinical Psychology, 49,* 927–939.

Guerney, B. G., Jr., Guerney, L., & Andronica, M. (1966). Filial therapy. *Yale Scientific Magazine, 40,* 6–14.

Guerney, B. G., Jr., & Stover, L. (1971). *Filial therapy: Final report on (MH) 18264-01,93.* State College: Pennsylvania State University Press.

Guerney, B. G., Jr., Vogelsong, E., & Confal, J. (1983). Relationship enhancement versus a traditional treatment. In D. Olson & B. Miller (Eds.), *Family Studies Review Yearbook* (Vol. 1). Beverly Hills, CA: Sage Publications.

Guerney, L. (1975). *Foster parent training: A manual for trainers.* State College: Pennsylvania State University Press.

Haley, J. (1973). Strategic therapy when a child is presented as the problem. *Journal of the American Academy of Child Psychiatry, 12,* 641–659.

Haley, J. (1976). *Problem-solving therapy.* San Francisco: Jossey-Bass.

Helfer, R., & Kempe, H. (1976). *Child abuse and neglect: The family and community.* Cambridge, MA: Ballenger.

Huberty, D. (1974, December). *Treating the adolescent drug abuser.* Paper presented at the North American Congress on Alcohol and Drug Problems, San Francisco, CA.

Hurd, P., Johnson, C. A., Pechacek, T., Bast, C. P., Jacobs, D., & Leupka, R. (1980). Prevention of cigarette smoking in seventh grade students. *Journal of Behavioral Medicine, 3*(1), 15–28.

Jenson, W. R., & Staff (1980). *CBTU Parenting program.* Salt Lake City, UT: Children's Behavior Therapy Unit, Salt Lake County Mental Health.

Jessor, R. (1975). Predicting time of onset of marijuana use. A developmental study of high school youth. In D. Lettieri (Ed.), *Predicting adolescent drug abuse: A review of issues, methods, and correlates* (DHEW Publication No. ADM 76-299). Washington, DC: U.S. Government Printing Office.

Jessor, R., & Jessor, S. L. (1977). *Problem behavior and psychosocial development: A longitudinal study.* New York: Academic Press.

Johnson, C. A., Graham, J., & Hansen, W. B. (1981). *Interaction effects of multiple risk-taking behaviors: Cigarette smoking, alcohol use and marijuana use in adolescence.* Paper read at American Public Health Association meeting, Los Angeles.

Johnson, C. A., Hansen, W. B., Flay, B. R., Graham, J., & Sobel, J. (1985, June). *Prevention of multiple substance abuse in youth.* Paper presented at National Prevention Network Conference, Nashville, Tennessee.

Kaufman, M. (1980). Myth and reality in the family patterns and treatment of substance abusers. *American Journal of Drug and Alcohol Abuse, 7*(3 & 4), 257–279.

Klein, N. C., Alexander, J. F., & Parsons, B. V. (1977). Impact of family systems intervention on recidivism and sibling delinquency: A model of primary prevention and program evaluation. *Journal of Consulting and Clinical Psychology, 45,* 469–474.

Krasnegor, N. (1979). *Behavioral analysis and treatment of substance abuse* (National Institute on Drug Abuse Research Monograph 25, DHEW Publication No. ADM 79-839). Washington, DC: U.S. Government Printing Office.

Kumpfer, K. L. (1975, May). *TBO: Therapy by objectives. A new clinical program for promoting change.* Symposium on new psychotherapy techniques for women, Rocky Mountain Psychological Association, Salt Lake City, UT.

Kumpfer, K. L., & DeMarsh, J. (1983a). *Strengthening Families Program: Parent training curriculum manual* (Prevention Services to Children of Substance-abusing Parents). Social Research Institute, Graduate School of Social Work, University of Utah.

Kumpfer, K. L., & DeMarsh, J. (1983b). *Strengthening Families Program: Family skills training curriculum manual* (Prevention Services to Children of Substance-abusing Parents). Social Research Institute, Graduate School of Social Work, University of Utah.

Kumpfer, K. L., & DeMarsh, J. (1984, February). *Prevention services to children of substance-abusing parents: Project rationale, description and research plan.* Technical report submitted to National Institute on Drug Abuse, Rockville, MD.

Kumpfer, K. L., & DeMarsh, J. P. (in press). Prevention strategies for children of drug-abusing parents. *Proceedings of the 34th Annual Congress on Alcoholism and Drug Dependence,* Calgary, Alberta.

Kumpfer, K. L., Williams, B., & Maldanado, D. (1985, June). *Evaluation of a Hispanic family substance abuse prevention program.* Social Research Institute, Graduate School of Social Work, University of Utah.

L'Abate, L. (1975a). *Manual: Enrichment programs for the family life cycle.* Atlanta: Social Research Laboratories.

L'Abate, L. (1975b). Pathogenic role rigidity in fathers: Some observations. *Journal of Marriage and Family Counseling, 1,* 69–79.

L'Abate, L. (1977). *Enrichment: Structured interventions with couples, families, and groups.* Washington, DC: University Press of America.

McAlister, A., Perry, C., & Maccoby, N. (1979). Adolescent smoking: Onset and prevention. *Pediatrics, 63,* 650–658.

Miller, S., & Wackman, D. (1968). *Couple communication: A marriage enrichment program.* Minneapolis: Interpersonal Communications Programs.

Millman, H., Schaefer, C., & Cohen, J. (1980). *Therapies for school behavior problems.* San Francisco: Jossey-Bass.

Minuchin, S. (1974). *Families and family therapy.* Cambridge, MA: Harvard University Press.

Moos, R. H. (1974). *Family environment scale.* Palo Alto, CA: Consulting Psychologists Press, Inc.

Olson, D., Sprenkle, D., & Russell, C. (1979). Circumplex model of marital and family systems. *Family Process, 15,* 3–15.

Patterson, G. R. (1974). Interventions for boys with conduct problems: Multiple settings, treatments, and criteria. *Journal of Consulting Clinical Psychology, 42,* 471–481.

Patterson, G. R. (1976). *Living with children: New methods for parents and teachers.* Champaign, IL: Research Press.

Patterson, G. R., & Fleishman, M. J. (1979). Maintenance of treatment effects: Some considerations concerning family systems and follow-up data. *Behavior Therapy, 10,* 168–185.

Perry, C. L., Killen, J., Telch, M. J., Slinkard, L. A., & Dannaher, B. S. (1980). Modifying smoking behavior of teenagers: A school-based intervention. *American Journal of Public Health, 70,* 722–725.

Pyramid. (1976). *Primary prevention research.* Unpublished report, Pacific Institute for Research and Evaluation, Walnut Creek, CA.

Richards, L. G. (1969, September). *Government programs and psychological principles in drug abuse education.* Paper presented at the annual meeting of the American Psychological Association, Washington, DC.

Rose, M., Battjes, R., & Leukefeld, C. (1984). *Family life skills training for drug abuse prevention* (DHHS Publication No. ADM 84-1340). Washington, DC: U.S. Government Printing Office.

Sager, C. J., Masters, Y. J., Ronall, R., & Normand, W. C. (1968). Selection and engagement of patients in family therapy. *American Journal of Orthopsychiatry, 38,* 715–723.

Schaps, E., DiBartolo, R., Moskowitz, J., Palley, C., & Churgin, S. (1981). Primary prevention evaluation research: A review of 127 impact studies. *Journal of Drug Issues, 11,* 17–43.

Seldin, N. E. (1972). The family of the addict: A review of the literature. *International Journal of the Addictions, 7,* 97–107.

Shapiro, I. S. (1976). Is group parent education worthwhile: A research report. *Marriage and Family Living, 18,* 154–161.

Slipp, S., Ellis, S., & Kressel, K. (1974). Factors associated with engagement in family therapy. *Family Process, 13*(4), 413–427.

Sowder, B., & Burt, M. (1978). *Children of Addicts and Nonaddicts: A Comparative Investigation in Five Urban Sites.* (Report to NIDA.) Bethesda, Md.: Burt Associates, Inc.

Sowder, B., Dickey, S., Glynn, T., & Burt Associates Inc. (1980). *Family therapy: A summary of selected literature* (DHHS Publication No. 81-944). Washington, DC: U.S. Government Printing Office.

Stanton, M. D. (1979). Family treatment approaches to drug abuse problems: A review. *Family Process, 18,* 251–280.

Stanton, M. D., & Todd, T. (1981). Engaging resistant families in treatment. *Family Process, 20,* 261–293.

Steinglass, P. (1975). Family therapy in alcoholism. In B. Kissin & H. Begleiter (Eds.), *Treatment and rehabilitation of the chronic alcoholic* (pp. 259–299). New York: Plenum Press.

Steinglass, P. (1980). A life history model of the alcoholic family. *Family Process, 19*(3), 211–226.

Streit, F. (1978). *Parents and problems.* Highland Park: Essence Publishers.

Swisher, J. D., & Hoffman, A. (1975). Information: The irrelevant variable in drug education. In B. W. Corder, R. A. Smith, & J. D. Swisher (Eds.), *Drug abuse prevention: Perspectives and approaches for educators* (pp. 49–62). Dubuque, LA: William C. Brown.

Szapocznik, J. (1983). *Family effectiveness training*. Unpublished final report. University of Miami Family Guidance Center.

Szapocznik, J., Kurtines, W., Hervis, O., & Spencer F. (1984). One person family therapy. In B. Lubin, & W. A. O'Connor (Eds.), *Ecological models: Applications to clinical and community mental health*. New York: John Wiley & Sons.

Szapocznik, J., Santisteban, D., Kurtines, W., Perez-Vidal, A., & Hervis, O. (1982). *Bicultural effectiveness training*. Miami: University of Miami Spanish Family Guidance Center.

Telch, M. J., Killen, J. D., McAlister, A. L., Perry, C. L., & Maccoby, N. (1982). Long-term follow-up of a pilot project on smoking prevention with adolescents. *Journal of Behavioral Medicine, 5*, 1–8.

Vaglum, P. (1973). The patient-centered family working group—A medium for collaboration with "unmotivated" family members: A mode and an example. *Scandinavian Journal of Social Medicine, 1*, 69–75.

Wegscheider, S. (1981). *Another chance: Hope and help for the alcoholic family*. Palo Alto, CA: Science and Behavior Books.

Wolfe, D., Kaufman, K., Aragona, J., & Sandler, J. (1981). *The child management program for abusive parents*. Winter Park, FL: Anna Publishing, Inc.

Ziegler-Driscoll, G. (1977). Family research study at Eagleville hospital and rehabilitation center. *Family Process, 16*, 175–189.

Mass Media, Youth and the Prevention of Substance Abuse: Towards an Integrated Approach

Lawrence Wallack, Dr. PH

ABSTRACT. Drug use rates among adolescents have declined in recent years but remain at high levels. This trend offers an excellent opportunity for reinforcing prevention efforts that focus on the context and conditions of use. Such an endeavor requires significant rethinking of the prevention process itself. This paper presents a series of principles which foster an integrated approach to prevention, and places the role of mass communications in that framework. Television programming, advertising, and mass media campaigns can all be used in an effort to change the message environment in which individuals behave.

INTRODUCTION

The early 1980s will be marked as a time when American youth moved away from the use of alcohol, tobacco and illicit drugs. Whether this movement will continue depends on several factors. Economic trends, social values, changing demographics and marketing developments all will have an effect on facilitating or inhibiting this encouraging direction. The

Lawrence Wallack, Assistant Professor, School of Public Health, U.C. Berkeley, Berkeley, CA 94720. Director, Prevention Research Center, Pacific Institute for Research and Evaluation, Berkeley, CA 94704.

The author wishes to express his appreciation to Kitty Corbett for her excellent editorial assistance. In addition, Ling Huse provided invaluable library support and Donna Elandt assisted with the referencing. Word processing was expertly done by Kathy Cole, Suzanne Gray and Paulette Comeau. Work on this paper was supported by a grant from the Henry J. Kaiser Family Foundation to the School of Public Health, University of California, Berkeley, and a National Alcohol Research Center Grant (#AA06282-03) from the National Institute on Alcohol Abuse and Alcoholism to the Pacific Institute for Research and Evaluation, Berkeley, CA.

153

current trend presents an excellent opportunity to reinforce the gains that have been made and begin to focus more on the conditions that contribute to the behaviors in question rather than just the behaviors. To further the goal of prevention, the individual behavior needs to be viewed in light of the broader behavior of the society. The two are inseparable.

Prevention efforts which include the broader context of substance use must address the effects and potential of mass communications, with attention to advertising, television programming and mass media campaigns. This paper will briefly review current trends in substance use, use of alcohol, tobacco and marijuana, as the backdrop to an overall integrated framework for future prevention efforts, and will discuss the role of mass communications in that framework.

CURRENT TRENDS

There appears to be consistent evidence from national high school (Johnston, O'Malley & Bachman, 1985) and household survey (Miller, 1983) data that there is an overall decline in drug use. The decline in use may not only reflect fewer youth initiating use but those already in the pool quitting (Johnston et al., 1985). Table 1 compares peak year data for high school seniors for any use in the last month with 1984 responses. Marijuana/Hashish use and cigarette smoking show considerable declines while the trend for alcohol use is not as dramatic. Frequent use, meaning at least 20 occasions in the past 30 days, has also declined across the board and is illustrated in Table 2. Clearly there has been a change in the drug-related behavior of high school seniors. Frequent drug use has by no means disappeared as part of the high school culture but students who entered high school in 1984 went into an environment with a much lower proportion of drug users than was the case in the late 1970s.

Trends from the household surveys are generally similar to those seen for high school seniors. Overall, as evidenced in Table 3, the proportion of those using marijuana at least once in the past month declined across all age groups. Since the peak year of 1977, use among those aged 12–17 has declined by almost one-third.

Table 1

Trends in Selected Drug Use
by
High School Seniors in Last 30 Days

	Peak Year	%	% 1984	Peak - Current	% Decline
Marijuana/Hashish	1978	37.1	25.2	11.9	32
Alcohol	1978	72.1	67.2	4.9	7
Cigarettes	1976	38.8	29.3	9.5	24

Source: Adapted from Johnston et al., 1985.

Table 2

Trends in Selected Daily Drug Use
by
High School Seniors in Last 30 Days

(20 or more occasions)

	Peak Year	%	% 1984	Peak - Current	% Decline
Marijuana/Hashish	1978	10.7	5.0	5.7	53
Alcohol	1979	6.9	4.8	1.3	19
Cigarettes	1976	28.8	18.7	10.1	37.5

Source: Adapted from Johnston et al., 1985.

Decreases in cigarette use can be seen in Table 4. Considerable reductions are apparent across all age groups, with smoking among those aged 12 and 13 seemingly almost disappearing in the past eight years. Overall, from 1974–1982, smoking among the group aged 12–17 appeared to decline by more than 40%. Alcohol use, as reflected in Table 5, has

Table 3

Trends in Marijuana Use
for
Household Sample by Age for Past Month

	Peak Year	%	% 1982	Peak – Current	% Decline
12–17	1979	16.7	11.5	5.2	31
12–13	1977	4	2	2	50
14–15	1979	17	8	9	53
16–17	1977	30	23	7	23

Source: Adapted from Miller, 1983.

Table 4

Trends in Cigarette Use
for
Household Sample by Age for Past Month

Age	Peak Year	%	% 1982	Peak – Current	% Declined
12–17	1974	25	14.7	10.3	41
12–13	1974	13	3	10	77
14–15	1974	25	10	15	60
16–17	1976	39	30	9	23

Source: Adapted from Miller, 1983.

also declined across age groups but not as markedly as the other substances. During the peak year of 1979, slightly more than 37% of those aged 12–17 had used alcohol in the past month, by 1982 slightly less than 27% were reporting use of alcohol.

Although the trends are encouraging, several caveats are appropriate. First, it is important to keep in mind that the data are based solely on self-reports with no validation methods used. It is not unusual to assume that underreporting of drug-related behavior, or any behavior perceived as deviant, is common. If the underreporting is consistent, then the general trend reflected may well be reasonably accurate. If there is reason to believe, however, that the level of underreporting is not constant, then the trends are highly unreliable.

Willingness to report accurately is in part dependent on one's perception of what is normative or acceptable behavior. Warner (1978), for example, found underreporting of cigarette use to increase as the social stigma on use increased and social acceptability declined. Johnson (1982) addressed the validity issue of a smoking decline among youth by pointing to two factors. First, he noted, in line with Warner, that self-reports of smoking reflect the perceived social acceptabil-

Table 5

Trends in Alcohol Use
for
Household Sample by Age for Past Month

Age	Peak Year	%	% 1982	Peak – Current	% Declined
12–17	1979	37.2	26.9	10.3	28
12–13	1979	20	10	10	50
14–15	1979	36	23	13	36
16–17	1979	55	45	10	18

Source: Adapted from Miller, 1983.

ity of the issue and not the actual behavior. Second, to support this point, he reported that other studies using some method for validating self-reports did not produce data supporting the decline in prevalence.

Another factor to consider in reviewing substance use trends is the increasing reports of smokeless tobacco use among youth (Wallis, 1985; Healy, 1985). Potentially, increases in this behavior could offset the reported decline in cigarette use.

The emergence of smokeless tobacco as a potential health problem of some significance is one of several possible counter trends. The possible reduction of the federal excise tax on cigarettes back to .08 per pack from .16 may have significant effects. Previous studies have indicated that price is a powerful determinant of onset of smoking behavior among youth (Lewit, Coate, & Grossman, 1981). Price can also be influenced by an increase in disposable income among teens that could result from an expanding economy. The reduction in the excise tax and a possible increase in disposable income could significantly lower the relative price of cigarettes, and have serious implications for smoking trends.

Alcohol consumption and driving, two behaviors that increase risk among youth, are linked to economic trends (Wagenaar, 1984). Survey data indicate that heavy drinking among high school seniors is positively associated with having a job and the number of hours worked per week. In addition, heavier drinking among high school students (10th–12th grade) is positively associated with the amount of weekly spending money (USHHS, 1984).

A recent increase in traffic fatalities has been linked to a change in driving habits resulting from a somewhat improved economy. Concern has been expressed that improving economic conditions may offset gains in public awareness and new legislation in the area of alcohol and seat belts (Staff, 1985).

Our concern here is with strategies involving mass communications. All specific approaches, however, must be responsive to certain principles of an integrated approach to prevention. Economic shifts and subsequent consequences cannot be controlled but can be anticipated. Prevention, to be effective, needs to be a broad enterprise that is comprehensive and coherent and addresses a wide range of individuals, social, cultural and economic variables related to the problems of drinking, smoking and drug taking. Excise tax changes, restrictions on the physical availability of substances, and advertising restrictions are examples of strategies that can be planned and promoted as part of a broad approach to prevention.

PRINCIPLES OF AN INTEGRATED FRAMEWORK FOR PREVENTION

Prevention is fundamentally concerned with keeping people well or problem-free and thus obviating the need for treatment. Primary prevention is an effort to reduce the incidence or numbers of new cases of a problem, disease or condition. Other strategies that focus on early casefinding are considered secondary prevention and will not be considered here. Casefinding, treatment, and rehabilitation are nonetheless recognized as greatly important in society's effort to address alcohol and drug problems.

Health-related behaviors do not take place in a vacuum but occur in a social, economic and cultural context. The usual practice in attempting to understand behaviors is to remove them from all or part of this context. This has at least two consequences. First, the problem or behavior is simplified by limiting the number of variables that need to be addressed. For example, behaviors that are connected to a family or community context are understood as personal problems rather than family concerns or community issues.

Second, behaviors that are removed from the more complicated context in which they exist and reduced to properties of individuals are much better suited to available "technology" in prevention programming. For more than a generation, social science (and biomedical science) has primarily sought explanations for social problems at the individual level (Gregg, Preston, Geist & Caplan, 1979). This has the effect of limiting solutions to that level and reinforcing the need to gain greater knowledge of the individual to further refine the solution. The result is a reification of "programs" and a tendency to leave the context or the environment of the problem untouched.

This program approach to prevention is popular for many reasons but mostly because it benefits all parties involved, except the person with the problem (Caplan & Nelson, 1973). The research process uncovers a deficiency that is thought to explain a behavior. The deficiency is recast as a need that is congruent with the assumptions and skills of bureaucrats, planners, program developers and researchers. Bureaucrats are satisfied, as are politicians, because these programs usually satisfy a desire to "do something" while remaining safe, but they do little to alter existing arrangements. Educators and other program interventionists can develop programs that fit the needs uncovered as perceived by the researchers. This usually entails providing more of something such as communication skills, self-esteem or sometimes just knowledge. Some researchers can evaluate the outcome of these programs, while others can seek greater and greater precision regarding the relevant factors and perhaps find new factors internal to the individual that are more strongly correlated with the problem behavior. The tobacco industry, pharmaceutical drug industry, or alcohol industry are pleased because the problem has been placed on the individual and the product from which the industry derives their profits has been excluded from the problem definition (Wallack, 1984). The narrow definition of the problem leads to narrow, limited solutions.

For the individuals with the problem, a few will gain some long-term benefit and most will likely have a short-term good feeling. Some will likely be bored. For the great majority, there will be no long-term effect either positive or negative. For the society, programs may serve a ceremonial purpose in that programs are a "good thing" to do. The program, in a sense, helps the society to meet an ethical obligation to help people help themselves. Yet, society's drug problem can only partially be addressed by addressing individuals because the problem exists as a function of the interaction of the behavior and the broader social context. Society's drug problem is not equal to or the same as the aggregation of individual problems. It is greater and different.

Programs tailored to the individual level are important but only as part of a broader effort to address problems. An integrated approach to prevention develops programs, social policies, and organizational structures to address problems. In this approach, there is substantial attention to the well-being of the whole as well as the individual parts.

The social and individual behavior that contributes to alcohol, tobacco, and drug problems is complex. Such behavior is a function of various interlocking components of a broad system. For example, production, marketing, and distribution practices of the tobacco and alcohol industries are clearly related to individual and community problems with these substances. The marketing of pharmaceuticals and over-the-counter drugs has been linked to the reinforcement of a "drug culture" and thus may indirectly affect the use of various substances. Laws, regulations, and restrictions are another component in this broader system as well as the reasons and motivations of individual behaviors.

The business structure, government regulatory structure, individual motivational structure, and the structure of community norms, standards and expectations are all part of the context of the problem and thus part of the problem. The challenge is to address the problem across these different segments of society. To progress in this endeavor, prevention efforts would do well to proceed from a specific set of principles. These principles, applicable at different levels, form the basis for an integrated approach to prevention.

1. Public health problems such as alcohol, tobacco, and drug use among youth are clearly complex. It is important to resist the temptation to simplify such problems by reducing them to individual behaviors. An analysis based on an approach that reduces problems in this way cannot lead to an adequate understanding of the problem and hence will result in partial or inadequate solutions.

Awareness programs, also sometimes referred to as educational programs, are an example of an oversimplification of the problem. The explicit logic of these programs is that the problem is caused by a lack of awareness; thus providing accurate information or increasing awareness to overcome this deficiency will solve the problem. These programs can vary from slogans such as "Just say no!" (the current drug message) to "Drinking and Driving Don't Mix." These efforts have not been successful and when used in isolation hold little promise for seriously addressing the problem. Nonetheless, increased awareness is a necessary part of the prevention process.

Programs that emphasize skill development have been

somewhat more successful. Apparent initial successes in the area of smoking (Telch, Killen, McAlister, Perry & Maccoby, 1982; Botvin, Eng & Williams, 1980; Botvin & Eng, 1982) are now being replicated with preliminary hopeful results in drug and alcohol areas (Botvin, Baker, Botvin, Filazzola & Millman, 1984). A range of methodological problems necessitate considerable caution in assessing the validity of these results. Nonetheless, these findings provide some hope that school-based programs based on sound social-psychological principles can be successful.

The social skills programs like the more general education and awareness programs suffer from a significant conceptual flaw. These programs reinforce a view of problems as properties of individuals rather than social systems. Individuals as a critical component of a broad social and economic system need to be an important, but not sole, focus. Because these problems are linked to the environment of institutions, norms and community life, it is in this broader context that such problems must be understood. A school program, whether based on an informational or skills approach, might well emphasize the role of advertising as part of the overall problem. Such programs provide students with resistance skills to help reduce the influence of these ads. Yet, the advertisements per se and the regulatory mechanisms that could be applied to make these ads more responsible are left untouched. When problems are defined at the individual level, there is little rationale for focusing on aggregate level strategies.

2. An integrated approach to prevention emphasizes a shared responsibility for addressing problems. Because these problems have many contributory causes that emanate from different sectors of the community, the responsibility for these is distributed across various groups. Many programs are based on an implicit assumption that the person with the problem bears sole responsibility for change. This approach has come to be known as "blaming the victim" after the work of Ryan (1976).

"Blaming the victim" strategies, or at least strategies that fail to acknowledge a shared responsibility, raise serious ethical concerns as well as effectiveness issues. If many contribute to the conditions that give rise to and sustain public health problems, then it is reasonable that the burden for prevention should be proportionately shared (Beauchamp, 1976). Further, because the group or community, as well as the individual, stands to benefit either directly or indirectly from the increased quality of life that results from lower levels of public health problems, it is legitimate and proper for many to contribute to the solution.

Individual level strategies can have a serious unintended consequence of stigmatizing the person with the problem and increasing the complexity of the situation. Health promotion strategies often call on all to make the same change, but all do not have the same resources to draw on to help with the necessary change. The result can be a concentration of lifestyle behaviors that detract from health in lower social status groups. This has clearly happened in the area of cigarette smoking which is quickly becoming a lower class behavior (Hall, 1985). The risk is that as behaviors become concentrated in those with the least political as well as personal resources, the likelihood of increased sanctions, legal and economic, against the behavior increases. Providing non-smokers with reduced insurance rates, for example, must result from an increase in the premiums for smokers. These people may already have the most difficulty getting insurance at affordable rates because of their employment status. Thus the penalty not only falls on smokers but those who are most in need because of their SES position and higher risk health. These people are probably least able to achieve insurance coverage. The ethical as well as practical implications of prevention policies and strategies need to be carefully reviewed as a matter of course.

3. An integrated approach to prevention emphasizes long-term planning as well as addressing short-term crisis interventions. It is fairly typical for our society to respond to crisis situations but be less willing to plan to prevent these situations from evolving. Longer-term planning is appropriate to the prevention of substance use problems because of the degree to which they have a history of intransigence to a range of varied strategies. In addition, a longer-term approach contributes to more realistic expectations regarding the level of effort and time that is necessary to stimulate meaningful change.

It is also important to institutionalize prevention efforts as part of the ongoing concerns of the group or community.

Prevention efforts, though well intentioned, often are brief in their life span. The lack of adequate funding, expectations for immediate change, a crisis intervention orientation and a categorical or isolated view of substance use problems all contribute to an issue-oriented type of prevention where the actors disband after token initial effect or resistance. Oftentimes the previous state of the problem quickly returns, sometimes at a more entrenched level. In recent years, groups such as Mothers Against Drunk Drivers, parents' groups, and non-smoking activist groups have built existing social policy and prevention efforts. This has facilitated the movement.

Because substance use problems exist across different levels of the community and society, prevention efforts need to be considered as relative, rather than absolute. The effectiveness of school programs, for example, could be enhanced if planning were done in relation to policies and practices in the larger community. Yet, what actually happens is many school-based strategies are seldom reinforced by the social and physical environment outside the school. Indeed, factors such as advertising and other variables related to availability often are directly contrary to the message of education programs. Planning or program development on one level needs to be consistent with activities on other levels.

4. Education is necessary, but not sufficient, for stimulating change. A strong implicit assumption about prevention has been that education is equal to prevention. From the current reported success of school-based smoking prevention programs (Telch et al., 1982; Botvin et al., 1980), it can be hypothesized that success, in part, is based on the development of skills *as well as* knowledge, and the rapid evolution of supportive norms for non-smoking in the broader social environment. Recent accelerated declines in smoking among those in the larger community, as well as in schools, are in part explained by the doubling of the excise tax on cigarettes and increase in the relative price of the product. In many cases, however, planning on one level runs counter to that on other levels. Certainly producers seek ways to expand markets and increase consumption. In other cases, such as the excise tax increase, the congruency of planning is coincidental. It is likely that the excise tax increase resulted from economic rather than public health concerns.

Strategies that are considered absolute (sufficient alone)

and that are conceived and implemented in isolation have serious flaws. Such strategies are not consistent with the complex systems quality of the problem and will likely, if successful at all, be less successful than necessary to create change.

5. Comprehensiveness is an important part of an integrated approach. This concept does not, however, simply refer to "more of" as so commonly seems the case. Comprehensiveness refers to the qualitative relationship between the different components of an overall strategy. Oftentimes, "more of" something when that something didn't work in the first place (save for some dose-response relationships) can become part of the problem, a barrier rather than a solution (Watzlawick, Weakland, & Fisch, 1974).

Comprehensive approaches are based on a carefully thought out assessment of the relationship of the nature of the problem to resources, needs, goals and conflicting interests. Because the nature of the problem is often unclear, difficult to define, and difficult to get an agreement on, a comprehensive approach involves increasing the number and type of variables to be considered. Traditional approaches often seek to eliminate variables and thus seek precision rather than comprehensiveness (Churchman, 1979). Precision, appropriate for well structured problems, is unrealistic with the ill-structured (Ackoff, 1974) or "wicked" (Rittel & Webaber, 1973) problems that public health addresses. Thus, integrated approaches to prevention may have to include attention to variables such as social status and underlying social inequalities that are often "controlled for" or ignored because they tend to blur rather that clarify the process.

Overall, comprehensive approaches need to address the relationship between program, policy and major social institutions. This is necessary to insure that the approach is not simply more of the same, but balanced and consistent.

In sum, the principles of an integrated approach to prevention suggested here address the need to understand and respond to problems as properties of the broader social and physical environment in which individuals behave. Because the causes and consequences of substance use exist across different levels of the broader system, solutions need to be conceived of in relational rather than absolute terms. Approaches based on long-term planning rather than short-term problem solving are central to serious efforts to prevent substance use problems.

The mass communications system conveys a range of messages that have implications for public health. In order to strive for a consistency of purpose and action across the many levels on which problems exist it is important to attend to the nature of these messages and try to insure that they support rather than contradict prevention goals.

THE ROLE OF MASS COMMUNICATIONS IN PREVENTION

The mass communications system comprises an important part of the environment in which people behave (and children develop). The information, images and messages put forth may serve to inhibit or facilitate the development of a range of health-related behaviors. Because television is so pervasive in our society, its presence in a household is no more questioned than that of a chair or table, it is the medium that will receive greatest emphasis here. As a participant at the White House Conference on Families (1980) noted:

> Television has become another member of the family. We eat meals near it, we learn from it, we spend more time with it than any single individual. Television is central in our children's lives, as a tutor, babysitter, teacher and salesperson all rolled into one. (p. 92)

Television plays a major role in the lives of children. From the age of 2 years, ratings studies track viewing habits to help advertisers better target their messages. Based on the Nielsen Company October 1984 ratings, children aged 2-5 years watch almost 26 hours of television per week, while those aged 6-11 years watch approximately 22 hours per week. Male teen average roughly 21 hours per week compared to 18 hours for their female cohort (Traub, 1985).

Television is a significant source of socialization for youth and represents an important part of the physical and social environment from which children learn how to act, what and who to like, what to expect from various actions and how different parts of life relate to one another (Comstock, 1981). Television offers lessons for life, but they are lessons based on a finely crafted view of the world that is intended to suit the needs of a consumption-oriented society (Gerbner & Signorelli, 1982) rather than one concerned with the development of healthy children. George Gerbner has noted: "If you can write a nation's stories, you needn't worry about who makes its laws. Today, television tells most of the stories to most of the people most of the time." Concern about the power of storytellers and their influence on children extends back to Ancient Greece. Never before, however, has there been such a centralized, powerful, pervasive storytelling machine as there is today.

Television Programming

Television tells a particular story about alcohol, drugs and tobacco. It is a story that is changing, getting better in some ways and more problematic in others. Most of all, it is a story that leaves out significant pieces and consequently fails to fulfill an important opportunity to provide accurate information and education for the viewer.

Studies of alcohol, drug, and tobacco use on television date back to the early 1970s. Since 1970, all but six of the prime-time television seasons have been analyzed for at least one substance by researchers (Winnick & Winnick, 1976; Smart & Krakowski, 1973; McEwen & Hanneman, 1974; Greenberg, Fernandez-Collado, Graef, Korzenny, & Atkin, 1979; Greenberg, 1981; Lowry, 1981; De Foe, Breed & Breed, 1983; Wallack, Breed & Cruz, 1985).

In general, smoking has been very rare over this period though there is some evidence of a recent upturn (Cruz & Wallack, 1985). Alcohol portrayals have been frequent and of questionable accuracy. The most recent data suggests that alcohol use is greater than in past studies, averaging more that 10 "acts" per hour. Greenberg (1981) estimates that the average viewer too young to drink will be exposed to about 3,000 drinking acts per year. In the past, the messages associated with these acts have not been sound from a health perspective. The most recent data suggest increasing frequency of alcohol portrayals but in a much more neutral way—higher risk and heavier drinking, for example, being rare. While the viewer is likely to see a lot of alcohol, s/he is not likely to see very heavy or irresponsible drinking (Wallack & Breed, in press).

None of the studies indicates a significant number of drug-related acts. Even though there was great concern over the national drug crisis, McEwen and Hanneman (1974) found very little on television about licit or illicit drugs, a finding supported by the other studies. References to illicit drugs outnumbered drug using acts and were consistently negative. Smart and Krakowski (1973) reported, "The major impact of television on the drug problem would appear to be to encourage primarily the use of beer, and household nostrums" (p. 21).

The common theme across the various content studies is the lack of any information about drugs and tobacco, reflected by the virtual absence of these substances. In a sense, television has addressed the marijuana and smoking issues by not presenting information of any kind, although references to drugs, when made, are generally negative. The drug traffic seems to be gaining more attention in the recent crop of action-adventure police shows. Yet society's drug problem is not addressed in a meaningful way. Alcohol issues likewise are not being addressed. Excessive consumption and blatant examples of alcohol misuse appear to have declined (Wallack & Breed, in press). Nonetheless, the strong association with alcohol in an array of settings may well contribute to a normalization of alcohol use that suggests a taken-for-granted nonchalance about the drug. This in turn could create a reticence to question the appropriateness of widespread availability of alcohol.

Advertising

The effects of advertising have long been a controversial issue and research has not been able to provide sufficient answers. In the area of alcohol, there have been two major series of studies. Work by Strickland and his colleagues (Strickland, Finn & Lambert, 1982; Finn & Strickland, 1982) has failed to find a basis for concern about either content or effects of advertising. Breed and De Foe (1979), to the contrary, have reported that the content of magazine ads is highly misleading, using images of sex, wealth and prestige to appeal to consumers. A team of Michigan State researchers have found a positive relationship between alcohol advertising and consumption (Atkin, Hocking & Block, 1984; Atkin, Neuendorf & McDermott, 1983; Atkin, 1985). Regarding adolescent drinking, their data indicate that the typical teenager is exposed to approximately 1,000 alcohol ads each year. These ads contribute to the ongoing legitimacy of alcohol use in an increasing array of situations and are a source of socialization about alcohol for youth. In particular, exposure to ads was significantly associated with current drinking and (for current abstainers) intentions to drink (Atkin, Hocking & Block, 1984).

Research has contributed little to increasing our understanding of the effects of drug advertising on licit or illicit drug use. In the early 1970s, there was considerable concern that over-the-counter (OTC) drug advertising on television was contributing to a drug oriented culture (Kramer, 1973). A major study to assess the effects of television drug advertising on OTC and illicit drug use of teenage boys was conducted by researchers from the National Broadcasting Company (NBC). The study found a negative association between television ad exposure and use of illicit drugs and a weak positive relationship to use of proprietary drugs (Milavsky, Pekowsky & Stipp, 1976). It is estimated that the average child between the age of 8 and 12 is exposed to 718 proprietary medicine ads per year (Robertson, 1980). Tobacco ads, not allowed on television, are heavily promoted in print. The effect of these ads, individually or collectively, is unknown. The purpose of these ads, however, is clearly to legitimize the use of the product through highly positive and attractive images. There is little or no concern with the possible negative consequences of the products. This raises an issue about the accuracy, fairness and potential misleading quality of these ads.

Another significant study of that period found that exposure to drug advertising was not related to positive attitudes toward illicit drugs. The study of 256 fifth, sixth and seventh graders found those who were more heavily exposed were more likely to think people: got sick "a lot"; should take medicine when they get sick; will get better faster; and worry about getting sick more often (Atkin, 1978). Overall, exposure to drug advertising was associated with slightly negative attitudes towards illicit drugs. Perceptions of levels of sickness, medicine use, and effectiveness of medicine, however were positively associated with exposure.

In his review of this literature, Robertson (1980) reported a lack of a relationship between OTC advertising and illicit drug use but also indicated that doubt persists. He identified a range of methodological shortcomings in the three major and half dozen or so related studies. Although making some excellent points about needed research, he fails to address key issues relating to the very nature of advertising and the broader cultural meanings that inform the socialization process in our society—particularly those meanings and values around sickness, health, treatment, and prevention.

Mass Media Campaigns

The use of media as a means for reducing alcohol, tobacco or drug use has a history dating back over a century (Wallack, 1981). Mass media efforts have relied on a set of assumptions reflecting an understanding of the problem to be addressed as a fundamental lack of information. These programs, historically, use a definition of the problem that is most consistent with the values of the larger society. This is a view that confuses information with education, and education with prevention.

There have been a number of reviews assessing the effectiveness of using mass media to change alcohol, drug or tobacco related behavior (Wallack, 1981; Flay, 1981; Hochheimer, 1981) and to alter general health behavior (Atkin, 1983; Solomon, 1982). At best, the reviews have presented guarded optimism about the potential of mass media efforts to stimulate significant change. At worst, the serious methodological flaws in the evaluations have been cited as the primary reason for not being able to say much of anything.

Campaigns that only use media are generally working against great odds. There are a great many more messages in the media that model the use and misuse of alcohol and cigarettes than messages that model non-use. Educators are often limited in the types of media formats that they have access to, especially if there are limited funds for production and for distribution. Often, adolescents are exposed to parents, friends and role models in the broader community who model behaviors that are counter to prevention (e.g., teachers who smoke, parents and friends who drink, etc.) (Flora, 1985). A clear indication from the mass media campaign experience is the need to link such efforts with broad-based community organization efforts (Farquhar, Maccoby & Solomon, 1984; Wallack, 1981; Flay & Sobel, 1983).

REVIEW

Television is a major part of the mass communications system and may contribute to how people behave in relation to alcohol, drugs and tobacco. Any cohesive, realistic story about any of these substances is absent from the prime-time television that young viewers watch. The absence of drug and tobacco use on television should not be seen as an indicator of responsible practices by the television industry but as a failure to take up the challenge to treat these issues in a serious ongoing way. This is not to say that there have not been several isolated programs that have been very important. Yet, these few excellent efforts, whether in existing programming or special programs, serve to highlight the enormous opportunity for television to provide valuable insights and information to its viewers and contribute to a legal and ethical responsibility to serve the public interest.

It is unlikely that sufficient research will be conducted to establish a causal relationship between viewing drugs or alcohol on television and increased use. (One current preliminary study supporting this view regarding alcohol has been done (Rychtarik, Fairbank, Allen, Foy & Drabman, 1983).) Clearly the relationship with increased use is complicated and television effects would be contributory but not causal. Flay and Sobel (1983), however, explain that such a causal relationship, is "highly likely" for the following reasons: (a) learning theory principles; (b) documented effects of anti- and pro-social programming on children's behaviors; (c) documented effects of advertising on children's consumer behavior; and (d) the finding that adolescents not yet using drugs seek information on them from mass media" (p. 8).

Mass media campaigns seldom have the resources to be successful. There is a tendency to fall victim to a "magic of media" syndrome. This includes vastly unrealistic expectations about the effects of "getting on television," lack of sophistication about campaign planning issues, and underutilization of formative research as a key ingredient in the planning process.

FUTURE DIRECTIONS

The general strategy being proposed here is to change the message environment in which indiviuals behave. This is part of an overall approach and should be considered in relation to other approaches. Clearly, television programming, advertising and mass media campaigns are not the only places that generate messages about substance use. The assumption is, however, that these are important sources that need much greater attention.

Cooperative Consultation

Television, as other media, is a significant actor in society. It is reasonable to demand that television, in line with its legal responsibility to serve the public interest, should strive to present accurate information about a wide range of health issues. In the area of substance use, this involves insuring that when alcohol, drugs and tobacco are involved in the storyline, it be done with the greatest possible accuracy. In addition, because the absence of these issues from television is not responsible, it is incumbent on the television industry to generate relevant programs.

A process called cooperative consultation has been developed as a means for working with writers, producers and directors in a constructive way to enhance the accuracy and usefulness for viewers of televised portrayals of alcohol (Breed & De Foe, 1982). This procedure has also been used with other media such as newspapers and comic books. The process is based on the assumption that television personnel will be responsive to legitimate concerns when approached in a tactful, thoughtful and knowledgeable way.

Cooperative consultation is a four-part process. *First,* Breed and De Foe (1982) conducted detailed *content analysis* of drinking on television over a period of several years, researched television production methods so they would be able to frame their findings and suggestions in an acceptable way, and became well-informed concerning issues related to alcohol problems and alcoholism. From research, the process moved to *general education of industry personnel.* This included a series of presentations to the Standards and Practices Offices of two of the three networks, extensive personal contacts with writers, and the development of a newsletter on alcohol topics that was widely distributed to industry people. The *next stage* is *specific education.* This happens when an industry person requests further information, which often takes the form of requests for help on specific problems related to scripts addressing alcohol issues. To meet these requests, De Foe, a member of the Writers Guild, offers a series of alternatives that serve the purpose of moving the script along but not at a cost of inaccurate alcohol information being used. The *final part* of the process is getting *feedback* from the industry in order to refine the process and facilitate effectiveness.

The apparent success of the technique stems from the way that they have carefully developed their project as a resource that serves the needs of the industry. In this case, both the industry and the viewer benefit. This process of research, general and specific education, and feedback fits well with a constructive, proactive prevention approach. It has been effective in attaining change in media portrayals of alcohol use. Several excellent examples of the outcome of this process are available (Breed & De Foe, 1982).

An approach to doing cooperative consultation with local newspapers is based on the same basic principles: know the problem; know the content; know the nature of the medium; be a valuable resource; have reliable information. Specific suggestions for approaching local media are discussed in Wallack and Breed (in press).

Cooperative consultation has been applied only to alcohol. It is clearly applicable, however, to drugs and tobacco. If the television industry is interested in addressing the issues of drugs in society as well as the individual manifestations of these problems, then a process such as cooperative consultation is valuable. Well-known actors and actresses proclaiming their support for non-drug use and being involved in prevention is important and praiseworthy. Nonetheless, these people do not necessarily have any special expertise in this area nor do they understand the complex social arrangements that contribute to these problems. Their efforts should represent part of the industry's responsibility in this area.

In sum, cooperative consultation should be used to increase the accuracy of existing incidental and purposeful portrayals of alcohol, drugs and smoking in regular television programming. In addition, special programs dealing with issues related to these substances can be initiated and developed through this process.

Advertising Activism

Advertising on television elaborates 30-second dramas that present problems and solutions. The effects of advertising are elusive; yet, the lack of *definitive* knowledge should not preempt action. Such action should follow at least two avenues. First, a renewed effort of content analysis of television ads regarding alcohol and over-the-counter drugs is necessary. A basic understanding of content is an essential step for any further debate. Content analysis can serve as a facilitator of increased rationality in the necessary public discussion that needs to accommodate this issue. Related to this, small experimental studies regarding advertising's influence on the perception of children of the causes of health problems and possible solutions are called for. The contribution of these ads to a reinforcement of health, and substance abuse, as strictly an individual concern needs to be addressed. Because future prevention models must evolve from a systems rather than an individual approach, the socialization of youth about health and disease, causes and responsibilities is important.

The second avenue of action is for parents and educators to become more involved in the process of questioning the practice of advertising as it relates to children. They can do this by forming their own viewing groups, developing goals in relation to working with key decision-makers and legislators, and supporting and participating in consumer action groups. Action for Children's Television (ACT) is an organization that seeks to eliminate advertising aimed at children and increase the amount of quality programming for children. Center for Science in the Public Interest (CSPI) has been very active in generating interest in more responsible alcoholic beverage advertising. As a result of their national petition drive in which one million signatures were obtained, and the support of organizations such as the National Parent-Teachers Association, congressional hearings on alcoholic beverage advertising have been held.

Advertising is a public health issue. It is an important part of the mechanism that fuels the economy. Yet, the consumption that advertising motivates may well have serious implications for the public health. Advertising is a social policy issue and as Rein (1976) notes, "Social policy is, above all, concerned with choices among competing values, and hence questions of what is morally or culturally desirable can never be excluded from the discussion." The answer to what kind of advertising for alcohol, over-the-counter drugs, cigarettes or smokeless tobacco is acceptable can only be answered by considering the role that such promotions play on the broader social agenda. Do such advertisements facilitate or inhibit the pursuit of public health goals? It is a public debate that demands broad participation from a range of perspectives.

Mass Media Campaigns

The use of mass media campaigns can keep issues regarding substance use uppermost on the public agenda. Such efforts can contribute to an overall message environment more conducive to informed decision making about the use of alcohol, tobacco, and drugs.

Education and behavior change efforts directed through the media should focus on at least three target groups. First, those who are at risk for using and having problems must be addressed. Second, those around the person at risk who might be used to alter the high risk situation are an important audience. Third, policy makers and opinion leaders, those who make decisions that affect the lives of others, represent a group requiring extensive attention.

Depending on the group, the messages and calls for action will vary. There are, however, three key messages. First, it is important to provide information on signs and symptoms of problems and where to get help. Second, the role of other people and the various environmental factors regarding use must be elaborated. Following from this will be specific skills that people can use to intervene in the drug-using *situation* of others. Third, a clear message about the social nature of drug, alcohol and tobacco use must be elaborated. Problems associated with these drugs are not random, but linked to other community problems and to people at less advantaged strata of society. Thus the link between these problems and other community and social issues must be made explicit.

The legacy of past mass-media efforts to change behavior may simply be that we've learned such efforts are more complicated than they appear. The Communication-Behavior Change model (Farquhar, Maccoby & Solomon, 1984) combines a variety of social-psychological as well as communications theories and processes to develop community-based education programs. One important component of the CBC model is the elaboration of a series of steps: moving from thinking about a problem, to trying out new behavior, to behavior maintenance. The process includes the following steps:

1. Agenda setting: getting the public thinking about the issue;
2. Information: education that makes the issue interesting, understandable, and personally meaningful;
3. Incentive: elaboration of the positive personal and social benefits;
4. Skills: providing step by step instruction and resources;
5. Action: education to trigger the trial adoption of new behaviors; and
6. Maintenance: developing social and other support for continuing of the changed behavior.

The CBC model is then subjected to a "social marketing analysis" to "package" and "deliver" the intervention. Social marketing is guided by the "4 P's"—the planning variables—of commercial marketing: the right Product at the right Price available in the right Place with the right Promotion. Solomon (1982) and Farquhar and his colleagues (1984) have reinterpreted these variables for a given issue and frame the planning process in the context of broader economic, political, technological, and cultural factors—thus merging social marketing and communications theory. As they define it, social marketing offers some useful tools such as market segmentation, a more holistic approach, and attention to issues in the larger environment.

While social marketing, however, may be a very useful addition to campaigns on social issues, it is far from a golden mean. Social marketing campaigns concerning health and social problems have not been shown to be successful. One such example is the "Winners" campaign (Wallack & Barrows, 1983). Although the theory of social marketing as an approach to prevention assumptions is consistent with public health understanding of primary prevention (especially as used by Fox & Kotler, 1980–81), the major barriers to prevention are not overcome by the *practice* of social marketing (Wallack, 1984a). A focus which is almost solely on the individual as the point of intervention, neglect of the conditions that give rise to the problems and an ethical stance that "blames the victim" characterize social marketing campaigns. Furthermore, the environmental variables deemed so important by social marketing are often beyond the reach of such efforts.

Well-developed communications and social psychology theory combined with the tools of social marketing may well result in innovative community programs to address substance use among youth. But the key here is community programs. Though mass media will have a role in these programs, community organizations and interpersonal contact will be important components, reinforcing and being reinforced by rigorously developed mass media messages as well as supporting printed materials.

CONCLUSION

Prevention is a long-term, complex undertaking. There are no magic slogans or magic medicines that can inoculate the population. Prevention is a process that starts with questioning why a problem happens and then moves back to understand not only the problem but the conditions that contribute to and sustain the problem. Mass media and the broader communication system in which they are housed are part of the conditions that contribute to the problem and are also part of the solution.

Television programming, advertising, and planned mass media campaigns all play a role in society's substance use problems.

This paper has suggested some ways that mass media could play a more enhanced role in prevention efforts. Mass media are, de facto, health educators. Those who determine content of television programming, create advertisements and plan health promotion and prevention campaigns have an important responsibility to serve the public interest. This is a challenge that those who think about the appropriate role of the mass media in prevention need to consider carefully.

REFERENCES

Ackoff, R. (1974). *Redesigning the future.* New York: Wiley-Interscience.

Atkin, C. (1978, Autumn). Effects of drug commercials on young viewers. *Journal of Communication*, 71–76.

Atkin, C. (1983). Mass media information campaign effectiveness. In R. Rice & W. Paisley (Eds.), *Public Communication Campaigns.* Beverly Hills: Sage Publications.

Atkins, C. (1985, Feb. 7). Testimony before Subcommittee on Alcoholism and Drug Abuse. Committee on Labor and Human Resources, U.S. Senate.

Atkin, C., Hocking, J., & Block, M. (1984, Spring). Teenage drinking: Does advertising make a difference? *Journal of Communication*, 157–167.

Atkin, C., Neuendorf, K., & McDermott, S. (1983). The role of alcohol advertising in excessive and hazardous drinking. *Journal of Drug Education*, 13(4), 313–325.

Beauchamp. D. (1976). Public health as social justice. *Inquiry*, 12–14.

Botvin, G., Baker, E., Botvin, E., Filazzola, A., & Millman, R. (1984). Prevention of alcohol misuse through the development of personal and social competence: A pilot study. *Journal of Studies on Alcohol*, 45(6), 550–552.

Botvin, G., & Eng, A. (1982). Efficacy of a multicomponent approach: The prevention of cigarette smoking. *Preventive Medicine, 11*, 199–211.

Botvin, G., Eng, A., & Williams, C. (1980). Preventing the onset of cigarette smoking through life skills training. *Preventive Medicine, 9*, 135–143.

Breed, W., & DeFoe, J. (1979). Themes in magazine alcohol advertisements: A critique. *Journal of Drug Issues, 8*, 339–353.

Breed, W., & DeFoe, J. (1982). Effecting media change: The role of cooperative consultation on alcohol topics. *Journal of Communication*, 32(2), 88–89.

Caplan, N., & Nelson, S. (1973, March). On being useful: The nature and consequences of psychological research on social problems. *American Psychologist*, 199–211.

Churchman, C. W. (1979). *The systems approach and its enemies.* New York: Basic Books.

Comstock, G. (1981). Influence of mass media on child health behavior. *Health Education Quarterly, 8*, 32–38.

Cruz, J., & Wallack, L. (1985). *Trends in tobacco use*, Unpublished manuscript, Prevention Research Center, Berkeley, CA.

De Foe, J., Breed, W., & Breed, L. (1983). Drinking on television: A five-year study. *Journal of Drug Education*, 13(1), 25–38.

Farquhar, J., Maccoby, N., & Solomon, D. (1984). Community applications of behavioral medicine. In W. Gentry (Ed.), *Handbook of behavioral medicine.* New York: Guilford Press.

Finn, P., & Strickland, D. (1982). A content analysis of beverage alcohol advertising, II: Television advertising. *Journal of Studies on Alcohol, 43*(9),964–989.

Flay, B. (1981). On improving the chances of mass media health promotion programs causing meaningful changes in behavior. In M. Meyer (Ed.), *Health education by television and radio*. Munich, Germany: Saur.

Flay, B., & Sobel, J. (1983). The role of mass media in preventing adolescent substance abuse. In T. J. Glynn, C. G. Leukefeld, & J. P. Ludford (Eds.), *Preventing adolescent drug abuse: Intervention* strategies (NIDA Research Monograph No. 47, Department of Health and Human Services). Rockville, MD: National Institute on Drug Abuse.

Flora, J. (1985). Personal Communication. Stanford Heart Disease Prevention Program, Stanford University.

Fox, K., & Kotler, P. (1980–1981). Reducing cigarette smoking: An opportunity for social marketing? *Journal of Health Care Marketing, 1*,8–17.

Gerbner, G., & Signorielle, N. (1982, October). The world according to television. *American Demographics,* 15–17.

Greenberg, B. (1981). Smoking, drugging and drinking in top rated TV series. *Journal of Drug Education, 11*(3), 227–233.

Greenberg, G., Fernandez-Collado, C., Graef, D., Korzenny, F., & Atkin, C. (1979). Trends in use of alcohol and other substances on television. *Journal of Drug Education, 9*(3), 243–253.

Gregg, G., Preston, T., Geist, A., & Caplan, N. (1979). The caravan rolls on: Forty years of social problems research. *Knowledge, 1,* 31–61.

Hall, T. (1985, June 25). Smoking of cigarettes seems to be becoming a lower class habit. *New York Times.*

Healy, M. (1985, July 26). Chewing over the problems of tobacco. *USA Today.*

Hochheimer, J. (1981). Reducing alcohol abuse: A critical review of educational strategies. In M. Moore, & D. Gerstein (Eds.), *Alcohol and Public Policy: Beyond the shadow of prohibiting.* Washington, DC: National Academy Press.

Johnson, C. (1982). Untested and erroneous assumptions underlying antismoking programs. In T. Coates, A. Petersen, & C. Perry (Eds.), *Promoting Adolescent Health.* New York: Academic Press.

Johnston, L., O'Malley, P., & Bachman, J. (1985). *Use of licit and illicit drugs by America's high school student, 1975–1984* (DHHS Publication No. ADM 85–1394). Washington, DC: U.S. Government Printing Office.

Kramer, E. (1973). A review of literature relating the impact of the broadcast media on drug use and abuse. In National Commission on Marijuana and Drug Abuse. *Drug use in America: Problem in perspective: Vol.11. Social response to drug use* (The Technical Papers of the Second Report of the National Commission on Marijuana and Drug Abuse). Washington, DC: U.S. Government Printing Office.

Lewit, E., Coate, D., & Grossman, M. (1981). The effects of government regulation on teenage smoking. *Journal of Law and Economics, 24,* 545–569.

Lowry, D. (1981, Spring). Alcohol consumption patterns and consequences on prime time network TV. *Journalism Quarterly,* 3–8.

McEwen, W., & Hanneman, G. (1974). The depiction of drug use in television programming. *Journal of Drug Education, 4*(3), 281–293.

Milavsky, J., Pekowsky, B., & Stipp, H. (1975–76, Winter). TV drug advertising and proprietary and illicit drug use among teenage boys. *Public Opinion Quarterly, 39,* 457–481.

Miller, J. (1983). *National survey on drug abuse: Main findings 1982* (DHHS Publication No. ADM 83–1263). Washington, DC: U.S. Government Printing Office.

Rein, M. (1976). *Social science and public policy.* New York: Penguin Books.

Rittel, M., & Webber, H. (1973). Dilemmas in a general theory of planning. *Policy Sciences,* 155–169.

Robertson, T. (1980). The impact of proprietary medicine advertising on children. In R. Adler, G. Lesser, L. Meringoff, T. Robertson, J. Rossiter, & S. Ward (Eds.), *The effects of television advertising on children.* Lexington, MA: D.C. Heath & Co.

Ryan, W. (1976). *Blaming the victim* (rev. ed). New York: Vintage Books.

Rychtarik, R., Fairbank, J., Allen, C., Foy, W., & Drabman, R. (1983). Alcohol use in television programming: Effects on children's behavior. *Addictive Behaviors, 8,* 1922.

Smart, R., & Krakowski, M. (1973, Spring). The nature and frequency of drugs content in magazines and on television. *Journal of Alcohol and Drug Education, 3,* 16–22.

Solomon, D. (1982). Health campaigns on television. In D. Pearl, L. Bouthilet, & J. Lazar (Eds.), *Television and behavior: Ten years of scientific progress and implications for the eighties* Vol. II (DHHS Publication No. ADM 82–1196). Washington, DC: U.S. Government Printing Office.

Staff. (1985, July). Auto deaths on increase after three years of decline. *The Nation's Health, XV,* 1ff.

Strickland, D., Finn, A., & Lambert, M. (1982). A content analysis of beverage alcohol advertising: 1. Magazine advertising. *Journal of Studies on Alcohol, 43*(7), 665–682.

Telch, M., Killen, J., McAlister, A., Perry, C., & Maccoby, N. (1982). Long-term follow-up of a pilot project on smoking prevention with adolescents. *Journal of Behavioral Medicine, 5*(1), 1–7.

Traub, J. (1985). The world according to Nielsen. *Channels, 4,* 26–29ff.

U.S. Department of Health & Human Services. (1984). *Report on the National Conference for Youth on Drinking and Driving* (DHHS Publication No. ADM 84–1356). Washington, DC.

Wagenaar, A. (1984). Effects of macroeconomic conditions on the incidence of motor vehicle accidents. *Accident Analysis and Prevention, 16,* 191–205.

Wallack, I. (1981). Mass media campaigns: The odds against finding behavior change. *Health Education Quarterly, 8*(3), 209–260.

Wallack, L. (1984a). Social marketing as prevention: Uncovering some critical assumptions. In T. Kinnear (Ed.), *Advances in Consumer Research: Vol II.*

Wallack, L., & Barrows, D. (1983). Evaluating primary prevention: The California "Winners" alcohol program. *International Quarterly of Community Health Education, 3*(4), 307–335.

Wallack, L., & Breed, M. (in press). Mass media and alcohol: Some opportunities for change. In B. Forster (Ed.), *Alcohol and drug abuse patterns: Prevention and treatments.* New York: Wadsworth Press.

Wallack, L., Breed W., & Cruz, J. (1984). *Alcohol on prime time television: Findings from the Fall 1984 season.* Berkeley, CA: Prevention Research Center.

Wallis, C. (1985, July 15). Into the mouths of babes. *Time Magazine.*

Warner, K. (1978). Possible increases in the underreporting of cigarette consumption. *Journal of the American Statistical Associates, 73,* 314–318.

Watzlawick, P., Weakland, J., & Fisch, R. (1974). *Change: Principles of problem formation and problem resolution.* New York: W. W. Norton Company.

White House Conference on Families. (1980, October). *Listening to America's families: Action for the 80's.* Report to the President, Congress and Families of the nation.

Winick, C., & Winick, M. (1976). Drug education and the content of mass media dealing with "dangerous drugs" and alcohol. In R. E. Ostman (Ed.), *Communication Research and Drug Education.* Beverly Hills: Sage Publishing.

Comprehensive Community Programs for Drug Abuse Prevention

C. Anderson Johnson, PhD
William B. Hansen, PhD
Mary Ann Pentz, PhD

ABSTRACT. This paper describes both a pilot and a larger research effort to implement and evaluate a comprehensive community-based approach to drug abuse prevention. Since heart disease is a side effect of youth and adult chemical abusers, models for community-based prevention in the heart disease prevention area are discussed as well as issues that are specific to the area of drug abuse prevention. Criteria for successful community drug abuse prevention programs are outlined that include the necessity for employing a step-wise multi-component approach involving school, media, parent, and community organization programs. Implications of the initial results of the pilot for future community prevention programs are also described. Entry, community support, and long-term community ownership of prevention are emphasized.

There are several reasons why sustained, highly integrated, multi-component community programs should be preferable to single component programs or campaigns for drug abuse prevention. School-based programs can be effective with the population they reach, but the potential of any solely school-based program is severely limited by a number of factors.

1. The majority of a youth's day is spent outside of school. Even in school, attention to drug abuse prevention consumes only a small amount of curriculum time. In addition, most opportunities to use drugs occurs outside of school.

Requests for reprints should be sent to C. Anderson Johnson, Health Behavior Research Institute, USC, 35 N. Lake Street, Pasadena, CA 91101.

Preparation of this chapter was supported in part by grants DA 03046-03, CA 35596-01, a grant from the W.T. Grant Foundation, and a project funded by the Kauffman Foundation.

181

2. The major portion of a young adolescent's time is still spent in the home (as much as 17 hours per day, more on weekends) and in front of the television set (four to six hours on the average per day). The potential influences of family and mass media are enormous.

3. Substantial time is spent by the young person in predictable out-of-school locations, such as diners, movie theaters, video arcades, and other recreational sites. These could become sources of considerable positive influence.

4. The young people at highest risk to drug use onset are least likely to be at school on the days that prevention programs are delivered. Absenteeism and dropout rates are known to be highest among drug users.

5. Adolescence is not the only risk period for onset of drug abuse. Other transition periods during adulthood are also periods of vulnerability. Beginning college, entry into the work force, the beginning of parenthood, midcareer, changing jobs, separation and divorce, moving to a new location, loss of a loved one are examples of stressful life events that may also represent significant transitions likely to increase one's vulnerability to drug abuse (Pentz, 1983).

For these reasons, an optimal drug abuse prevention program would utilize not only school systems for delivery, but also families, mass media, and community organization. Any such program should be comprehensive and highly integrated with each component contributing according to its unique potential. Every intervention component should be soundly based on theory and research findings.

Recent studies in heart disease prevention have demonstrated that comprehensive community programs sustained over several years can bring about meaningful health behavioral changes, including reduction in drug abuse (cigarette smoking and alcohol use) in whole populations (Blackburn, Carleton, & Farquhar, in press). The North Karelia (Finland) Project (McAlister, Puska, Salonen, Tuomilehto & Koskel, 1982), has produced significant reductions in cigarette smoking, dietary fat intake, hypertension and serum cholesterol levels in what was, at the onset of the program, the leading in the world in heart disease mortality (Puska et al., 1985). As a consequence of reductions in drug use and related health behavioral changes, cardiovascular mortality has declined significantly over the last 10 years, both in reference to the baseline and in comparison to the rest of Finland (including a country matched for comparison)(Puska, Tuomilehto & Salonen, 1981b; Puska, Vienola, Kottke, Salonen & Neittanmaki, 1981a; Puska, 1981).

Similar results have been obtained in other studies, including a less comprehensive community study in Oslo, Norway (Holme, 1980; Holme, 1982). Large reductions in cigarette smoking, serum cholesterol, and blood pressure were achieved in the Multi Risk Factor Intervention Trial (MRFIT) in the United States, although this trial has not yet produced mortality reduction in comparison with a control group (for which smaller but important behavioral changes also occurred (Hughes, 1981)). Small but significant effects for alcohol consumption were also produced (people were told that one way of controlling obesity was by curbing alcohol intake). The Stanford Three Community Study, with heavy emphasis on mass media, also produced significant reductions for all targeted risk factors with important effects being realized for cigarette smoking (Farquhar, 1978; Maccoby, 1981; Farquhar, Magnus & Maccoby, 1981).

Several additional studies in Europe and Australia have produced similar health behavior changes (Egger, 1983; Gutzwiller, Junod & Schweizer, 1979). These studies have all used various types of community activation, in some cases involving mass media and schools, to bring about and maintain health behavior changes in whole or at-risk populations. When interventions have been sustained, behavioral changes have been maintained, as in North Karelia. Where interventions have ceased, behavior has tended to revert to pre-intervention risk levels, as in the MRFIT study (Hughes, Hymowitz, Ockene, Simon & Vost, 1981). Program continuity, therefore, is important to success.

These findings in heart disease prevention are highly relevant to drug abuse, as are the experimental school based drug abuse prevention program. These are factors surrounding drug abuse, however, that call for special attention. For example, it should be recognized that not all drug abuse begins as social behavior. The dynamics of drug abuse onset in adulthood are somewhat different than during adolescence. During adulthood, social factors may be less directly influential, and drug use as a coping strategy may be more important (Flay, Hansen, Johnson & Sobol, 1983). Components of community programs for drug abuse prevention should be directed at these periods of increased risk during adulthood. Programs teaching self management and stress coping skills can be implemented in churches, civic clubs, parent groups and other groups, and supported by voluntary health organizations and other civic groups. These might follow the models of community organization for heart disease prevention developed in the heart disease prevention programs.

The active participation of health practitioners, supported by their professional societies, is important for comprehensive community prevention of drug abuse. Too often, abuse during adulthood begins as sequelae to medical care. Abuse of amphetamines, tranquilizers (especially benzodiazapines), and barbiturates begins this way for substantial segments of the population. Persons who would never consider using an illegal drug become the victims of dependence or addiction under the well-meaning care of physicians. Community prevention programs should include training programs for physicians, dentists, pharmacists, nurses, psychologists, and other health professionals, as well as plans for involving and documenting their active participation in a coordinated community program for drug abuse prevention.

Law enforcement officials and the courts can and should be included in planning for comprehensive community prevention programs. Policemen may be viewed as positive role models by young children in many communities. The Los Angeles Police Department sponsors a program wherein carefully selected officers are trained to deliver a program developed at the University of Southern California in conjunction with the Los Angeles Unified School system to elementary school children (Project DARE, unpublished). That program is carried out with younger children not only because officers' credibility may be greatest with this age group, but also to separate educational efforts from the enforcement responsibilities of the department. Although the effectiveness of the program in preventing the onset of drug abuse is not known, this program provides a good example of positive police action in a coordinated program for drug abuse prevention.

The mass media can and have been used effectively for drug abuse prevention, with the best documentation occurring for prevention and control of cigarette smoking (Danaher, Berkanovic, & Gerber 1982; Atkin, 1979; Flay, d'Avernas, Best, Ketsell & Ryan, 1983; Flay, et al., 1985). Mass media effects are greatest when combined with, and used to complement, other community activities (e.g., family involvement mobilized through coordinated school programs)(Pentz, 1985a). Television and radio can be especially effective tools. The role of the printed media will probably be limited until means have been developed to overcome the considerable censorship exerted by the tobacco manufacturers over drug (specifically tobacco) related articles. Most popular magazines and newspapers depend heavily on tobacco advertising revenues. The tobacco industry's use of this dependence to profoundly limit publication of tobacco related materials has been well documented (Warner, 1985). Comprehensive community intervention might include steps to countermand the censorship of drug related material in the mass media.

Community organization for drug abuse prevention should involve major components of the community, including schools, families, mass media, and community organizations. Health professionals and their societies, voluntary health organizations and civic groups, businesses, churches, existing community agencies and groups concerned with drug abuse control should all be involved in planning and program implementation. Existing community structures are especially responsible for program continuation, which is so important for maintenance of program effects. Municipal and county governments should be involved from the beginning, especially to facilitate planning for and implementation of policy changes and inforcement supportive of prevention.

In the remaining pages of this paper, we describe the initial results of a completed pilot study, and a five-year project for comprehensive community drug abuse prevention in youth and their families. The pilot project focused on developing methods for mobilizing multiple program channels, community resources, and community ownership of drug abuse prevention. The 5-year project is testing the feasibility of a long-term comprehensive community effort.

Both projects have at their core the training of youth to exercise drug resistance skills. This training is derived from several social-psychological developmental behaviors, including social learning theory, attribution theory, attitudinal in-oculation, and diffusion of innovation theories (Bandura, 1977; Fishbein & Ajzen, 1975; Pentz, 1985; Rogers, 1962, Rogers & Shoemaker, 1972). Research based on these theories has demonstrated that active resistance skills training as taught in this study, that is, training to resist peer and other social pressures to use drugs, can be highly successful in reducing and preventing drug use in youth and their families (Pentz, 1983). As described above, additional theory and research suggest that program effects may be enhanced and diffused by the inclusion of other channels (in addition to school) that also affect youth and their families on a daily basis, including family, media, and community organizations (Brown, 1984; Flay, in press; Johnson & Solis, 1983; McAlister, et al., 1982).

The projects presented here have employed all four of these channels in sequence, both to maximize prevention impact and provide the capability for evaluating separate channels, a capability not previously available in community prevention projects (Howe, 1982). The projects also have utilized community resources by organizing community leaders and other representatives of community agencies for dissemination of prevention information and referrals throughout the general population. Finally, community "ownership" has been addressed by tailoring program components to each community and by matching federal project funding with community-based funding.

PILOT PROJECT

The pilot project was an 18-month study designed to meet four specific objectives: (a) identification of community-level demographic and drug use-related data for use in assignment of whole communities to experimental conditions, by level of drug use risk; (b) development of a health promotion council for drug abuse prevention in a median-risk-level community; (c) development and feasibility testing of short-term interventions and family assessments for drug abuse prevention; and (d) development of a large-scale, long-term experimental project for drug abuse prevention, involving multiple communities. The pilot project focused on communities in Southern California.

Method

Community and Participant Selection

Data for community risk scores were collected on Los Angeles and Orange County cities from October through December, 1983. A pilot community was selected, based on median scores for drug-use related items, and median scores for county-level demographic statistics. Tustin, the selected community, had a population of 40,000, with a mean age of 33 years, 77% White, 10% of families with children between the ages of 10 and 15, and an average of 3.4 persons/family. From January through February, 1984, a community health promotion council was selected to facilitate the implementation of research objectives for *health screening, prevention workshops,* and a *community campaign.*

Between March and May, 1984, two methods were used to recruit families for health screening (including drug use): a community health fair, open to everyone in the community, and a newsletter distributed in randomly-selected classrooms of students in two middle schools.

Prevention workshop participants were solicited through their respective organization newsletters and the local community newspaper. Workshops included health professionals, business, parents, and mass media leaders in planning community support for drug abuse prevention.

The samples used for analysis included 61 families with youth between the ages of 10 and 15 who participated in health screening (N = 188); 81 adults who were evaluated in a health professionals' workshop (N = 17), a parent workshop (N = 18) or a business and media representatives' workshop (N = 13) for community drug abuse prevention, and matched controls (N = 42); and 18 community leaders who served on a community health promotion council developed for this project.

Research Design and Measures

Because the pilot project was intended as a small-scale descriptive project to develop methods for family-based health screening, short-term community interventions, and community organization for drug abuse prevention, only small sample sizes were used and no formal experimental tests were conducted. The health screening sample was tested in a single group pre-post design, with an initial health screening and an annual phone survey follow-up. The workshop sample was evaluated in a quasi-experimental, posttest only two-group design, with experimental and matched control groups evaluated in an annual phone survey follow-up. The community leader sample was interviewed at one time only, at six months following project termination (1984). Interview items included retrospective reports of prevention involvement in 1983, and reports of ongoing involvement in 1984.

Results

Identification of Data for Community Stratification and Selection

Information sources included census tract data on socioeconomic status (occupation, education, income, poverty level), race/ethnicity, mobility (rentals, residence change, commuting, census tract population change), and size of family and community; California state government statistics on alcohol- and drug-related offenses and cigarette sales tax; DAWN data on regional hospital admissions related to drug use; county data on drug abuse and prevention service utilization; community police data on drug-related arrests; and school district survey data on student drug use. The data were publicly available from libraries, government offices, and school district offices at no cost.

The search yielded fifteen variables that were significantly related to the variables we had used for assignment of schools to experimental conditions on the basis of drug use risk (Graham, Flay, Johnson, Hansen, & Collins, 1984): occupation, income, education, poverty status, single parent families, community size, family size, race/ethnicity, English-speaking, school drug use (a standardized and summed measure of cigarette, alcohol, and marijuana use), school achievement scores, mobility (a standardized and summed measure of residence change, commuting, and rentals), working women with children, prevention service utilization, proportion of convenience stores and liquor outlets, proportion of high school drop-outs. These data allowed for meaningful comparison of communities in a number of dimensions. We believe that these data which are readily available to communities throughout the United States should provide the primary data set for available analysis in community-based epidemiological studies of drug use, and stratification of communities to establish comparability for assigned to experimental continuity intervention.

Development of a Health Promotion Council

Thirty-seven community leaders were interviewed using a snowball sampling technique (Bloom, 1977). The leaders represented each of the four proposed prevention program channels for youth (schools, family groups, media, community agencies), as well as local government, church, and health groups. The major question addressed by this objective was whether community leaders from diverse backgrounds outside of drug abuse prevention could be mobilized to facilitate the implementation of specific short-term prevention activities.

Twenty-five leaders subsequently agreed to serve on a health promotion council that would meet monthly with HBRI staff to develop short-term intervention strategies for community drug abuse prevention. Eighteen of these leaders participated in 75% or more of council meetings; these leaders constituted the sample for the community leader follow-up survey. Fifty-six percent of community leaders reported a great increase in their organization's participation in drug abuse prevention in 1984 (intervention year) relative to 1983. Most of these leaders (i.e., 70%) represented school and family groups. Eighty-four percent of leaders reported at least a moderate increase in community awareness of drug abuse prevention in 1984. Only 26% reported perceiving a decrease in community drug use behavior in 1984. Ninety percent of these leaders expected to maintain a high level of participation in 1985.

As might be expected, organizations exhibiting a high degree of prevention participation in 1984 (versus some or little) expected a greater amount of participation in 1985 (X (4) = 17.34, p < .002). A content analysis of type of organizations represented by community leaders showed that the organizations with consistently high levels of participation from 1983 through 1985 were those associated with school and parent/family groups (e.g., school board, PTO, Parents Who Care). The findings from these analyses suggest that: (a) Participation in prevention by community leaders can be increased to a high level and with promise for maintenance at that level, and (b) the organizations most committed to prevention involvement are those which represent two of the major prevention program channels for youth, school and family.

Tests of Approaches to Health Screening

The purpose of the tests of approaches to family health screening was to evaluate the validity and reliability of family measures of drug use and related health behaviors, and to assess participation rates in alternative procedures. A secondary goal was to assess the relationship between drug use and other health behaviors and behavior-related variables.

Intra-familial reliability and concurrent validity assessments of drug use reporting demonstrated that family members' reports of drug use were highly valid and reliable. There were no differences in reliability or validity between families assessed in a mass data collection at the health fair and individual families that were assessed individually by appointment following the health fair. Individual family data collection, however, yielded more complete data (35/39 or 90% versus 26/40 or 65% of families with complete data).

Subsequent analyses were based on the pooled sample of 61 families with complete data (N = 188 individuals). Only 20% of these families reported any awareness of drug prevention activity in the community prior to the health screening. All but three families (95%), however, ranked drug abuse as the leading health issue in the community (cancer was rated second, heart disease third).

A secondary goal of the family health assessments was to evaluate the relationship between drug use and other health behaviors and behavior-related variables, including exposure to drug use (availability of drugs, parent, spouse, and peer use of drugs, drug-related offenses), physical health (physical health status, nutrition, exercise, sleeping patterns); psychological health; social/behavioral health (social support, extracurricular activity); health care utilization; and exposure to health communications. Composite scores were developed by standardizing and summing individual items from the same scales on the self-report measures. Common factors analysis of all health and drug items yielded six health factors for adults: (a) drug use, (b) extracurricular activity, (c) overall fitness, (d) medical problems, (e) communications, and (f) mental health. In contrast, youth data yielded only three major health factors: (a) drug use influences, (b) communication with parents, and (c) media exposure. Consistent with findings from developmental research, these results suggest that drug use and health behaviors are more complex and differentiated in adults than in youth (Pentz, 1983).

Common factors analyses were also conducted separately on youth drug use scores. Five factors were derived: (a) drug use, (b) drug use environment (availability, setting), (c) consequences, (d) parent smoking influence, and (e) parent reaction. The factor structure suggests that parents play a considerable role in their children's drug use behavior. Other research suggests that these influences are mediated primarily through peer associations (Hansen, Graham, Sobel, Flay & Johnson, 1985).

We are encouraged in regards to the reliability and validity of the measures. Participation ratios, however, were unacceptably low. We concluded that the two methods used, health fairs and invitations to come to a central site for health screenings, are inadequate for assessment of an attendance of 4,000 families/year. Each of 15 community agencies donated the time of three persons over the course of the three-day fair; at any one time, four to six persons staffed the booth. Each family attending the booth was given a resistance skills button and a prevention practice pamphlet if its members successfully completed two drug resistance role-plays with booth staff. At the end of the fair, 750 buttons with pamphlets had been distributed. Thus, 750/4,000 or 19% of families attending the fair were trained in drug resistance skills.

Development of a Longitudinal Community Drug Abuse Prevention Project

A proposal for a large-scale, longitudinal community project was developed and approved by NIDA in Spring, 1985. The project has already begun as a private foundation funded program in one midwestern city, and is expected to continue with Federal funds for a five-year period. The design and methods for this project are described below.

Conclusion

All of the six goals were met, at least in part. We demonstrated to our satisfaction that community leaders from diverse backgrounds who previously had not been engaged in drug abuse prevention efforts could be brought together in the existing drug treatment and control groups to develop a self-sustaining and coherent program for community drug abuse prevention. Assessment of program effectiveness in preventing drug use onset was beyond the scope of this project. Low cost strategies for assessment of family health and drug use behavior (health fairs and recruitment to a central testing site) proved to be inadequate. Home visits, bolstered by telephone surveys, will probably be necessary in order to assess a representative sample of families in the community.

THE FIVE-YEAR PREVENTION PROJECT

The 5-year comprehensive community drug abuse prevention project will involve three large metropolitan areas (n = 838,000–1,500,000/city) including a total of 45 district communities in a test of strategies for community organization for drug abuse prevention. In this study, school district boundaries define the unity of community. A five year study calls for phased-in experimental comparison of intervention components within communities, as well as lagged comparison between communities. The program in each city includes implementation of school programs to first year junior high or middle school students in half the communities, and implementation of a family program in half of these. Second year includes school program implementation in all communities in the city, extensive parent involvement and beginning of media involvement. Media involvement and community organization peak in years three and four, and communities assure full responsibility for program implementation and continuation over years four and five. The objective of the project is drug abuse prevention in youth 10–15 (the first risk period for drug use onset) and their families.

Method

Participants

Approximately 45,000 youth and 5,500 adults are surveyed annually for drug use and drug use risk behaviors, including related attitudes, drug availability, and community norms for drug use. The study population is approximately 73% White, 18% Black, and 9% other minority groups.

Research Design

At the city level, the design is quasi-experimental, with two cities assigned non-randomly to immediate or a two-year lagged intervention, and one city assigned to a no-intervention condition. Within intervention cities, at the community level, the design is experimental with communities assigned randomly to intervention and a two-year lagged replication against the no-intervention control. Separate 2 × 2 factorial designs will be used to test the effects of grade of program implementation (6th or 7th) and programs that are introduced sequentially each year within the overall intervention (components testing), including the school program (yes or no), parent organization (yes or no), community organization (yes or no), and use of policy change strategies (yes or no).

Measurement Design

The major design is cohort-sequential with successive cohorts of 6th and 7th grade students added in each of the first four years of the study. Five student samples, two parent samples, and one community resident sample will be evaluated.

Results

At the close of the first year of implementation with one-half of the communities receiving school programming in the first city, the first wave of each of the student data sets has been collected, cleaned, and entered. Preliminary incidence and prevalence data are available. Rates of drug use in youth are for middle school transition year students (based on data from a sub-sample (N = 3), 165 6th- and 7th-grade students analyzed by the Greater Kansas City Mental Health Foundation): 6.95% smoked at least one cigarette weekly, 4.30% took at least one alcoholic drink weekly, and 2.90% smoked marijuana at least once a week. Results, while slightly lower than in the Los Angeles area, are consistent with data from other HBRI studies, and with Johnston's data on student drug use in the Mid-West (Johnston, O'Malley, & Bachman, 1983).

Program process and implementation data are also available from the 60% of teachers who implemented the school program in one-half of the Kansas City schools (45/75). Sixty-one percent of these teachers reported that session-by-session delivery went "very well", and 39% reported that it went moderately "well"; 74% reported that students were very interested in participating. Program implementation data showed that 37.5% of the teachers taught the program exactly as written; 44.5% deviated from the program in the direction of extending the written program beyond the planned number of class periods, and 18.0% in the direction of conveying program material in fewer sessions. The primary reasons for extension included more practice in difficult role-plays, and extended discussion of role-play situations.

The questions to be addressed in this first year of school programming in the first city are the following: (a) Does training affect the stage of drug use? (b) Does training affect drug use incidence? (c) Does training affect drug use prevalence? (d) Does random versus preferred assignment to conditions affect outcome? (e) To what extent does the school program diffuse to older student populations? and (f) Do spontaneous community events affect drug use prevalence in youth?

The Five-year project has already addressed two of the

major issues confronting community level prevention research, use of available resources and community ownership. The first involves obtaining high-level, widespread support and resources to ensure that all communities within a metropolitan area are willing to participate. In this project, high level support is most visible in the form of major businesses that are recognized for civic involvement. These businesses are approached early in the project for support in the form of matched funding, as well as for verbal and written support disseminated throughout the community. High level support from a leading corporation and foundations in the community has produced a 100% involvement rate by schools in the intervention communities, and a 95% individual participation rate of teachers in intervention schools. Community ownership is assured by sponsorship of the program by a leading corporation in the community. Other issues that are currently being addressed include acceptance by communities of a phased-in versus and immediate full program approach to prevention, and methods for ensuring complementarity of extant environmental control approaches to prevention with the skills-based approach used in the project.

DISCUSSION

A technology for drug abuse prevention through school-based programs now exists. School-based programs, however, fail to reach those at highest risk to drug abuse, and are limited in their ability to influence those at moderate risk. Comprehensive prevention programs are based on existing technology from smoking prevention research and heart disease prevention offer the best hope for drug abuse prevention and control. The Tustin pilot project demonstrated that community leaders from diverse fields can be organized to plan and implement community drug abuse prevention activities on a short-term basis, and that collection of drug use and health data on an individual appointment basis with families is feasible, valid, and reliable. The results, however, also raise several questions. One is *enduring* community ownership of drug abuse prevention. Whether one major agency or several agencies will be responsible for future programming is still at issue. A local grass roots parent group, while perceived by the community as the most logical organization to promote prevention, suffers from lack of adequate funding, regular access to prevention specialists, and high level business sponsor contacts to ensure that programming will continue to be implemented. In contrast, the large midwestern city in the Five-Year Study has identified one major business sponsor for the project. The sponsor has exceptional civic service credibility with the city, funding for long-term programming, access to prevention professionals, and contacts with the business community. A previous multi-city self-study conducted in the U.S. has suggested that a primary business organization may provide the strongest identity and credibility for health-related programs, combined with ongoing credibility and resources provided by health professional groups (Wilson, 1970).

A question posed by both the pilot and the longitudinal project, is whether program (and research) integrity can be maintained (Sechrest, 1979; Sechrest, 1981). The campaign mounted by the Health Promotion Council in the Tustin pilot project demonstrated that paraprofessional leaders could be trained to deliver resistance skill role-play training to the public. The extent, however, to which the role-play demonstrations were effective, or had different effects as a function of characteristics of the demonstrator or length of the role-play, were not measured. These factors, along with other considerations, such as differences in length of programming, could seriously affect the outcome and interpretation of a community program (Kornitzer, 1984; McFarland, Norman, Streiner, Roy & Scott, 1980; Puska et al., 1981). To address this issue, the longitudinal project will include extensive process and program implementation assessments throughout all years. Results will be analyzed both descriptively and statistically to determine: (a) What exactly constitutes a community program for drug abuse prevention? and (b) How person, situation, assessment, and program environment characteristics interact to affect program outcome (Biglan, McConnell, Severson, Bavry & Ary, 1984; Huba et al., 1983; Mechanic, 1980; Sechrest, 1981; Webb, 1981)? Answers to these two questions will help determine the long-term diffusion potential of the approach.

REFERENCES

Atkin, C. K. (1979). Research evidence on mass mediated health communication campaigns. In D. Nimmo (Ed.), *Communication Yearbook 3.* New Brunswick: Transaction.

Bandura, A. (1977). *Social learning theory.* Englewood Cliffs: NJ.

Biglan, A., McConnell, S., Severson, J. J., Bavry, J., & Ary, D. V. (1984). A situational analysis of adolescent smoking. *Journal of Behavioral Medicine.*

Blackburn, H., Carleton, R., & Farquhar, J. (in press). The Minnesota Heart Health Program: A research and demonstration program in cardiovascular heart disease prevention. In J. Matarazzo, S. M. Weiss, J. A. Herd, & N. E. Miller (Eds.), *Behavioral Health: A handbook of health enhancement and disease prevention.* New York: Wiley.

Bloom, B. L. (1977). The assessment of community structure and community needs. *Community Mental Health.* Monterey, CA: Brooks/Cole.

Danaher, B., Berkanovic, E., & Gerber, B. (1982, July). Media-based quit smoking program (NCI Report). *Final report: Community cancer control of Los Angeles.*

Egger, G., Fitzgerald, W., Frage, G., Monaem, A., Rubenstien, P., Tyler, C., & McKay, B. (1983). Results of a large scale media antismoking campaign in Australia. *British Medical Journal, 287,* 1125–1128.

Farquhar, J. W. (1978). The community-based model of life style intervention trials. *American Journal of Epidemiology, 108*(2), 103–111.

Farquhar, J. W., Magnus, P. F., & Maccoby, N. (1981). The role of public information and education cigarette smoking control. *Canadian Journal of Public Health, 72*(6), 412–420.

Fishbein, M., & Ajzen, I. (1975). *Belief, attitude, intention, and behavior.* Reading, MA: Addison-Wesley.

Flay, B. R., d'Avernas, J. R., Best, J. A., Ketsell, M. W., & Ryan. (1983). Cigarette smoking: Why young people do it and ways of preventing it. In P. McGrath, & P. Firestone (Eds.), *Pediatric and adolescent behavioral medicine.* New York: Springer-Verlag.

Flay, B. R., Hansen, W. B., Johnson, C. A., & Sobel, J. L. (1983). *Involvement of children in motivating smoking parents to quit smoking with a television program.* Paper presented at the 5th World Conference on Smoking and Health, Winnipeg, Canada, July and the Annual Convention of the American Psychological Association, Anaheim, CA, August.

Flay, B. R., Ryan, K. B., Best, J. A., Brown, K. S., Kersell, M. W., d'Avernas, J. R., & Zanna, M. P. (1985a). Are social psychological smoking prevention programs effective? The Waterloo study. *Journal of Behavioral Medicine, 8*(1), 37–59.

Flay, B. R., Ryan, K. B., Best, J. A., Brown, K. S., Kersell, M. W., d'Avernas, J. R., & Zanna, M. P. (in press). Psychosocial approaches to smoking prevention: A review of findings. *Health Psychology, 4*(5).

Gutzwiller, F., Junod, B., Schweizer, W. (1979). Prevention des maladies cardio-vasculaires. *Les cahiers medico-sociaux,* 23 eme anne, 23(2), 79–144. Geneva, Switzerland.

Hansen, W., Graham, J., Sobel, J., Flay, B., & Johnson, C. A. (1985, Sept.). *A test of hierarchial psycho-social models of adolescent drug abuse.* Paper presented at the 93rd annual meeting of the American Psychological Association, Los Angeles.

Holme, E., Helgeland, A., Hjermann, I., & Leren, P. (1982). Socio-economic status as a coronary risk factor: The Oslo study. *Acta Med Scand,* Suppl 660, 147–151.

Howe, H. L. (1982). Increasing efficiency in evaluation research: The use of sequential analysis. *American Journal of Public Health, 72,* 690–697.

Huba, G. J., Wingard, J. A., & Bentler, P. M. (1983). Applications of an interactive theory of drug use to prevention programs. *Journal of Drug Education, 10,* 25–38.

Hughes, G. H., Hymowitz, N., Ockene, J. K., Simon, N., & Vogt, T. M. (1981). The multiple risk factor intervention trial (MRFIT) V. Intervention on smoking. *Preventive Medicine, 10*(4), 476–500.

Johnson, C. A., & Solis, J. (1983). Comprehensive community programs for drug abuse prevention: Implications of the community health programs for future research. In T. Glenn, C. Lukefield, J. Ludford, & R. Jessor (Eds.), *Preventing adolescent drug abuse: Intervention strategies Monograph No. 47.* Rockville, MD: National Institute on Drug Abuse.

Johnston, L. D., O'Malley, P. M., & Bachman, J. G. (1983). *Highlights from drugs and American high school students (1975–1983).* The University of Michigan Institute for Social Research (NIDA). U. S. Department of Health and Human Service, Alcohol, Drug Abuse, and Mental Health Administration.

Kornitzer, M. (1984). Why those differences between the U. K., and the Belgian heart disease prevention project results? *Preventive Medicine,* 13, 136–139.

McAlister, A., Puska, P., Salonen, J. T., Tuomilehto, J., & Koskel, K. (1982). Theory and action for health promotion. Illustrations from the North Karelia Project. *Amercian Journal of Public Health,* 72, 43–50.

McFarlane, A. H., Norman, G. R., Streiner, D. C., Roy, R., & Scott, D. J. (1980). A longitudinal study of the influence of the psychosocial environment on health status: A preliminary report. *Journal of Health and Social Behavior, 21,* 124–133.

Maccoby, N., & Solomon, D. S. (1981). Heart disease prevention: Community studies. In R. E. Rice, & W. J. Paisley (Eds.), *Public communication campaigns* (pp. 105–125). Beverly Hills: Sage Publications.

Mechanic, D., & Cleary, P. D. (1980). Factors associated with the maintenance of positive health behavior. *Preventive Medicine,* 9, 805–814.

Pentz, M. A. (1983). Prevention of adolescent substance abuse through social skill development. In T. Glynn, & D. Lettieri (Eds.), *Preventing adolescent drug abuse: Intervention strategies.* Rockville, MD: National Institute on Drug Abuse.

Pentz, M. A. (1983b). Prevention of adolescent substance abuse through social skills development. In T. Glynn, C. Leukfeld, & J. Ludford (Eds.), *Preventing Drug Abuse Monograph, 47.* Washington, DC: National Institute on Drug Abuse.

Pentz, M. A. (1985a, March). *Developmental transitions and smoking prevention.* Paper presented at the meeting of the Society of Behavioral Medicine, New Orleans, LA.

Puska, P. (1981). *Community control of cardiovascular diseases: Evaluation of a comprehensive community programme for control of cardiovascular diseases in North Karelia, Finland, 1972–1977.* Copenhagen: World Health Organization Regional Office for Europe.

Puska, P., Nissenem, A., Tuomilehto, J., Salonen, J. T., Koskela, K., McAlister, A., Kottke, T. W., Maccoby, N., & Farquhar, J. W. (1985). The community-based strategy to prevent coronary heart disease: Conclusions from ten years of the North Karelia project. *Annual Reviews of Public Health.*

Puska, P., Tuomilehto, J., & Salonen, J. (1981b). The North Karelia Project: Evaluation of a comprehensive community program for control of cardiovascular diseases in North Karelia, Finland, 1972–1977. [Monograph] Copenhagen, WHO/EURO.

Puska, P., Vienola, P., Kottke, T. E., Salonen, J. T., & Neittaanmaki, L. (1981a). Health knowledge and community prevention of coronary heart disease. *International Journal of Health Education, 2*(Suppl. 24), 1–10.

Rogers, E. V., & Shoemaker, F. (1972). *Communication of innovation.* New York: Free Press, 1972.

Sechrest, L., West, S. G., Phillips, M. A., Redner, R., & Yeaton, W. (Eds.). (1979). *Some neglected problems in evaluation research: Strength and integrity of treatments. Evaluation studies review annual* (Vol. 4). Beverly Hills, CA: Sage Publications.

Sechrest, L., & Cohen, R. Y. (1981). Evaluating outcomes in health care. In G. C. Stone, F. Cohen, & N. E. Alder (Eds.), *Health Psychology.* San Francisco: Jossey-Bass.

Webb, E. J., Campbell, D. T., Schwartz, R. D., Sechrest, L., & G., Grove, J. B. (1981). *Non-reactive measures.* Boston: Houghton Mifflin.

PART III: INTERVENTION

Introduction

Intervention assumes that it is possible to prevent the continuance of symptoms of a disease prior to the onset of the actual diseased state. Within the field of chemical abuse, researchers and practitioners have investigated a variety of methods for intervening in the processes which continue the abuse of chemicals. This section serves to identify interventive methods which comprehensively encompass the environment of youth and also discusses the various treatment approaches applicable and available to youth.

Ezekoye provides the pluralistic application of a Multicultural Model in prevention. She promotes culturally specific strategies and community involvement in the prevention effort. Beschner discusses the treatment strategies available to youth and makes note of the scarcity of programs for youth below age twelve. Kumpfer et al. summarize the issue and discuss future prevention possibilities.

The Multicultural Model in Chemical Abuse Prevention and Intervention

Stephanie Griswold-Ezekoye, MEd, MPH

ABSTRACT. This paper focuses on the concept of multiculturalism in relation to the development of chemical abuse prevention and intervention programs. It includes a model for implementation and describes projects that have a similar conceptual base. The author acknowledges the cultural foundations for developing the individual's positive self-understanding and builds on this to promote the development of culture-specific prevention strategies.

INTRODUCTION

For too long the concept of multiculturalism has been misunderstood, underdeveloped, inappropriately applied and unnecessarily restricted to a "Minorities Only" status. This paper seeks to stimulate thought about multiculturalism and its application in the field of chemical abuse.

A recurring statement among prevention trainees has been: "Why bother with prevention; people are going to use chemicals anyway." At the risk of appearing idealistic in a world threatened with extinction by man, the response given by the author is: "Because as humans, we have to care about what happens to other humans or we lose the distinction between ourselves and other forms of animal life." A part of that caring includes making judgements about the behavior of our fellow humans in relation to the common good.

Stephanie Griswold-Ezekoye has been a private design and training consultant in the field of chemical abuse for eight years. She is currently executive director of the Addison Terrace Learning Center of Pittsburgh, Inc., a community-based chemical abuse prevention/intervention agency, 2136 Elmore Square, Pittsburgh, PA 15219.

The common good is a nebulous concept, as human society includes many distinctly different groups each with their own peculiar definition of the common good. American society exemplifies this through the many subcultures that coexist and the various special interests they promote. Yet, as a society, we still strive to maintain some general understanding of what is in our common interest. When the common good is threatened, we respond as a group to eradicate the threat. Unfortunatly, we do not always effectively reflect the differences between groups or cultures when implementing solutions. Many groups, therefore, within the society continue to experience the threat.

Chemical abuse is a threat that has received much attention with minimal results. For over two decades, the prevention of chemical abuse has been a concern of enlightened policymakers, health professionals and educators; yet, an effective process for providing prevention services that are appropriate to all groups has eluded us. The current level of abuse in America, especially among youth, remains a threat to the foundations of the society. It challenges the ability of generations to provide an increasingly better quality of life, and threatens the evolution of positive interpersonal interaction. People have become increasingly alienated, and the fear associated with chemical abuse has contributed to this alienation. The years invested in addressing this issue do not appear to have impacted the problem significantly.

With so much attention given to the field of prevention over the past twenty years, one wonders why some practitioners and funding sources continue to ask: "What is the appropriate approach?" Has the field been saturated with so much information that it is unable to sort out appropriate methods, or has it been so dissected that researchers, practitioners and funding sources have not come together to share critical information that would answer fundamental questions?

At some point, field practice and research must come together (Dembo, 1979). Although several studies have supported the use of both a psychosocial and sociocultural approach to prevention for the most effective results (Kandel, 1975; R. Jessor & S.L. Jessor, 1977; Brooks, Lakoff & Whiteman, 1977), field practice still appears to be arguing the issue. Chemical abuse involves such a wide range of human attitudes and values that whether a person with a disturbed personality is abusing or whether a person is reflecting the perceived values of their community, it is ultimately a matter of decision about what the use of a particular chemical does for the user. A discussion of how this issue relates to treatment may clarify the direction of prevention.

If an individual's abuse of chemicals is symptomatic of an underlying personality disorder, then the psychosocial approach may indeed by the most effective. But if the abuse is a function of the survival or value system of the individual within his or her environment, then a psychosocial approach would only treat the individual's symptoms during an intervention or treatment process; the underlying sociocultural factors would remain unchanged. The individual might show signs of recovery due to abstinence during treatment, but he or she would likely return to use after terminating professional care. The high rates of recidivism for many treatment programs suggest that some important factor has not been addressed during treatment or follow-up. If this is true, then it is reasonable to assume that within prevention the use of one or two approaches to cope with a variety of causal factors may be inadequate. Continued controversy between the various approaches only serves to confuse the issues of appropriate service to the appropriate population. There is no panacea that is applicable across the board to all individuals or populations (Dodson, 1983); yet, there is an effective model that can encompass them all.

Currently practitioners tend to shape their prevention programming into molds that fit the prescriptions of funding sources, at times without regard for the service population. For example, one state's regulations defining prevention/intervention services categorizes prevention as education/information activities (those that increase cognitive and affective development skills) and alternative activities (those recreation/leisure activities that are provided as alternatives to getting high). Intervention activities are defined as drop-in centers and hot lines. Within the restrictions of those who interpret the regulations for application in the field, there occur difficulties in offering services like tutoring, GED, economic development, and home or community support without experiencing definitional conflicts with the funding source; yet, these activities are effective prevention/intervention services for low-income minority communities (Payton, 1981). The confusion that arises from the inflexibility of funding sources tend to feed the debate over approaches and to increase the cost of service. What appears to be lacking in our good intentioned efforts to address the problem effectively is a model that permits flexibility in the approach and individualization in application. The Multicultural Model can provide this vehicle if applied appropriately.

FOUNDATIONS OF THE MULTICULTURAL MODEL

Intracultural Issues

In light of the historical relationship between chemical use and cultural traditions and rituals, this section focuses on the presuppositions of the Multicultural Model. Cultures are living entities that reflect the history of a group of people and influence their basic value system, identity development, and decision-making processes (Geertz, 1973). They, therefore, impact significantly the behavior of most persons regarding chemical use. Within the United States, there are a minimum of two cultures, the culture of origin and the primary culture, that influence each individual. American society is an amalgamation of many cultures of origin. Over a period of time, these have evolved into a new primary culture to which all others are subjected. The various cultures of origin coexist with the newly evolving primary culture; and this interaction may create conflicts which serve to more accurately define the traditions and rituals of both. They exist independently and interdependently as each shapes the future of the other. Since most of the cultures of origin were developed around an agrarian economy with a homogeneous frame of reference and worldview, their adaptation to an industrial (and post-industrial), culturally heterogeneous society has been a slow process. Their values, traditions, and rituals do not always coincide with the primary culture, yet, they are the first learning experiences of children during their most impressionable years. Both the personal family culture and the culture of the community impact on a youth prior to his or her introduction into the primary culture. If we are to believe that the future problematic behavior and psychiatric intervention needs of humans are predictable, based on the interaction of mother and infant (Broussard & Hartner, 1971; Broussard, 1976), then it is also reasonable that that the essence of an entire culture, which is mediated through mother, can be predictable. The use of chemicals usually derives from family practices, role models in the community, rituals of the culture, and the example and persuasion of peers. Youth who are exposed to traditions and models of abuse that imply acceptance tend to imitate those behaviors and pass them on to younger members of the community (Dembo, 1979; Dembo, Farrow, DesJarlois, Burgos & Schmeidler, 1981).

Szasz (1971) has suggested that the psychiatric or disturbed personality base found in some addicts is really a moral problem that has been misdiagnosed to meet the survival needs of the practitioners and health organizations. If Szasz is correct, then sociocultural factors play a much greater role in abuse and addiction than is currently accepted because morality is intricately bound to cultural values (Geertz, 1973). This theory receives continued support through the field observations and studies of chemical abusers within African-American (Black) cultures of origin in the United States (Gordan, 1982; Dembo, 1979; Trader, 1981). The subjects of these studies showed a much stronger influence from their cultures of origin than from a disturbed personality.

The author does not suggest that inherent defects exist within cultures of origin and that these precipitate problems of chemical abuse. For some individuals, however, the interaction of unresolved historical conflicts between the traditions and rituals of cultures of origin and those of the primary culture increase the susceptiblity of individuals to chemical abuse. Since no formalized research has been conducted on this issue, theorists should investigate its implications for application in the field.

Culture is an accumulation of the historical experiences of a group and, therefore, is animate and continually evolving (Dodson, 1983). This evolution is reflected in the language, worldview, interpersonal interactions, religions, economics and values of the members. Chemical use has always been a part of this evolution within most cultures of origin either medically or socially; yet, the use has also been tied to its function within a specific ritual or within the culture as a whole. Currently, within the United States, the traditions and rituals of many cultures of origin that provided guidelines for the meaningful use of chemicals are disintegrating. For example, the rites of passage ceremonies which served to guide a youth in the socially acceptable norms of behavior in cultures of origin are not practiced consistently within the American society and in some communities they are not practiced at all. Mixed messages about chemical use are presented through the media, literature, and music. These messages from the primary culture, along with the disintegration of the traditions and rituals of the cultures of origin, serve to validate, confuse or conflict with the child's perceptions of appropriate use. The immediate models for the child, such as mother, father, older siblings, close relatives, neighbors and peers (depending on which is most significant in the child's life), many times do not clarify these perceptions; and the child is left to his or her own musings.

Socioeconomic Factors

Another variable considered significant in the use of chemicals among youth is socioecomonic background. Since the access to money and resources in the United States provides a wider variety of opportunities in experience, it should not be overlooked. Yet, a review of United States history demonstrates that despite the theoretical opportunity for access to money and resources, there continues to be a disproportionately lower percentage of members of the African-Asian based cultural groups within the higher socioeconomic strata (1980 census). If we accept that current culture reflects the historical experiences of a people, then we must investigate this factor in the context of how the lack of money and resources has impacted the cultural evolution of groups and then how existing cultural influences impact the chemical use of group members. This issue becomes important as we study persons who were raised within cultures of origin that have experienced a lack of money and resources in disproportionately larger numbers from generation to generation. The sociocultural influences on the types of chemicals used, the attitudes and values about recreational use, and the economics surrounding the culture's adaptation to a tolerant, if not accepting, chemical life-style are significant (Gordon, 1982; Dembo & Shern, 1982).

The economic history of groups within the United States is also reflected within the job market. This arena of interaction between the cultures of origin and the primary culture has a direct impact on the chemical abuse of youth. The employment issues that influence chemical use include the importance placed on the amount of money earned, the amount of time within a day spent at the job site, the stress related to job seeking and job satisfaction, and the relationship of all the above to the psychological well-being of the individual (Griswold, 1984).

These concerns often carry over into the home and manifest themselves through spousal abuse, child abuse, and chemical abuse. This is particularly true for persons who have difficulty procuring employment. The frustrations and low self-esteem exhibited by persons who have experienced long-term unemployment tend to increase their susceptibility to the abuse of chemicals. A survey conducted by the Addison Terrace Learning Center (refer section: Prevention Intervention Projects) on the age at onset of use, types of chemicals used, and the reasons for use in the adult target population, revealed that 64% of those assessed as regular users of chemicals (once a week or more) indicated "frustrations of unemployment" and "nothing better to do" as the most frequent reasons for their use of chemicals (Griswold, 1982).

Among cultural minorities within the United States, historically there have been higher rates of unemployment and poverty level existence. Payton (1981) acknowledges and discusses the characteristics and stresses of poverty, such as feelings of hopelessness, alienation, and powerlessness, as high correlates to chemical abuse within African-American communities. Youth raised in these communities are often subjected to a culture of origin that appears to tolerate and support the trafficking and use of chemicals for nonmedical purposes. These youth more frequently are seeking identification with various aspects of the culture that they perceive as valuing chemical use rather than escaping from the realities of their environment (Jordan, 1980). This does not imply that all members of low income communities succumb to or tolerate the abuse of chemicals. In fact, the majority of people in these communities do not. Yet, in terms of prevention or intervention program development, the visibility and accessibility of trafficking and use does impact the cultural and lifestyle evolution of many of these communities. It is evident historically that the trafficking of illegal chemicals within minority communities has served to fulfill some of the economic needs of a population that was systematically and legally ostracized from the job market. Over time, the culture has adapted to a situation thrusted upon them but not accepted by the majority.

For members of the higher socioeconomic strata, research tends to support the dominance of psychosocial factors as deciding variables in the abuse of chemicals; yet, we have neglected to investigate the strength of ties between the culture of origin and the individual. A study of alcoholism within a middle-class Jewish population indicated that a strong sense of commitment and identity with the traditions and rituals of the Orthodox sect tended to decrease their susceptibility to chemical abuse. It also indicated that members who were less traditional in the practice of their culture were more susceptible to chemical abuse (Zimberg, 1977). Other studies point out that as more opportunities open for members of the African-Asian based cultural groups to enter higher socioeconomic levels, they experience more cultural conflicts and frustrations which, when unresolved, tend to increase their susceptibility to chemical abuse (Gordon, 1982; Wilcox, 1973). These findings suggest that there are still cultural undertones to the problems of chemical abuse for members of higher socioeconomic groups, and that a stronger identification with the culture of origin or a resolution of the conflicts between the traditions and rituals of the cultures of origin and the primary culture may minimize the susceptibility to chemical abuse.

Intercultural Factors

There are many factors that correlate with chemical abuse in youth across cultures; for example, the dependency of a parent, guardian, or significant other places the offspring at the highest risk of becoming an abuser (Ackermen, 1983). If not provided with appropriate and functional methods of coping and understanding their own self-determining abilities, and strategies for distinguishing the positive and negative aspects of their environment, many of these youth begin to experiment with chemicals at an early age and eventually become regular users by the time they reach middle-school or high-school age. The recent furor over the needs of this population has just begun to stimulate processes for the indentification and provision of services for these youth; yet, problems of identification occur in the issues of confidentiality which surround the provision of services to dependent persons. Since clients in treatment are guaranteed confidentiality, it is difficult to procure information from the treatment agencies about their client's children. Prevention provider agencies are forced to depend on less efficient methods of identifying these children. They use indirect methods of identification such as teacher assessment of abnormal classroom behavior, child abuse centers, recreation centers, community task forces, and juvenile justice services. These indirect processes are not only unreliable but also costly in the use of manpower to assess the validity of referrals. An extremely vulnerable segment within this population are children of teen parents.

The issues of teen pregnancy and parenthood as they relate to chemical abuse span a wide range of concern, from the current physical health of the mother and child to the impact of unguided teen parenthood on the future susceptibility of their offspring to chemical abuse. For most adolescents, coping with their own emotional, physical, social, and economic needs during this period of maturation is a full time concern. The introduction of a pregnancy and resulting child into this arena usually serves to complicate and sometimes inhibit the developmental process for the teen mother (and the fathers who choose to be involved). Since the majority of teens are not married, do not possess skills for gainful permanent employment, and do not have the life experience or mature judgment necessary to raise a child, teen mothers tend to experience more difficulties than women who become first-time mothers at a later age. They tend to be economically less marketable, more prone to prenatal and birth difficulties, and are more likely to live in poverty after childbirth (Children's

Defense Fund, 1984). This is particularly true of African-American teen mothers.

Teen fathers do not become involved with the parenting of their offspring for a variety of reasons which include, but are not limited to, lack of parenting skills and a perception that childrearing is the duty of the mother. For many African-American teen fathers, the latter perception has been reinforced by the increasing number of single-female parent households within African-American communities and the fact that many of these fathers were raised by a single-female parent. In a document prepared by the Children's Defense Fund and presented to participants of the 1984 conference to "Prevent Children Having Children", the following issues were discussed: (a) approximately one-third of the babies born in 1982 were born to teen mothers, (b) over 50% of all black children are born to a single mother and 40% of these births are to black women in their teens, (c) the median income for female headed families is $7,458, and (d) pregnancy is the primary reason given for girls who drop out of school.

All of these issues emphasize the concern that providers must have in the correlating problems of teen pregnancy and chemical abuse. It is generally accepted within the chemical abuse and addiction field that there is no single causal factor in abuse; yet, there are correlates that appear dominant among most addicted persons. Some of these correlates are also related experiences for teen parents and therefore impact the resulting issue of chemical abuse for their offspring. For teen mothers, especially African-American teen mothers, the majority of whom would fall under the poverty line, susceptibility to chemical abuse appears to be evident. The factors associated with poverty and abuse, such as feelings of frustration, powerlessness, and hopelessness, are also dominant experiences of the teen mother and father. Services to these parents and their children as a family is an important step in prevention for this group. In many instances, the cultural traditions and norms developed around a poverty existence tend to be tolerant of the abuse of chemicals; and if an intervention process is not implemented, chemical abuse may become the culturally transmitted norm from generation to generation.

Although little research has been conducted to support this theory, there is evidence in field practice that this process has already begun among teen parents who are themselves the offspring of teen parents. Fifty percent of the teen mothers who participate in the Single Parent/Toddler Chemical Abuse Prevention/Intervention Program of the Addison Terrace Learning Center of Pittsburgh are offspring of teen parents themselves. Formalized research would give information on how many of these teen parents were raised by chemically abusing teen parents within a culture or community that tolerated the open abuse of chemicals.

Self-Understanding

Another factor that crosses cultures and has been present consistently among addicted persons is a lack of positive self-understanding (self-concept). This term has been used erroneously in many situations and needs definition. For this paper, self-understanding means "the individual's conscious and functonal awareness of his or her values, actions, reactions, abilities, and identity with the physical, social, mental, and spiritual environment in which he or she operates." In simpler terms, it is the functional understanding of who one is and the capabilities one possesses in relation to the world around oneself. Addicted, and many times abusing, individuals either have not developed a positive self-understanding or over a period of time have not been encouraged to use it. In either case, self-understanding is usually acquired through the reward-and-punishment processes within the traditions of the family, community, and culture; and depending on which is the greater influence for the individual, a lack of positive self-image development may occur when there is inconsistency, conflict or confusion in the nurturing process.

In light of this information, theorists and providers should seek methods of prevention and intervention that can address a wide variety of issues and that influence the ability of persons to make healthier decisions about their use of chemicals, regardless of the extrinsic influences on their daily lives. The mere fact that the majority of persons do not succumb to the harmful use of chemicals, even under living environments comparable to those who do, does not negate the importance of the cultural factor rather it suggests that there must exist certain processes, attitudes, or behavior patterns that are useful in minimizing their effect. The author suggests that this "immunizing" agent lies within individuals' self-perception as a capable, lovable, and loving human being who is able to interact positively with the life situations in which he or she is involved. Since this self-image initially develops through the family and community cultural traditions and rituals, providers need to address those traditions in relation to their function as an encouragement or discouragement to abuse.

The Multicultural Model of prevention/intervention seeks to incorporate the approaches to service delivery that are appropriate to the specific culture targeted. It also works with those aspects of the culture or community that have guided the majority of the members to reject the abuse of chemicals. It allows for the idiosyncratic changes that are necessary to tailor the service to the target group or individual, and it is also applicable and replicable in most cultures of origin and within the primary culture. The following section outlines the components of this approach.

COMPONENTS OF THE MULTICULTURAL MODEL

This Model is a component of a comprehensive multicultural approach to prevention, intervention and treatment (Griswold-Ezekoye, in press). It recognized the following in providing prevention services: (a) the existence of a variety of living and evolving subcultures in the United States; (b) the significance of the historical relationship between the individual, culture, and chemical abuse; (c) the current impact of culture on chemical abuse; (d) the evolving, interactive, and overlapping systems that influence the individual's age at initial use, the types and amounts of chemicals use, situations that encourage use, and the duration of use; (e) chemical use and abuse does not occur in a vacuum but has a system of subtle yet coersive mechanisms that maintain its existence; and (f) the development of positive self-understanding will influence decisions in the use of chemicals, and this development occurs first through the family and community cultural traditions. The unique marketable and replicable qualities of this model are couched in its process, the role of the client (whether group or individual) and the characteristics of self-determination.

The emphasis on the Multicultural Model ultimately is to

impact the chemical use decisions of the individual, either directly or indirectly, through increasing his or her identity with the positive elements of the culture of origin, assisting the positive resolution of cross-cultural conflicts that may exist, influencing change within the significant systems that impact the environment, providing concrete mechanisms for constructive acceptance or rejection of events that occur beyond their locus of control, and guiding the development of positive self-understanding. To accomplish this, general knowledge of the culture and perceptions of the individual or group in relation to the use of the chemicals is essential. The findings from this information will allow the provider to establish: (a) an appropriate means for assessing the abuse patterns and correlates of the community or individual, (b) a reliable network for identifying youth and families at risk, (c) a culturally based prevention/intervention strategy system, (d) an ongoing community-based support network, and (e) an ongoing feedback process in order to effect the appropriate changes as needed.

Developing an advisory board is the first step in implementing this model. The following section details the importance, structure, and role of this group.

Advisory Board

Unlike most Advisory Boards, this group is to be a working force within the community, not just an advising body. Its recruitment, structure, reinforcement, and implmentation processes must reflect the community it represents and all members of the community must have access to it. There is debate within the field as to the effectiveness of an advisory board in low-income minority communities because of the difficulty in maintaining consistency and reliability among the members and because of their inherent powerlessness. They have been perceived, by the community, as a quasi-elite group that succumbs to the pressures and demands of the provider agency and has no authority itself. This model demands an alternate focus for the Advisory Board; its goal is autonomy and self-determination. When structured and implemented appropriately, it has proven to be a most effective community force (see discussion of Addison Terrace Learning Center). The effectiveness of the group lies with its active working role, rather than its passive advisory role, within the community. It is a culturally focused advisory board and as such impacts all areas of community life.

Structure

The Board should be open to all members of the community who have been residents for a minimum of three years. This provides a balance in the perspectives of current issues, historical changes, and special interest needs. There should also be at least one youth and one senior-citizen representative who have contact with a broader base of persons within their age-groups. This can happen by recruiting a representative from an already established group in the community or by establishing auxiliary youth and senior citizen groups who appoint a representative to the board. In mixed culture communities, it is important to have a representative for each culture among the residents, despite the numbers of person within the community who represent that culture. This tends to eliminate the problems experienced by many groups who find themselves relatively uninfluential within their home communities. It is also advisable to include one representative from the business, religious, health, and social service sectors of the community. The Ideal structure will be as follows:

Homogeneous Culture Community

—Six unaffiliated community residents (18 years and older)
—One Business Representative
—One Religious Representative
—One Health Representative
—One Social Service Agency Representative
—One Youth Representative
—One Senior Citizen Representative

Heterogenous Culture Community

—The number of unaffiliated community residents is determined by the number of cultures in the community.
—One Business Representative
—One Religious Representative
—One Health Representative
—One Social Service Agency Representative
—One Youth Representative
—One Senior Citizen Representative

This is a volunteer body and as such should be given the flexibility needed to grow as a group. Although the above structure is not unlike many other advisory boards, its rules of recruitment and operation differ significantly.

Recruitment

The recruitment of members to a volunteer group is difficult, at best, in the most ideal situation. But careful planning can facilitate this process. When the service area is a homogeneous low-income urban community, members tend to be skeptical about the permanence and appropriateness of the services provided and the effectiveness of prevention. Even though the majority of the community is against trafficking, another obstacle may be the perception of some community members that the illicit trafficking of chemicals is a necessary evil to provide supplemental income for unemployed families. Recruitment should be done face-to-face, where the provider secures one person to take responsibility for recruiting the board. This person can be identified through other agencies in the community. In most communitities, it is also beneficial to contact a health organization (hospital, clinic, doctor's office) that will be able to confidentially recruit persons who may be interested in serving on the advisory board because of their personal involvement with an addicted family member. It is not necessary for the drug-and-alcohol-treatment provider to violate confidentiality to recruit these most valuable volunteers.

Rules of Operation

As a working culturally focused body, this group must exercise firm adherence to the following goals: (a) to identify any aspect of community life that impacts the individual's, family's or community's decision about chemical use; (b) to implement activities and programs that provide an opportunity for youth of the community to participate in and that reinforce their identity with the positive aspects of their cultures of origin; (c) to implement activities that provide youth opportunities to participate in traditions and rituals from a variety of cultures (within mixed cultural communities), equal participation in (exposure to) the various cultures is essential; (d) to implement an internal ongo-

ing reinforcement system for the Board and a community-rein-
forcement system that award youth and families participation in
the preceding goals; (e) to network with already established
agencies, organizations, or community groups to implement the
first three goals; (f) to participate in all training necessary to
accomplish the goals of the group; (g) to network with other
community agencies, businesses, organizations, and groups to
establish a system of identification, intervention, referral, and
support for youth and families with current chemical abuse
problems and those who are in high-risk groups; and (h) to
maintain an effective record-keeping and feedback system for
the planning and evaluation of ongoing activities.

This group functions in conjunction with personnel of the
prevention-provider agency. It is not an auxiliary group but
rather the heartbeat of the provider's service to the community. It is the provider's responsibility to give technical assistance, direction, and support (financial, resources, access) to
the Board. The Board recognizes the ability of the community
or organization to determine and implement its own solutions
and redefines the role of the provider to be more supportive
and directional than total direct service. This model does not
demand that the entire membership of the board be recruited
prior to the implementation of planning and strategies.
Rather recruitment of members should be an ongoing process
that facilitates not impedes progress. There are many communities in which recruitment and board functioning are more
realistically accomplished simultaneously because the actions
of the board are the catalyst for involvement by otherwise
uninvolved community members.

Training the Board

Initially, this occurs as needed and is conducted by the
provider agency to give basic information and strategies employed in chemical abuse prevention. After the initial training, advisory board members become the trainers of other
members, using the provider for technical support and guidance. Training is crucial in this process because it provides
board members with the skills necessary to accomplish their
goals. It also increases the confidence of the board in their

ability to address the task at hand. It includes the following: communication skills (intrpersonal and group), identifying cultural traditions and rituals that impact chemical use, organizing and rewarding a community group, chemical abuse as a disease (pharmacology, issues of family, codependency enabling and community control), team building, sensitivity to youth and adolescent issues, the economics of chemical use, developing a personal positive attitude toward prevention, and identifying youth at risk and networking.

Reinforcing the Board

An important aspect of a successful volunteer advisory board is an ongoing self-determined reinforcement system. The essential ingredient is that the board determines for itself the type of reinforcement since the reward needs will vary from individual to individual, community to community, and culture to culture. The assumption behind this strategy is that board members are better able to determine their own needs and will be more likely to build on this process with others when it is completed by them. The reinforcement should benefit all members and meet a pressing need for them as individuals. Examples of some reinforcers may be recreational trips or retreats, free job skill training, less costly access to a food coop, established periodic awards ceremonies or access to free concert tickets.

The advisory board becomes cost-effective through its networking, co-sponsorship, and incorporation of other community groups, agencies, and business in the prevention effort. It allows the provider's funds to be utilized in the most beneficial and cost-effective manner and assists direct-service personnel in accomplishing their duties. They generate their own capital needs outside those utilized for training and reinforcement. Once the group has established itself, the costs for both training and reinforcement will be minimized. Through the Advisory Board, the provider will plan and implement activities at five levels of impact: the individual, the family, the community-at-large, community organization, and the society-at-large. The focus of these levels is as follows:

Individual. They will provide: (a) culturally based participatory activities for youth that are enjoyable and rewarded by the community, (b) an identification and referral process for youth that adheres to the established processes of seeking help within the community, and (c) the opportunity to partici- pate in cultural activities that can be implemented within the home as well as within community programs and that have a feedback and reward system for participation.

Family. They will prove or sponsor activties that encour- age: (a) total family participation, (b) family interaction within the home, and (c) the establishment or reestablishment of family cultural activities within the home, and (d) increase the families' awareness of chemical abuse issues which effect the family as a unit.

Community-at-Large. They will implement activities that can: (a) increase the awareness of the community at large to the specific cultural traditions that both encourage and dis- courage chemical abuse, (b) encourage participation in the solution of community problems, (c) increase the commu- nity's awareness of prevention strategies, and (d) increase awarness of positive cultural norms.

Community Organizations. They will implement activities that can: (a) encourage networking between groups, and (b) increase the awareness of organization members of their role in chemical abuse prevention.

Society-at-Large. They will implement activities that can: (a) increase the awareness of the society-at-large to the spe- cific needs of the community in relation to chemical abuse prevention and (b) foster the maintenance, change, or estab- lishment within the community of services that are needed to address chemical abuse.

Phases of Implementation

After recruitment of the advisory board, both the board and provider work cooperatively through the phases outlined below.

Phase 1: Information Gathering

To determine the focus and apply the appropriate strategies, basic information about the culture, community, and lifestyles is necessary. The data is gathered through observation, nominal group process, personal interviews, and surveys. It includes answers to the following questions: (a) What is the cultural/community process for teaching acceptable use? (b) What is the cultural/community process for teaching non-use? (c) How has the culture/community historically coped with members who break the rules of chemical use? (d) What aspects of the culture/community life do the members perceive as encouraging chemical abuse? (e) How does the community maintain the passing of traditions and rituals from generation to generation? (f) What aspects of the culture/community life do the members perceive as discouraging chemical abuse? (g) What seems to be the dominant attitude in the community toward distribution and use of recreational chemicals? (h) How does the culture/community implement changes in traditions and rituals? (i) What are the issues of the culture/community that indirectly affect chemical use? (j) How does the culture/community determine and procure services it needs from the society at large? (k) How does the culture/community as a unified entity reward its members for maintaining traditions? (l) How do the youth in the community perceive the traditions of the culture/community? (m) How does the community facilitate the youth's transition from their traditions within their respective cultures of origin to the traditions of the primary culture? and (n) Which culture/community traditions are carried over into the primary culture lifestyle? and which are not?

These questions suggest that an anthropological study should be conducted. Although formalized research, however, can be established, it is not necessary for program implementation. Most of the information required can usually be ascertained from the members of the advisory board if it is structured adequately.

Phase 2: Focus

This process enables the advisory board and provider to utilize the information gathered in Phase 1 in a systematic way. It also identifies the cultural traditions and rituals that are within the realm of influence of the board and provider and which should be maintained, encouraged or discouraged to facilitate prevention and intervention. Determining the focus is essential because it may vary from culture to culture and community to community. It is also important to note that within the United States, there are increasing numbers of culturally mixed communities and that using a one-person-one-vote system to decide the focus will neither meet the needs of the population nor provide effective service. As discussed in the section on the advisory board, the board is strategic and should not be permitted to alienate any culture that is represented within the resident population.

The date from Phase 1 is categorized as follows: (a) traditions that encourage abuse of chemicals, (b) traditions that discourage the abuse of chemicals, (c) traditions that encourage the culturally accepted use of chemicals, (d) traditions that discourage conformity to cultural/community norms, (e) traditions that assist in the development of self-understanding. Each of the categories are then rank ordered from those most within the influence of the Board and provider to those least within their influence. The group then begins developing programs and activities for the category ranked as most within their sphere of influence.

Phase 3: Planning and Evaluation

These processes, although distinctly different, are interdependent; therefore, they are developed simultaneously. They are essential steps in establishing measurable objectives, appropriate reinforcement, and reliable changes as the prevention/intervention services evolve. The Strategies developed incorporate the information gathered on the various changes as the prevention/intervention services evolve. The strategies developed incorporate the information gathered on the various processes used by the culture/community to accomplish specific goals and set a measureable time frame for the provider to evaluate effectiveness, process and outcome. They are tailored to the culture/community by the culture/community itself. The group uses the category identified as primary in Phase 2 and develops strategies for each of the levels of impact: individual, family, community at large, community organizations, and society at large. They establish concrete community reinforcement strategies for each of the levels and a vehicle for youth, both as individuals and as a group, to consciously identify with and physically participate in.

Phase 4: Implementation

This phase is the culmination of the prevention/intervention process. The board and the provider must ensure consistency in implementation and flexibility to change when necessary. Time frames established for feedback must be enforced to determine if the strategy is meeting the designated goal.

PREVENTION INTERVENTION PROJECTS

The following projects exemplify the concepts of the Multi-cultural Model.

Addison Terrace Learning Center
of Pittsburgh (ATLC)

This nonprofit chemical abuse prevention agency began in 1982 to provide programming to improve the living environment of youth ages 8 through 12 who were being raised within the Addison Terrace public housing community of Pittsburgh, Pennsylvania. It was an outgrowth of "Operation Build", a project of the U.S. Department of Housing and Urban Development. Although no federal funds were allocated for its start-up, ATLC was established through the efforts of a steering committee organized by the Housing Authority of the City of Pittsburgh. The steering committee consisted of representatives from local public and private health and human service agencies within Pittsburgh and Allegheny County along with a representative group of the Addison Terrace community. The Junior Tenant Council of the target community had determined that the most pressing threat to the healthy development of their youth was chemical abuse; therefore, the center began as a chemical abuse prevention/intervention agency.

After eighteen months of providing prevention services as prescribed by the regulatory agency with minimum results, ATLC assessed that it was not feasible to expect significant results unless they could impact the total environment of the youth. This included expanding the target area and population to include the entire Hill District in which ATLC was located. All activities were then restructured under the auspices of the Community Mobilization Project (CMP). This is a comprehensive cultural based, outreach project that enables the community to define its own strategies for prevention and intervention and incorporates all aspects of community life in the prevention process. The CMP operates through networking groups that plan and implement strategies that focus on the individual, family, community, and society. Following, is a description of these groups.

Prevention Advocacy Group

The advisory board of the center consists of residents of the community eighteen years of age or older. They identify youth and families in need of chemical abuse services; set policy for the center in conjunction with the board of directors; plan and implement individual, family, and community activities independently and in conjunction with other groups in the project; and develop prevention campaigns. One of the major ongoing programs planned and developed by the Prevention Advocacy Group is the Single Parent/Toddler Chemical Abuse Prevention/Intervention Program. It is an intergenerational, two-phase program that focuses on adult and teen single parents. In the first phase, both adult and teen mothers participate in focus support groups and/or individual support counseling for the development of personal goals and the implementation of strategies to meet them. The toddlers participate in a developmental chemical abuse prevention program four hours a day, five days a week. In the second phase, teen mothers are paired with adult mother parenting partners and adults mothers are paired with female senior citizens for ongoing networking and support.

Prevention Agency Group

This group consists of youth recreation, health, and human service agencies that service the target community. They are trained to identify youth and families in need of service, to incorporate prevention activities within their established programs, and to network with other groups in the project to execute various communitywide activities.

School Group

This group is trained to identify and refer youth in the classroom who exibit chemical abuse problems (both users and children of dependent persons). They also implement intraschool activities in prevention.

Youth Council

A community based group for youth between 14 and 18 years of age who network primarily with the Prevention Advocacy Group and are trained to identify, refer, and act as peer counselors for youth with chemical abuse problems.

Auxiliary Group

This group consists of representatives from the churches, businesses, and police of the community. Their function is to identify, refer, and support the activities of the other groups within the project.

The Addison Terrace Learning Center has projected a five-year development period for all aspects of the Community Mobilization Project to be in operation and to produce significant results. Further information about the Community Mobilization Project is available from Addison Terrace Learning Center, 2136 Elmore Square, Pittsburgh, Pennsylvania, 15219.

The Floating Classroom

This is a remedial tutorial program for low socioeconomic persons designed by Dr. Winfred Coachman of the Pittsburgh Public School System. Although not originally intended as a chemical abuse prevention program, during its five years of operation as a pilot program, with the Pittsburgh public school system (1971–1976), it proved to be one of the best prevention efforts for a low-income inner-city population. The Floating Classroom provided the opportunity for the total community to address the problems of poor academic achievement through pairing youth in need with community tutors or counselors. It serviced between 700 and 1,000 elementary and middle school students annually and employed approximately 367 high school and college students, community parents, and professional staff.

Since it is difficult to determine whether poor academic achievement is a causal or resulting factor in chemical abuse, it would be erroneous to state that this program directly impacted abuse. Since it had a significant impact, however, on the academic achievement of long-term poor achievers, it would be unwise to overlook its possible indirect impact on chemical abuse. A unique quality of the Floating Classroom is that it encouraged youth to continue their academic development within the community after school and also encouraged the community to support this continuance. As has been the case for many excellent programs, a lack of funding closed the doors of the Floating Classroom in 1976. Information about the program can be obtained through Dr. Winfred Coachman at the Pittsburgh Board of Education, 341 S. Bellefield Street, Pittsburgh, Pennsylvania 15213.

The Chemical People Institute

This is a local outgrowth of the national and regional Chemical People Public Television Project which aired during 1982 and 1983. The original concept was a public-private partnership with the goal of increasing awareness of chemical abuse problems, promoting community involvement, and combating community denial of chemical abuse issues. This was accomplished through the establishment of community task forces who would carry out prevention efforts within the suburban middle- and upper-class communities, but not within the urban low-income ethnic communities. Many members of these inner-city communities perceived the project as being directed only toward a middle-class population because it did not address the problems of abuse as they existed within their communities and also it did not include representatives of these populations in the planning of the project. Despite this controversy, the Chemical People concept was the first successful privately initiated effort to increase public awareness and to utilize lay community members in the continuance of activities for the prevention of chemical abuse.

The Institute was established in 1983 to continue the work of the task forces within Western Pennsylvania. Although this project was not founded on a cultural base, its emphasis on the community task force is similiar to that of the advisory board in the Multicultural Model and can be utilized by inner-city communities to tailor prevention and intervention strategies to the particular needs of their communities. To avoid the pitfalls of being labeled a middle class organization, the institute, has incorportated a number of persons from various professional and cultural backgrounds into a professional advisory committee. This group functions individually or as a group, and provides necessary technical assistance to program planning and implementation. CPI is also developing a training component to provide ongoing technical assistance, direction, and support to the task forces and the community at large. More information about the institute can be obtained by writing The Chemical People Institute, Duquesne University, Canevin Hall, Pittsburgh, Pennsylvania, 15282.

The Minnesota Institute on Black Chemical Abuse

This program concentrates on a community approach to chemical abuse prevention and incorporates businesses, agencies, and community members within the activities. It uses community education, support groups, and family counseling techniques designed to meet the needs of the African-American as vehicles. The institute also provides programming for children of chemically dependent persons. The institute has received national recognition and can be replicated in similar cities throughout the country. For more information contact Mr. Peter Bell, Executive Director, Minnesota Institute on Black Chemical Abuse, 2616 Nicollet Avenue, Minneapolis, Minnesota 55408.

Shalom, Inc.

Shalom is a school-community partnership program that began as a pilot prevention program with catholic high schools in Philadelphia, Pennsylvania. Shalom offers family focused prevention/invervention activities and will begin programming within catholic elementary schools in the near future. Further information can be obtained from contacting Shalom, Inc., 311 South Juniper Street, Suite 900, Philadelphia, PA 19107.

The National Partnership

This is a project initiated by the U.S. Department of Juvenile Justice and modeled after the National Chemical People Project. It incorporates the resources of major television networks, corporations, and national and local organizations to implement a nationwide prevention and intervention project. The project is presently in the process of identifying pilot cities for implementation of the project. For further information contact Wendy Keefe, Juvenile Justice Clearing House, NCJRS, 1600 Research Blvd., Rockville, MD 20850.

SUMMARY

In light of the diverse and complex issues involved with chemical abuse, it is necesary to expand the scope of models used to address them. The Multicultural Model has application in a broad range of issues that impact chemical abuse and is adaptable to most individuals, cultures, communities, socio-economic levels and systems. It does not assume the priority of one approach or strategy over another, but encompasses within its structure a variety of approaches. Through the individualized strategies developed by the advisory boards, the Multicultural Model enables a community to campaign and distribute information under a public health approach (refer to the therapeutic setting under the psychosocial approach), influence cultural change under the sociocultural approach, address the societal/legal standards of use under the moral/legal approach, and incorporate all of the above comprehensively under a systems approach.

REFERENCES

Ackerman, R. (1983). *Children of alcoholics: A guide to educators, therapists, and parents*. Holmes Beach, FL: Learning Publications.

Brooks, J. S., Lukoff, I. F., & Whiteman, M. (1977). Peer, family, and personality domains as related to adolescents drug behavior. *Psychological Reports, 41*, 1095–1102.

Broussard, E. R., & Hartner, M. S. S. (1971). Further considerations regarding maternal perception of the first born. In J. Hellmuth (Ed.), *Exceptional Infant: Vol. 2. Studies in Abnormalities* (pp 432–449). New York: Brunner/Mazel.

Broussard, E. R. (1976). Neonatal prediction and outcome at 10-11 years. *Child Psychiatry and Human Development, 7* (2), 85–93.

Children's Defense Fund (1984). *Preventing children having children.* Paper presented at the 1984 Conference on Children having Children, Washington, D.C.

Dembo, R. (1979). Substance abuse prevention programming and research: A partnership in need of improvement. *Journal of Drug Education, 9,* 139–208.

Dembo, R., Farrow, D., Des Jarlais, D., Burgos, W., & Schmeidler, J. (1981). Examining a causal model of early drug involvement among inner city junior high school youths. *Human Relations, 34,* 169–193.

Dembo, R., Farrow, D., Schneidler, J., & Burgos, W. (1979). Testing a causal model of environmental influences on the early drug involvement of inner city junior high school youths. *American Journal of Drug and Alcohol Abuse, 6,* 313–336.

Dembo, R., & Shern, D. (1982). Relative deviance and the processes of drug involvement among inner city youths. *The International Journal of the Addictions, 17*(8), 1373–1399.

Dodson, J.E. (1983). Black families: The clue to cultural appropriateness as an evaluative concept for health and human services. In A. E. Johnson (Ed.), *The black experience: Considerations for health and human services* (pp. 41–52). Davis, CA: International Dialogue Press.

Geertz, C. (1973). *The interpretation of cultures.* New York: Basic Books.

Gordan, T. (1982). The black adolescent. *Mental Health, 25,* 114–133.

Griswold, S. (1982). *Survey of attitudes toward prevention in an inner city African-American community.* Pittsburgh, PA: Addison Terrace Learning Center, 2136 Elmore Square, Pittsburgh, PA 15219.

Griswold, S. (1984, April). Drug and alcohol abuse in industry. *Technotimes* (p. 4). Pittsburgh, PA: United Technology Inc.

Griswold-Ezekoye, S. (in press). *The multicultural approach: A culture specific model of prevention/intervention and treatment of chemical abuse.* Pittsburgh, PA: Addison Terrace Learning Center, 2136 Elmore Square, Pittsburgh, PA 15219.

Jessor, R., & Jessor, S. L. (1977). *Problem behavior and psychosocial development: A longitudinal study of youth.* New York: Academic Press.

Jordan, V. (1980). *Setting the stage for prevention planning.* Paper presented at the Multicultural Prevention Planning Symposium, Arlington, VA, Center for Multicultural Awareness.

Kandel, D. B. (1975). Some comments on the relationship of selected criteria variables to adolescent illicit drug use. In D. J. Lettieri (Ed.), *Predicting adolescent drug abuse: A review of issues, methods and correlates* (Research Issues No. 11). Rockville, MD: National Institute on Drug Abuse.

Payton, C (1981). Substance abuse and mental health: Special prevention strategies needed for ethnics of color. *Public Health Reports, 96* (1), 20-25.

Szasz, T. (1971). The ethics of psychiatry. *The American Journal of Psychiatry, 128* (5), 541–546.

Trader, H.T. (1981). Black family life and life styles. In A. E. Johnson (Ed.), *The black experience: Social, cultural and economic considerations* (pp. 123–138). Chapel Hill, NC: School of Social Work, University of North Carolina.

United States Bureau of Census. (1985, July) *Labor force and disability characteristics, 1980* (pp. 10,14). Washington, DC: United States Department of Commerce.

United States Department of Labor. (1985). *Civilian unemployment rate: Blacks age 16 and over.* Washington, DC: Bureau of Labor Statistics.

Wilcox, P. (1973). Positive mental health in the black community: The black liberation movement. In C. Willie, B. Kramer, & B. Brown (Eds.), *Racism and mental health* (pp. 463–524). Pittsburgh, PA: University of Pittsburgh Press.

Zimberg, S. (1977). Sociopsychiatric perspectives on Jewish alcoholism: Implications for the prevention of alcoholism. *American Journal of Drug and Alcohol Abuse, 4* (4), 571–579.

Treatment for Childhood Chemical Abuse

George Beschner, MSW

ABSTRACT. This article describes intervention and treatment services available to youth and adolescents with chemical abuse problems and discusses the necessary components of a comprehensive approach in serving youth with these problems. The author also discusses research on treatment outcomes within the various types of programs along with research on the treatment models employed.

Although childhood chemical (drug and alcohol) abuse is acknowledged to be a major national problem, little is known about treatment programs for young chemical abusers. There have been few controlled, prospective research studies to determine the effectiveness of programs and services for such youngsters.

Young boys and girls who sense that they have a chemical abuse problem are not likely to know where to turn for help. Parents of young chemical abusers do not know where they can go for help. Teachers and school administrators are perplexed when it comes to finding assistance for such youngsters and their families. Courts generally refer young chemical abusers who come to their attention to probation officers who, in turn, refer them to the custody of parents. Even private physicians and clinicians in health care systems have difficulty identifying appropriate treatment resources for young chemical abusers.

Drawing from the literature and current research, this article reviews what is known about treatment programs for chemical abusers 12 to 19 years of age. Special attention is given to: the types of programs that serve young chemical

George Beschner, Chief, Technology Transfer Branch, Division of Prevention and Communications, National Institute on Drug Abuse, Room 10A37, 5600 Fisher's Lane, Rockville, MD 20857.

231

abusers, what has been learned about these programs and
their effectiveness, the factors that influence treatment outcomes, and promising treatment models that have been
tested.

TREATMENT SERVICES

A study conducted by the National Association of State
Alcohol and Drug Abuse Directors, Inc. (Burynski, Record
& Yates, 1985), shows that in recent years a growing number
of younger persons with substance abuse problems have been
entering treatment. It is conservatively estimated that more
than 65,000 youngsters (17 years and under) entered drug and
alcohol facilities in 1984. Yet, few drug and alcohol treatment
programs in this country are designed specifically to serve
youngsters. Of the 3,018 substance abuse treatment facilities
identified in the United States in 1982, only 155 (5.1%) had
adolescents as their main clientele (i.e., at least 50% 19-years
of age and under, NIDA 1983a).

In general, three treatment settings are available: inpatient,
outpatient, and residential. If young chemical abusers are not
sufficiently motivated for treatment (and most are not), and if
they cannot be controlled by their parents, there are few options available. They can be, however, legally committed to a
hospital inpatient program. Hospital inpatient facilities provide medically-based diagnostic services and psychological
counseling. Unfortunatly, inpatient chemical abuse treatment
services are scarce, very expensive,, and in some states it is
difficult to work out involuntary commitment procedures. In
recognition of the growing need for adolescent inpatient facilities, private inpatient programs for adolescent substance
abusers have been established in many communities across
the country. These programs, however, average over $10,000
per patient, per month (Kusnetz 1985), and, therefore, are
available only to families with comprehensive health insurance or the means to pay the high inpatient costs. Some states
and local governments support public inpatient treatment programs for young chemical abusers but the capacity of these
programs is limited. Most of the hospital programs offer only
short-term inpatient care essentially to treat crisis cases,

young men and women in need of detoxification, and those who appear to have serious psychological problems. It is difficult to determine how many young chemical abusers are being treated in hospital inpatient facilities because most of these programs are private and do not report regularly to state drug and/or alcohol authorities. One source of data indicates, however, that only 1.6% of young drug abusers (12 to 19 years of age) enrolled in publicly supported drug treatment programs in 1981 were treated in inpatient facilities (NIDA 1982).

Most young chemical abusers (75.2%) are admitted to outpatient programs which include a wide range of organizations from unstructured drop-in centers to highly structured family service agencies (NIDA 1982). Most outpatient programs generally offer at least one and usually a number of the following services: individual counseling, group counseling, family counseling, post-discharge follow-up and, when appropriate, referral to other modes of treatment. A youngster will usually attend this type of program one or more times per week spending one to three hours at each session for periods ranging from several months to two or more years. Almost all communities have outpatient drug/alcohol treatment and counseling programs or community mental health centers supported by state, county or city governments. These programs generally provide drug counseling services to adolescents in addition to treating a broad range of psychological and behavioral problems. Outpatient clinics have very few controls and relatively little structure. Thus, patients must be highly motivated to benefit from counseling provided and make a personal commitment to attend counseling regularly and participate actively. As in other treatment settings, generally family participation is needed for treatment to be effective but, unfortunately, few substance abuse outpatient programs serving adolescent have family therapists available on staff. Most outpatient programs charge a fee for service, usually on a sliding scale. The average cost for outpatient services is about $3,000 per year (Kusnetz, 1985).

Some 15.1% of young chemical abusers, 12 to 19 years of age, entered residential programs (NIDA 1982). These programs operate in facilities that provide enough space for therapeutic activities and living quarters. Unlike most inpatient facilities, young residential clients generally are confined or forced to participate in treatment against their will. Clients usually stay in residential treatment for six months to one year. Compared to inpatient programs, residential programs are far less costly, averaging between $8,000 and $9,000 per year (Kusnetz, 1985). Most residential programs provide individual and group therapy, educational classes, parent participation, confrontational meetings, recreational activities, and shared responsibility for managing the facility. They often lack the medical, psychological, and diagnostic services offered by inpatient programs (Kusnetz, 1985)

Compared to youngsters served in outpatient facilities, residential clients are: (a) lower in educational level, (b) more likely to have been referred to treatment by the criminal justice system, (c) more likely to have had previous treatment episodes, and (d) more likely to have been using drugs other than marijuana, such as heroin, other opiates, cocaine, hallucinogens, barbiturates, and inhalants (Friedman, 1983).

Few residential drug programs are specifically designed for youngsters, and, therefore, youths are likely to receive the same treatment as adults. In an effort to differentiate between the problems of residential youngsters and adults, and to develop suitable treatment programs the former, Holland (1983) compared the substance use patterns, consequences of use, and problems reported by young and adult drug abuse clients in residential programs. Young clients reported more family problems while growing up, were more likely to have a psychological problems, and were more likely to have attempted suicide. As might be expected, adults were more likely to have been arrested, convicted and jailed.

De Leon and Deitch (1985) observed the following differences between youngsters and adults in residential treatment centers:

1. Young clients have a higher incidence of disorganized family backgrounds.
2. Young clients receive psychological treatment at an earlier age, including treatment after suicide attempts.
3. When deciding whether to stay in treatment, youngsters are more likely to respond to pressures exerted by family and the fear of jail.
4. Educational needs, the need for parental and family

support, and the provision of educational assistance play a larger role in the treatment of young chemical abusers.

5. The impact of the negative consequences of substance abuse is more apparent for adults. Because they have abused drugs over longer periods, adults suffer more tangible losses in money, family, and in interpersonal relationships.

THE NEED FOR AFTERCARE

Most youngsters find it difficult to retain their newly learned lifestyle when they come back home after inpatient or residential treatment and are in contact with former peer groups, families, and school situations. Almost all, therefore, revert back to pre-treatment alcohol and marijuana use (Sells & Simpson, 1979; Hubbard, Cavanaugh, Graddock & Rachel, 1983). Even those who develop self-esteem, self-awareness, and coping skills find it hard to counteract the pressures in their old environments, and they are likely to require support and direction. Assistance may come, in part, from the family, if family intervention of some sort has been provided, or it may come from *aftercare programs* that have the capability of treating youngsters as they adjust to the community.

Aftercare is based on a recognition that the treatment process should not end abruptly at discharge from a day care, inpatient, or residential treatment. Aftercare programs usually have professional counselors or other support persons available to help when problems arise, anxieties build, and peer pressure or temptation to use drugs increases. Some aftercare programs make use of peer groups to provide support during the reentry process. These groups, consisting of other youngsters going through recovery, are organized and led by both professional or peer counselors. Youngsters often feel more comfortable talking openly to peers about their families, friends, and other relationships; also, they may be more receptive to feedback from their peers. Outpatient programs can be instrumental in providing aftercare for youngsters discharged from inpatient and residential programs.

IMPORTANCE OF FAMILY PARTICIPATION

Parent participation is very important during the treatment and aftercare processes. Unlike adult chemical abusers who have more independent control of their life situations, young chemical abusers, even after successfully completing an inpatient or residential treatment program, usually return to their families and their former living situations.

The love and understanding of the parents certainly will be tested. They must be prepared to respond with their time and patience, setting limits and giving ongoing support. In some cases, the parents themselves will need assistance in developing and maintaining an appropriate and positive parent-child relationship. In short, almost all parents of adolescent substance abusers, even those parents who are well/adjusted, will need support in coping as their children adjust to family, friends, and school.

In more difficult cases, youngsters may abuse drugs to gain attention in a family that otherwise ignores them. Family therapists who specialize in treating young chemical abusers have found that patients' families often are conflictual or disengaged, lack open communication, mutual respect, reasonable organization, or close loving relationships (Friedman, Pomerance, Sanders, Santo & Utada, 1980). The parents and children often are alienated; the parents may be poor models or overly controlling. In such cases, expert assistance is needed. Drug abuse itself must be of concern but cannot be treated outside the context of these other factors.

Findings produced by the National Youth Polydrug Study (Friedman, Santo & Glickman, 1983) show the direct relationship between family factors and adolescent and childhood drug abuse:

1. Youngsters whose parents had drug problems, alcohol problems, psychiatric problems, or problems with the law are more heavily involved in drug abuse than adolescents whose parents were not reported to have such problems.
2. There is a significant positive correlation between the number of problems reported in families and the number and types of drugs used by the offspring.

It has frequently been found that it is necessary to "insist" on the involvement of the parents since it is common for them to deny the nature and origin of chemical abuse by their child. It is important to assess the feelings and emotional state of the parents when a youth is entering treatment. The parent, most likely, will have experienced a degree of emotional upheaval comparable to that of their child and have lived through the child's rebellious antisocial and/or self-destructive acting-out behavior. The parent's emotions and feelings are also likely to be related to the weight of their problems as adults and to feelings of having failed.

In describing the parents of young clients at treatment entry, drug counselors report that the parents have conflicting, muddled, and/or confused feelings. Conflict between the two parents is often apparent. They have been so emotionally exhausted by the events leading to treatment that they present a sense of hopelessness and a "give up" attitude. At the same time, they tend to be overinvested emotionally in the problematic situation and to be desperately seeking guidance and direction (Friedman et al., 1980).

Even if it is assumed that the family environment did not significantly contribute to the development of the youngsters chemical problem, the family can assist the young chemical abuser to overcome the problem. In the more severe cases this may develop into a long-term endeavor, requiring patience, staying power, firmness, persistence and tolerance of frustration. For this reason, parents often find the support of a professional helpful during the treatment process.

YOUNG CHEMICAL ABUSERS IN OTHER TREATMENT SETTINGS

Many youngsters are seen for chemical abuse-related problems by one or more organizations not primarily invested in chemical abuse treatment, such as community mental health centers, hospitals, or family and child agencies. These institutions may be unfamiliar with chemical abuse and ill-equipped to treat it. Because these organizations are outside the normal drug treatment network, little is known about the number of youngsters they treat or the effectiveness of the treatment.

1. One study of a day school treatment program (operated exclusively for court-referred delinquents) found that the degree of current chemical use (except for heroin) at admission to treatment far exceeded that for youngsters in the state/federally funded treatment network. Twenty-five percent of the day school sample had been "drunk" 150 times or more during their short lives, and approximately one-half got "drunk" at least once a week (Gaus & Henderson, 1984).

2. A recent study conducted by the Office of Juvenile Justice and Delinquency Prevention found that more than half (50.5%) of 43,415 adolescents treated for delinquency in group homes had chemical abuse problems. In addition, many adolescents in other types of criminal justice facilities had drug and alcohol problems: status offender (45%), emotionally distrubed (39%), detention (38%), psychiatric care (27%), temporary shelters (23%), and dependent and neglected (14%) (Pappenfort, Young & Dore, 1983).

3. Many youngsters are treated in hospital emergency rooms for chemical-related episodes; yet, there has been little attempt to find out if these youngsters receive treatment after leaving the hospital. In 1982, the Drug Abuse Warning Network (DAWN) reported that 23,091 drug/alcohol emergency episodes involved patients 10 to 19 years of age (NIDA 1983b). Of these, 3,949 involved alcohol in combination with other drugs, 1,553 involved marijuana, and 1,311 involved amphetamines. Heroin/morphine and cocaine were mentioned less frequently (383 and 399 respectively) and most often by patients 18- or 19-years-old.

4. A national reporting system, which provides statistical information on a broad range of drug and alcohol treatment environments and units, shows that in 1982, 22% of the clients in the total NDATUS sample, 20 years of age and under, are treated in community mental health centers (CMHC) (NIDA, 1983a). In comparison, 14% of adults in the 21- to 44-year-old age category were treated in CMHCs. Depsite the evidence that large numbers of young chemical abusers are indeed treated in CMHCs, there is little information regarding the capacity of these centers to respond to the problem of adolescent chemical abuse.

COMPARISON OF OUTPATIENT
AND RESIDENTIAL PROGRAMS

A recent national survey compared 31 residential drug programs oriented to treat young people (18 years of of age and under) with 43 outpatient drug programs serving youth (Friedman et al., 1983) and learned that:

1. Outpatient programs devoted more staff time to counseling and psychotherapy than did residential programs (69% vs. 40%). Outpatient programs devoted more staff time to individual counseling, medial services, art therapy, vocational training, and IQ testing. The group counseling emphasis in residential treatment reflects the essential nature of residential programs, people who live together tend to work out their problems together.

2. When asked to specify the most important attributes for a counselor of young chemical abuse clients, both residential and outpatient program administrators selected the following three attributes more frequently than others on a list of possible attributes: (a) natural ability and ease in relating to adolescents, (b) an ability to project a positive model, and (c) several years of counseling experience. Having street savvy and experience as ex-drug abusers were rated higher as counselor attributes by residential administrators than by outpatient administrators.

3. Residential programs have a relatively higher percentage of black counselors, possibly related to having a greater proportion of black clients or to being in communities with greater numbers of Blacks.

4. A greater proportion of outpatient program counselors have master or high degrees than residential counselors (54% vs. 29%).

Significantly, counselors in both outpatient and residential programs most often endorsed the following treatment goals:

—to change clients' attitudes so that they are committed to working on their personal and situational problems in a positive way;

—to help clients stop or at least diminish the drug use that is complicating their lives; and

—to work toward involving the client's whole family in the

treatment as soon as possible, concentrate on establishing good parent-child relationships.

The counselors also identified what they considered to be the most effective counseling approaches:

—applying an understanding and empathetic attitude;
—confronting the client with his/her self-destructive/maladaptive behavior; and
—providing practical assistance in solving clients' real-life problems.

The outpatient and residential counselors were less in agreement on the most utilized therapy techniques, methods, and approaches (from a list of 23). Both groups reported reality therapy and modeling as most utilized. After these two, residential counselors selected confrontation, rap sessions and assertiveness therapy, while outpatient counselors selected long-term psychotherapy, values clarification, and gestalt therapy.

Counselors in both settings reported that at least half of their clients: (a) consider the use of marijuana and alcohol to be an acceptable and normal activity, (b) have psychological and situational problems which predate their drug use, (c) are failing in their formal societal roles, especially as students, (d) come to treatment nonvoluntarily, (e) do not come to treatment seeking help to stop taking drugs, and (f) feel they are helped by the drugs they take. Thus, counselors in both types of programs see young clients as very challenging.

TREATMENT OUTCOME STUDIES

There have been few systematic attempts to evaluate which treatment environments, program conditions, or treatment methods are most effective in treating young chemical abuser. The three largest studies (Hubbard, Cavanaugh, Graddock & Rachel, 1983; Rush, 1979; Sells & Simpson, 1979) all involve descriptive rather than controlled study; therefore, the findings should be viewed with caution.

Sells and Simpson (1979) assessed the progress made by

5,406 young chemical abuser (19 years of age and under) four to six years after they were admitted to treatment. These patients showed some favorable outcomes including significant reductions in the use of opiates and in criminal activities for all major types of treatment environments. In addition, youngsters remained in treatment (outpatient and residential) for longer periods than the older clients. Treatment failed, however, to influence the use of marijuana and alcohol; youngsters still used these two substances extensively one year after treatment. Marijuana use showed no change among Whites and an increase among Blacks; alcohol use increased slightly among Black 18 to 19 years of age. It is not clear to what extent treatment programs attempted to bring about a reduction in marijuana use and alcoholism, since the programs in this sample were primarily oriented to serve adult opioid abusers.

Rush (1979), who analyzed treatment data in Pennsylvania, found several characteristics of young clients that predicted treatment outcome at discharge, and these differed by modality. Retention (time spent in treatment) was positively related to, and was the best predictor of, improvement in "productivity" for youngsters in residential programs. The productivity criterion is an index score that combines education, training, and employment. The reverse was true for youngsters treated in outpatient programs, retention was negatively related to productivity gains. It was concluded that young outpatient clients who stay in treatment longer are likely to have more severe problems and be less capable of making constructive changes in productivity. In contrast, young clients who remained in the protective environment of residential programs were better able to restructure their lives and become productive at discharge. It should also be pointed out that Rush found that young outpatient clients had not been as heavily involved as residential clients in the drug use or criminal activities prior to entering treatment.

Hubbard and his colleagues (1983) interviewed 240 youngsters (age 12 to 17) in six cities, one year after treatment and considered only those who stayed in treatment at least three months. Findings were mixed. Among respondents in outpatient programs, there were: (a) more daily marijuana users at follow-up (54%) than in the year preceding treatment (48%),

(b) fewer heavy alcohol users (54% pretreatment vs 41% at follow-up), and (c) less involvement in criminal activities (53% before and 36% after). Large proportions of female clients (37%) and male clients (27%), in the 17 years of age and younger category, felt that treatment had not helped them reduce their drug use at all.

Youngsters treated in residential program fared better: daily marijuana users dropped (79% vs. 12% of the sample, before and after, respectively); (b) heavy alcohol users declined (from 56% to 29%); and (c) involvement in illegal acts declined (from 71% to 36%). Almost half of the residential clients were "very satisfied" with the treatment they had received. Two-thirds of the clients reported that treatment helped them reduce their drug use "a lot."

In spite of the relatively positive outcomes reported by these three large-scale studies, given the limitations of their research designs, the findings must be considered as less than conclusive. The continuing high levels of alcohol and marijuana use after treatment indicate that, on the average, treatment does not influence youngsters to stop using chemical substances.

EVALUATION OF TREATMENT MODELS

In recent years, several modest attempts have been made to evaluate treatment programs and services that have been developed and specifically oriented to serve young chemical abusers. Although these formative research efforts have been limited in size and sophistication, they provide a foundation for future treatment and research. They have produced important knowledge about programs, treatment process, and clients that otherwise would have been lost. They document how programs are formed, implemented, and take shape over time. They describe problems encountered early in the program and the research. They provide data that may be useful in interpreting what is learned later from more rigorous research. Through a development process they helped build and, in some cases, reconstruct treatment models that will be evaluated in the future. They identified clinical and research issues which future researchers will need to focus on in designing and conducting studies. In some ways, these studies broke the ice, providing clinicians and researchers to work with and gain respect for one another. Several examples of these formative research studies follow:

Using a quasi-experimental design, Grenier (1985) evaluated a comprehensive multidisciplinary adolescent chemical dependency unit (referred to as the *"AA-Family Model"*) located at Baton Rouge General Hospital, Louisiana. It was determined that youngsters treated in the unit were more likely than waiting-list controls to be abstinent at follow-up. The model consists of three phases: (a) evaluation (one week), (b) inpatient open treatment (one month), and (c) aftercare (up to two years). It includes elements of the Alcoholics Anonymous recovering process and ongoing parent involvement.

The Youth Environment Study (YES) in San Francisco tested the effectiveness of a neighborhood-based early intervention program in reaching and treating young chemical abusers. Applying ethnographic (field observation) techniques, the YES team was able to gather information about the chemical use patterns, lifestyles, and activities of youngsters in their natural communities and to apply appropriate intervention and referral strategies (Feldman, Mandel & Fields, 1985)

Researchers at The Door, a comprehensive treatment center in New York City, evaluated the effectiveness of an individualized alternative education model for young chemical abusers (Learning Laboratory). Unable after some effort to establish a control group, the effectiveness of the program was evaluated by measuring pretest vs. posttest (6-month follow-up) changes in three dimensions: (a) education, (b) chemical use, and (c) involvement in purposeful activities. At follow-up, 43% of the Learning Laboratory participants were involved in education or training programs, 56% had furthered their education, and 50% had decreased their chemical use (Mai, Pedrick & Greene, 1980).

Kukulu Kumuhana, a cultural enrichment program in Hawaii, proved to be effective in treating youths age 14 to 19 who were inhalant abusers (Winn, 1981). The program combined educational instruction, skills training, and group and individual counseling with a number of cultural activities. Six-month follow-up data showed that clients made significant gains in measures of self-esteem, psychological adjustment, and academic achievement. Even more encouraging, at follow-up, the evaluators found almost a total absence of inhalant use.

Results from a controlled pilot study indicate that social skills training may be effective in treating young chemical abusers. Based on prior work in the delinquency field, Hawkins (1984) evaluated a program designed to improve the problem-solving and social skills of young institutionalized chemical abusers. The program had little difficulty motivating youngsters to participate in videotaped role-playing sessions and problem-solving training but had problems recruiting parents to particpate. The investigators concluded that longer (more than 9 sessions) and more intensive skills training were needed to treatment outcomes.

In Bucks County, near Philadelphia, *the DeLaSalle Vocational School,* a day school rehabilitation program, assessed a "supportive life skills" and counseling program for delinquent and chemical-abusing court-referred boys, 14 to 18 years of age (Gaus & Henderson, 1985). The mean number of substances (different types) used in a lifetime was 5.87 for the evaluation study sample of 205 consecutively admitted boys. At time of admission, approximately half of the sample reported that they got "drunk" at least once per week. The experience-based life skills enrichment, an off-campus program offered on a volunteer basis, included: stress challenge, adventure learning, service learning (mostly helping children), and community culture and history. Follow-up evaluation, 17 months later, showed significant improvement in attitudes toward school and school adjustment, self-esteem, family role task behavior, and interpersonal maturity (Beverly-Grant Scale). In addition, there was a lessening of psychic symptomatology (Brief Symptom Inventory), illegal behavior, frequency of getting "drunk," and frequency of hallucinogen and PCP use.

Straight, Incorporated, a large private non-profit rehabilitation program for youthful chemical abusers, emphasizes positive peer pressure and active parent involvement. Founded in 1976, Straight treatment facilities are located in: Springfield, Virginia; Cincinnati, Ohio; Atlanta, Georgia; and the Tampa Bay area in Florida, and have the capacity to serve 700 clients. The program relies heavily on the participation of parents who attend open meetings and parents/rap sessions and provide host-home care (living arrangements for new clients and out-of-towners). According to findings produced by Straight, the program has a 62% completion rate (Oliver 1985).

In addition, there have been some attempts to evaluate school-based treatment programs which have been growing in number as a result of increase attention to student drug use, the influence of the parents movement, and the initiation of prevention programs in schools. Since 1979, the Westchester County Department of Community Mental Health (New York) has been studying the effectiveness of a large innovative school-based chemical abuse treatment program (Morehouse, 1984). The initial pilot study findings indicate that the county's Student Assistance Counseling Program is effective in reducing substance abuse, but that it has little impact on student attendance and academic performance.

The Montgomery County Department of Education (Maryland) provided support for an outside pilot evaluation of its school-based substance abuse program called the *Phoenix School*. This program places student substance abusers in a facility where they receive counseling and individualized academic training during the period when they would normally be in school. The evaluators (Enrich & Green, 1981) found that the program strengthened the commitment of students to education, promoted good school habits, and virtually eliminated chemical use during the school day. Student self-reports, however, showed that chemical use was still a problem for these youngsters when they left school or completed the program.

As pointed out earlier, it is important, and sometimes vital, to work with the parents of young chemical abusers, yet, until recently there was little attempt to study family treatment services in the drug field. A survey of 2,012 drug treatment programs by Coleman and Davis (1978) showed that a majority of programs are involved in some kind of family service.

A team of researchers at the University of Miami compared the effectiveness of two family therapy methods in treating young chemical abusers: conjoint family therapy (CFT) and one-person family therapy (OPFT). CFT involves the entire family while OPFT works primarily with individual clients on family and family-related problems. The study findings indicate that both types of therapy are equally effective in improving family functioning and reducing chemical use (Szapocznik, Kartines, Foote, Perez-Vital & Hervis, 1983).

CONCLUSIONS

More than 65,000 youngsters between 12 and 19 years of age entered chemical abuse treatment facilities in 1984. Countless others, identified as substance abusers, are treated in community mental health centers, juvenile justice agencies, and hospital emergency rooms. In addition secondary schools across the country have implemented alternative school programs for students identified as substance abusers.

Despite the growing numbers of young chemical abusers, there are relatively few programs specifically designed to treat them, and programs that do exist, have had mixed results. In addition, their services can be very costly and beyond the means of many families.

There are two important factors that must be considered in any attempt to provide treatment services to young chemical abusers. First, it is essential to involve parents in the treatment process, from the very beginning, if possible. Second, it is important to provide aftercare services to adolescents after they complete formal treatment and go back to the situation (family, friends and community) they were in when the chemical problem developed.

A number of exploratory studies, evaluating the effectiveness of promising adolescent treatment methods and approaches, have been conducted in recent years. Although somewhat limited in size and sophistication these studies represent a first step in the process of finding out what works for young chemical abusers.

There is a need for well-conceived and rigorously designed studies to: (a) determine the efficacy of different treatment options available to childhood substance abusers, (b) find out which youngsters profit most (and least) from particular treatments, and (c) identify those aspects of treatment which bring about the desired changes. This is no easy task. Program resources are limited, few young treatment agencies have the required research capacity, and it is difficult to conduct controlled studies in human service settings of this type.

For treatment to be successful, new commitments must be made. Administrators must be willing to provide the needed resources and support. Clinicians must be prepared to make investments beyond their normal responsibilities to client and agency. Investigators must be willing to explore research questions and design studies in clinical settings where it is difficult and sometimes impossible to control key variables.

REFERENCES

Butynski, W., Record, H., & Yates, J. (1985). *State resources and services related to alcolhol and drug abuse problms: An analysis of state alcohol and drug abuse profile data–FY 1984 (Contract No. 271-84-7314).* Rockville, MD: National Institute on Drug Abuse.

Coleman, S. B., & Davis, D. E. (1978). Family therapy and drug abuse: A national survey. *Family Process, 17,* 21–29.

De Leon, G. (1984). *The therapeutic community: Study of effectiveness* Treatment Research Monograph Seried (DHHS Pub. No. ADM 84–1286). Rockville, MD: National Institute on Drug Abuse.

De Leon, G., & Deitch, D. (1985). Treatment of the adolescent abuser in a therapeutic community. In A. Friedman, & G. Beschner (Eds.), *Treatment services for adolescent drug abusers* (DHHS Pub. No. ADM 85–1342). Rockville, MD: National Institute on Drug Abuse.

Enrich, R., & Green, P. (1981, December). *Evaluation of the Phoenix Pilot Drug Program.* Report prepared for the Montgomery County Public Schools, Maryland.

Feldman, H., Mandel, J., & Fields, A. (1985). In the neighborhood: A strategy for delivery early intervention services to young drug users in their natural environments. In A. Friedman, & G. Beschner (Eds.), *Treatment services for adolescent substance abusers* (DHHS Pub. No. ADM 85–1342). Rockville, MD: National Institute on Drug Abuse.

Friedman, A.S., Pomerance, E., Sanders, R., Santo, Y., & Utada, M. (1980, Fall). The structure and problems of the families of adosescent drug abusers. *Contemporary Drug Problems,* 327–356.

Friedman, A. S., Santo, Y., & Glickman, N. (1983). *The program characteristics that predict successful treatment of adolescent drug abusers.* Final report to National Institute on Drug Abuse, Rockville, MD.

Gaus, S., & Henerson, G. (1985). Supportive life skills aftercare program for court-committed adolescent substance abusers. In A. Friedman, & G. Beschner (Eds.), *Treatment services for adolescent substance abusers* (DHHS Pub. No. ADM 85–1342). Rockville, MD: National Institute on Drug Abuse.

Grenier, C. (1985). Treatment effectiveness in an adolescent chemical dependency treatment program: A quasi-experimental design. *The International Journal of the Addictions, 20* (3), 381–391.

Hawkins, D. (1984). *Adolescent drug abuse treatment and early intervention* (Grant No. R01 DA 03599). Rockville, MD: National Institute on Drug Abuse.

Holland, S. (1981, July). *Comparison of adolescent and adult clients.* Clinical Research Notes. Rockville, MD: National Institute on Drug Abuse.

Hubbard, R. L., Cavanaugh, E.R., Graddock, S. G., & Rachel, J. V. (1983). *Characteristics, behaviors and outcomes for youth in TOPS study*. Report submitted to NIDA (Contract No. 271-79-3611). Research Triangle Park, NC: Research Triangle Institute.

Kusnetz, S. (1985). An overview of selected adolescent substance abuse treatment programs. In A. Friedman, & G. Beschner (Eds.), *Treatment* services for adolescent substance abusers (DHHS Pub. No. ADM 85-1342). Rockville, MD: National Institute on Drug Abuse.

Mai, L., Pedrick, S., & Greene, M. (1980). *The learning laboratory treatment research monograph* (DHHS Pub. No. ADM 80-928). Rockville, MD: National Institute on Drug Abuse.

Morehouse, E. (1984). *Assessing and motivating adolescent drug abusers* (Grant No. H81 DA01657). Rockville, MD: National Institute on Drug Abuse.

National Institute on Drug Abuse. (1982). *Data from the Client Oriented Data Acquisition Process (CODAP)* (Series E, No. 21). Rockville, MD: Department of Health and Human Services.

National Institute on Drug Abuse. (1983a). *Main findings for drug abuse treatment units. Data from the National Drug and Alcoholism Treatment Utilization Survey* (NDATUS). Rockville, MD: Department of Health and Human Services.

National Institute on Drug Abuse. (1983b). *Data from the Drug Abuse Warning Network (DAWN)* (Series I, No. 2). Rockville, MD: Department of Health and Human Services.

Oliver, W. (1985). *Facts about Straight*. St. Petersburg, VA: National Office of Straight, Inc.

Pappenfort, D., Young, T., & Dore, M. (1983, April), *The national survey of residential group care facilities for children and youth*. Report prepared for the Office of Juvenile Justice and Deliquency Prevention, Washington, DC.

Rush, T. V. (1979). Predicting treatment outcomes for juvenile and young-adult clients in the Pennsylvania Substance-Abuse System. In G. Beschner, & A. Friedman (Eds.), *Youth drug abuse: Problems, issues and treatment*. Lexington, MA: Lexington Books.

Sells, S. B., & Simpson, D. D. (1979). Evaluation of treatment outcomes for youths in the drug abuse reporting program (DARP): A follow-up study. In G. Beschner, & A. Friedman (Eds.), *Youth drug abuse: Problems, issues and treatment*. Lexington, MA: Lexington Books.

Szapocznik, J., Kurtines, W., Foote, F., Perez-Vidal, A., & Hervis, O. (1983). Conjoint versus one-person family therapy: Some evidence for the effectiveness of conducting family therapy through one person. *Journal of Consulting Clinical Psychology, 51* (6), 889–899.

Winn, J. (1981). *A cultural enrichment program for you*. Treatment Research Notes. Rockville, MD: National Institute on Drug Abuse.

Future Issues and Promising Directions in the Prevention of Substance Abuse Among Youth

Karol L. Kumpfer, PhD
Joel Moskowitz, PhD
Henry O. Whiteside, PhD
Michael Klitzner, PhD

ABSTRACT. This concluding article first reviews environmental and public policy approaches to prevention not covered in the prior articles. Next, it provides a scheme for conceptualizing the various approaches to prevention in relation to the Public Health Services prevention model—the Host/Agent/Environment Triad. The difficulty in prioritizing prevention approaches and six major areas of research needed before this can be accomplished are discussed. The article concludes with speculation about the future of prevention, based on possible positive and negative changes in society and drug use patterns, and finally, recommendations are made for the most promising approaches.

Karol L. Kumpfer, Research Associate, Social Research Institute, Graduate School of Social Work, University of Utah, Salt Lake City, UT 84112. Joel Moskowitz, Associate Director for Research, Prevention Research Center, 2532 Durant Avenue, Berkeley, CA 94704. Henry O. Whiteside, Assistant Vice-President, Triad America Corporation, Salt Lake City, UT 84112. Michael Klitzner, Research Associate, Pacific Institute for Research and Evaluation, Bethesda, MD 20800.

Preparation of this article was supported in part by National Institute on Drug Abuse grant DA2758-01/02 and DA03888-01 (Dr. Karol Kumpfer, Principal Investigator), and National Institute on Alcohol Abuse and Alcoholism grant AA06282-03 (Dr. Joel Moskowitz, Principal Investigator). The authors wish to acknowledge Bonnie Anderson and Lorna Raty for their assistance in the preparation of this article.

INTRODUCTION

The prevention of substance abuse is a complex and difficult, but critically needed activity in our society. The abuse of alcohol and other drugs is not a new phenomenon. Use, misuse, and efforts to control the use of drugs are apparently as old as civilization. In recent years, there has been increasing interest in taking a proactive stance towards the prevention of alcohol and drug abuse. In the previous articles of this issue, some of the major approaches currently being used in the fight to prevent drug and alcohol abuse among youth have been examined. A variety of approaches to primary prevention were discussed utilizing the family (De-Marsh & Kumpfer), the schools (Bukoski), the community (Johnson, et al.), and the mass media (Wallack). Knowledge about the etiology of substance abuse was summarized by Hawkins and his associates, and Kumpfer and DeMarsh. A cultural model of prevention incorporating a number of approaches in an integrated community model was described by Ezekoye. Finally, Beschner discussed the scarcity of treatment services available for youthful substance abusers. Combined, these papers provide an excellent overview of the state-of-the-art in the prevention of substance abuse among children and youth.

ENVIRONMENTAL APPROACHES TO PREVENTION

Not all possible prevention approaches have been covered. For instance, specialists in the alcohol field have advocated numerous environmental and regulatory approaches to prevent alcohol-related problems. Recommended measures include regulating the content of alcoholic bevarage advertising (Mosher & Wallack, 1981), increasing the accuracy of portrayals of the consequences of alcohol use in the mass media (Wallack, 1984), increasing counteradvertising via industry funding (Wallack, 1984), increasing excise taxes and price (Mosher, 1982; Grossman, Coate, & Arluck, 1984) and decreasing availability by: (a) increasing the minimum age for legal purchase (Wagenaar, 1981, 1982, 1984; Vingilis & DeGenova, 1984; Williams & Lillis, 1985), (b) reducing the number of outlets selling alcoholic beverages for off-premise consumption (Mac-Donald & Whitehead, 1983; Hooper, 1983) (c) eliminating alcoholic beverage sales from gas stations, and (d) restricting sales at public events (Wittman, 1985).

Many of these prevention strategies entail public policy changes and are only appropriate for the prevention of abuse of a legal substance like alcohol. They are less applicable to the drug abuse prevention field except for over-the-counter and prescription drugs. Also, because these environmental and regulatory approaches tend to legislate personal choice, they often face public and private resistance (Bell & Levy, 1984) and raise ethical and moral questions (Roffman, 1982).

This concluding article will provide a scheme for conceptualizing the various approaches to prevention in relation to the Public Health Services prevention model—the Host/Agent/Environment Triad. Next, two different philosophies of prevention, namely prevention of causes versus consequences, are contrasted. The difficulty in prioritizing prevention approaches and six major areas of research needed before this can be accomplished are discussed. The article concludes with speculation about the future of prevention based on possible positive and negative changes in society and drug use patterns, and, finally recommendations are made for the most promising approaches.

PUBLIC HEALTH SERVICES PREVENTION MODEL

The Public Health Services (PHS) model of prevention, a triad of Host, Agent, and Environment, provides a method for categorizing substance abuse activities. Figure 1 depicts the primary sites of influence for various prevention approaches currently being advocated. Other reviews of substance abuse prevention that attempt similar groupings using the PHS prevention model may differ slightly because they focus on either the agent, environment, or host, and not on the interaction of the three (Schinke & Gilchrist, in press, b; Lauzon, 1977; Nathan, 1983). Approaches that attempt to influence the availability or accessibility of alcohol and drugs (i.e., licensing, drug control, triplicate prescriptions, limiting sales outlets, prohibiting sales in fast food or gasoline stations), and the attitudes and normative behaviors of society in relation to alcohol and drugs (such as advertising and the portrayal of alcohol and drugs in the mass media as discussed by Wallack) are place on the AGENT-ENVIRONMENT axis. Prevention strategies that work to decrease youth's interest or motivation to use alcohol and drugs (i.e., increasing minimum age laws; increasing penalties for use of illegal drugs, drinking while driving, or under-age drinking; increasing cost and taxes; increasing arrests and law enforcement), or to decrease amount consumed (i.e., decreasing strength of alcohol or drugs, and server education and liablility) are placed along the HOST-AGENT axis.

Most approaches, including those that the general public consider as prevention, lie along the ENVIRONMENT-HOST axis. The Kumpfer/DeMarsh VASC Model of Substance Abuse (explained in more detail in the Kumpfer and DeMarsh article in this issue) situates etiological influences along this axis on a continuum from the most distal—national, state, and local community; to intermediate influences from co-workers, peers, friends, role models, and teachers; to proximal influences from the family of origin and the immediate family or spouse (Kumpfer & DeMarsh, 1984). Chemical dependency programs can also be located along this traditional prevention axis by the primary site of influence, community, social network or school, family, or youth, as shown in Figure 1.

Community-focused prevention programs include examples discussed in the Johnson et al., Ezekoye, and Wallack articles of this issue, such as community prevention councils, health fairs, use of community volunteers, mass media campaigns, and coordinated community prevention campaigns. Social network or school-focused prevention programs include approaches discussed in the Bukoski article, such as education and prevention programs aimed at changing the attitudes and behaviors of peer groups in schools, colleges or universities, churches, neighborhoods, or social groups. Family-focused prevention programs include such approaches as parent training, family skills training, family relationship enhancement, and family alcohol and drug education programs, as discussed in the DeMarsh and Kumpfer article. Prevention interventions which appear to be focused primarily on the attitudes or

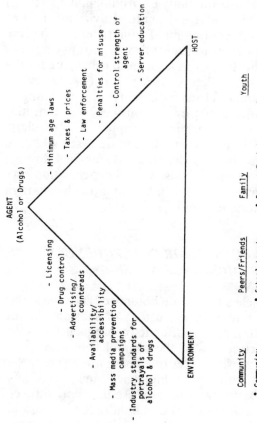

AGENT
(Alcohol or Drugs)

- Licensing
- Minimum age laws
- Advertising/ counterads
- Taxes & prices
- Availability/ accessibility
- Law enforcement
- Mass media prevention campaigns
- Penalties for misuse
- Industry standards for portrayals of alcohol & drugs
- Control strength of agent
- Server education

ENVIRONMENT

HOST

Community	Peers/Friends	Family	Youth
• Community Prevention Councils	• School-based Education	• Parent Training	• Social Skills Training
• Health Fairs	• Student Groups	• Family Skills Training	• Social Competency Programs
• Community Volunteers	• Parent Groups	• Family Relationship Enhancement	• Social Inoculation Programs
• Adopt-A-Family Programs	• Church Groups	• Family Alcohol & Drug Education	• Alternatives Programs
	• Fraternities/ Sororities		• Affective Education Programs

FIGURE 1. Categorization of prevention approaches by the Public Health Service model.

values and coping skills of youth include social skills training programs discussed in the Kumpfer and DeMarsh and Johnson et al. articles, and the alcohol and drug education, alternatives programs, and affective education programs discussed in the Bukoski article.

Some prevention programs have multiple sites of influence. For instance, national media counteradvertising campaigns (primarily classified as a community environmental approach) could have broad influence across the entire Environment/Host and Environment/Agent continuum. Training those who serve alcoholic beverages in ways to prevent their patrons or guests from becoming intoxicated, or at least from driving under the influence (Mosher, 1983; Peters, 1985), can impact several points on the Environment/Host continuum (i.e., local lounges, taverns, and restaurants; public events, business socials, fraternities/sororities; and friends or family members who regularly use alcohol or drugs to entertain). In addition, school-based programs that seek to involve the students' families through homework assignments and televised smoking cessation programs (Flay & associates, 1982, 1983a & b) or through volunteer efforts will impact multiple sites of influence.

ADDRESSING CAUSES OR CONSEQUENCES OF SUBSTANCE ABUSE

Prevention approaches can be dichotomized into those that attempt to modify or remove the causes of substance abuse versus those that attempt to buffer its consequences. Some researchers and practitioners in the alcohol field attempt to prevent the adverse consequences of alcohol use by creating a low-risk environment through technological and social engineering. They seek better ways to decrease the approximately 100,000 deaths (Ravenholt, 1984) and hundreds of thousands of injuries that occur each year due to encounters between drinkers and high-risk environments. Advocates of this approach (Wittman, 1985; Moore & Gerstein, 1981) point out that current prevention policy often places the onus for substance abuse problems solely on the individual despite scientific information clearly implicating the environment (Beauchamp, 1976; Ryan, 1972).

Environmental risk reduction strategies have been quite successful in the public health field. Removal of lead from paint to protect babies from lead poisoning and control of air pollution are examples of cost-effective risk reduction strategies. In the alcohol field, recommended measures to mitigate alcohol-related motor vehicle accidents include mandatory seat belt and air bag laws, ignition starter control devices that require skills needed to drive safely, increasing the penalties and enforcement for driving under the influence or while intoxicated, increasing liability and education of servers (Mosher, 1983), and Students Against Drunk Driving (SADD) contracts for parents to drive teenagers home who have been using alcohol or drugs. Other environmental risk reduction policies include public intoxication legislation, which attempts to remove public inebriates from parks and abandoned buildings and house them in safe, supervised settings like walk-in and detoxification centers (Moore & Gerstein, 1981).

Certain consequences of chemical dependency such as family violence, child neglect and abuse, decreased worker productivity, and increased crime, accidents, and fires are addressed by various programs that are not specific to substance abuse, such as employee or student assistance programs (National Institute on Alcohol Abuse and Alcoholism, 1984), crime prevention programs, and family violence and neglect prevention programs. Many of these programs are not the primary activity of substance abuse agencies, but of other social service or juvenile justice agencies.

PREVENTION RESEARCH

The research support underlying most approaches currently advocated in the substance abuse prevention field is weak. Educational programs that are strictly informational or that employ "scare tactics" appear to be ineffective (Bukoski, 1979; Wepner, 1979). Educational programs that teach decision-making skills and have students apply those skills to issues regarding alcohol and drug use appear to be counterproductive in that they stimulate experimentation with alcohol and drugs (Goodstadt et al., 1979; Schlegal, Manske & Page, 1984). Affective educational programs that target the correlates of substance abuse (e.g., self-esteem), but do not directly address substance use are of questionable value. Their indirect approach in conjunction with the difficulty of implementing them in the classroom with fidelty or intensity yields little impact on even the correlates of substance abuse (Schaps, Maskowitz, Malvin & Schaeffer, 1984). Alternative programs have also had disappointing evaluation results (Cook et al., 1984; Malvin et al., 1985). An evaluation of Channel One, a nationwide program in which high-risk youth are involved in community recreation and business projects, revealed that it failed to prevent short-term increases in frequency of drunkenness and drug use (Stein, Swisher, Hu & McDonnell, 1984).

Much of the recent research on school-based prevention has focused on preventing cigarette smoking through enhancing students' social competencies. Two major approaches have been tried. The "social influences" approach (sometimes called "saying no" social inoculator or peer resistance strategies) focuses on family, peer, and media influences to smoke and helps students develop counterarguments and skills to resist social pressures to smoke. This approach was initially developed by Evans et al. (1978, 1981). A broader "life" or "social skills" approach was developed by Botvin and Eng (1980, 1982) and by Pentz (1982, 1983). Various antismoking programs utilizing these approaches have been developed and evaluated by a number of research teams in the United States, Europe and Australia, including those of McAlister (1979, 1980), Perry (1980a, b), Tell (1984), Vartianinen (1983), Schinke and Gilchrist (1983; in press-a), Pentz (1982, 1983), Johnson (1984), Flay (1982, 1983a, b, c, 1985), Fisher (1983), Dielman (1984a, b), and Biglan and Severson (1985). Most programs appear to be effective in decreasing the onset of cigarette smoking among nonsmoking early adolescents. Unfortunately, each of the evaluations suffers from serious metodological shortcomings, so it is impossible to recommend any single program (Moskowitz, 1983). In a recent comprehensive review of this research, Flay (in press, b) concludes:

> Overall, the findings from the most rigorous studies to date suggest that the social influence approach to smoking prevention can be effective some of the time. How-

ever, this conclusion seems somewhat fragile, given the considerable differences between studies in the patterns of reported results. Also, at least two plausible alternative interpretations of the reported effects remain—namely, effects of testing (or screening), and the Hawthorne Effect.

Prevention practitioners and researchers have begun to express concern about the practical significance of these findings (as opposed to their statistical significance). For instance, because of the high rate of attrition (25% to 64%) in these school-based programs, the often reported 50% reduction in youth in experimental schools who begin to use cigarettes can mean very few youth when percentages are translated to actual numbers. Furthermore, the impact found in this select group of students is probably not generalizable to higher risk students who are excluded from the study because they were more transient, were absent more often, or were smoking at pretest. Because of their high cost and intrusiveness into the daily academic schedule of schools, these programs do not at this time appear to be cost-effective. Also, without substantial teacher training and careful classroom monitoring, it is questionable that these programs can be disseminated and implemented in classrooms with any fidelity or efficacy.

Whether the social competency approach can be effectively applied to drug and alcohol education is currently being investigated. Unfortunately, we have little knowledge about *why* the earlier "saying no" programs were effective in preventing cigarette smoking. It is possible that reported effects are largely due to eliciting the existing anticigarette smoking attitudes of early adolescents in a supportive group setting that reinforces their own antismoking attitudes. Hence, this procedure may help these students to more correctly assess their peers' attitudes towards smoking. Students generally overestimate the percent of their peers who use or are favorable about substance use (Johnston, O'Malley & Bachman, 1985). When an entire grade-level cohort in a school participates in the program, the normative climate within the school is thus affected. If this hypothesis is correct, the teaching of specific skills like assertiveness (or teaching how to say no) may not be essential to the program's efficacy (Moskowitz, 1983).

If the above normative change hypothesis is valid, a multi-substance social competency curriculum may not be as successful in preventing alcohol or drug abuse as anticigarette programs have been in preventing cigarette smoking. Cigarettes serve different psychosocial functions, and there is much greater consensus among both adults and youth as to what constitutes a reasonable prevention objective—namely abstinence (Moskowitz, 1983). Furthermore, we fear that youth are more likely to *perceive* that the other two gateway drugs, alcohol and marijuana, can be used in a relatively safe recreational manner. Hence, there is greater risk of the program stimulating some students to experiment with these substances (Moskowitz, 1983). Caution is warranted as mixed or negative behavioral effects have been fairly common outcomes of prior alcohol and drug education courses (Goodstadt, 1980).

On a more positive note, substance abuse prevention research is in its infancy. Although pilot studies began as early as 20 years ago, systematic evaluation research began quite recently. In addition, prevention research has been hampered by inadequate funding and the high cost and difficulty of conducting large scale, applied research projects. The majority of the funding has been for school-based approaches; hence, little research exists on the effectiveness of the multitude of different strategies discussed at the beginning of this article.

Recommendations for Future Prevention Research

Befor public agencies can begin to prioritize prevention approaches, more information is needed in the areas listed below.

1. The Etiology of Substance Abuse

More knowledge is needed about the risk factors and protective factors that influence substance abuse, particularly those that are possible targets for change in prevention programs. This research will require funding of prospective, longitudinal studies in which low and high risk children are followed for several years to determine the early childhood correlates and also biological markers for substance abuse.

Once there is an improved understanding of why children do or do not become abusers, prevention programs can be better designed to address those causes of substance abuse.

2. The Efficacy of Prevention Programs

Prevention researchers and the general public need to understand why prevention programs work or fail. Unfortunately, few prevention evaluations adequately assess whether the programs were implemented as planned. Hence, studies should include better qualitative and quantitative process evaluations assessing important intermediary variables as well as analyzing the program's impact on outcomes (Patton, 1980). As discussed by Flay (in press-a), few prevention programs have been subjected to the stringent series of research levels needed to determine if they are effective under optimal, standardized conditions (efficacy trials), let alone under weaker, and generally less standardized conditions of wide dissemination to general prevention practitioners or volunteers (treatment effectiveness trials or implementation effectiveness trials).

3. Awareness of Side Effects

Policy makers and program administrators need better information about the effects and side effects of prevention policies and programs. Few evaluation studies to date have been comprehensive. Generally, data are collected on a limited set of variables related only to narrow research hypotheses. Hence, it is often not possible to anticipate additional effects that a prevention strategy may have. One of the best examples of unintended, *positive* side effects in the prevention field involves reduced substance use in prevention program volunteers (Merrill & Boswell, 1975), and the spread of prevention effects by community volunteers to those other than the targer population, as documented in the National Institute on Alcohol Abuse and Alcoholism (NIAAA) evaluation of alcohol prevention programs. *Negative* side effects are also possible. For example, raising the price of alcohol may include economic deprivation for children of alcoholics, or the adoption of increased bootlegging and home stills, which during prohibition were associated with increased mortality. Special school programs for children of alcoholics or drug abusers could increase stigmatization by other children and teachers.

4. Cost-Effectiveness or Cost-Benefit of Prevention Programs

Increased assessment is needed of the costs of prevention programs in relation to their potential benefits. Public and private funding agencies are becoming increasingly cost conscious. Cost-benefit analyses are complex and often difficult to accomplish, particularly before data determining effectiveness are available. Even simple unit cost estimates need careful record keeping and rely on a number of debatable assumptions. Nevertheless, best available estimates can at least help to inform policy makers' preliminary decisions about which prevention approaches to pursue with additional funding. Hence, analyses to determine which prevention approaches are likely to produce the largest positive outcomes for the investment made are needed, realizing that such analyses are complex and not completely accurate until more research is done on the efficacy of prevention approaches.

5. Clearer Definitions of the Goal of Prevention Programs

Should alcohol and drug abuse agencies be concerned with prevention of the causes or the consequences of alcohol and drug abuse, or both? Should the goal of prevention be to prevent use or abuse. What constitutes use and abuse? These questions require considerable study and debate.

A decade ago, prevention professionals generally believed that the goal of prevention was to teach the responsible use of substances. Today, responsible use is little mentioned, and many professionals believe that, at least for illegal substances, no use can be considered responsible. Similarly, traditional approaches to the prevention of alcohol-related problems focused on the individual, while more recent approaches have focused on the environment in which the individual operates. These changes in orientation and perspective illustrate the difficulties in developing a consensus concerning the goals of prevention. Yet, without such consensus, both program planning and program evaluation are problematic. Questions concerning the goals of prevention are largely matters of public policy and prevailing standards and norms, yet these questions must be answered if research and program development are to proceed in an integrated and focused way.

6. Theory-Driven Prevention and Increased Use of State-of-the-Art Change Technologies

Practitioners in the substance abuse prevention field should keep abreast of new research findings in related fields on theories and techniques for influencing knowledge, attitudes, norms, and behaviors. Much research in educational technology, social learning theory, developmental and social psychology, mass communication and social marketing, and organizational behavior is applicable to the development and delivery of prevention programs. In addition, successes in the prevention of allied health and social problems should be continually monitored for their applicability to substance abuse prevention.

7. Increased Analysis of Natural Experiments and Existing Data Bases

Rapid funding mechanisms should be established at the federal level to assist state and local governments in evaluating the impact of major prevention programs or public policy changes. The current federal research review process is too lengthy to allow for evaluation of these prevention efforts, and the states are rarely interested in funding research or evaluation. These prevention efforts are also very important because they represent locally designed programs that may have particular relevance to many states and communities. Although it is often difficult to conduct controlled experiments in naturally occurring settings, some local programs may occur in isolated communities (e.g., military bases, rural towns), which would allow for some control of independent variables.

If prevention is to be effective, more public funding of research on prevention of substance abuse will be needed. Although the economic consequences of alcohol, tobacco, and drug use are comparable to those of heart disease and cancer, 35 times more public research funds are spent on cancer and 15 times more public research funds are spent on heart disease (Institute of Medicine, 1984). In the total National Institute on Alcohol Abuse and Alcoholism (NIAAA) and National Institute on Drug Abuse (NIDA) FY 85 extramural budgets for research, prevention research represents only 8% and 9%, or $3.2 million and $5.1 million, respectively. In addition, a majority of these research funds are spent on only one approach to prevention, namely school-based social competency prevention programs. Broader research funding of the whole spectrum of prevention approaches is needed.

FUTURE ISSUES IN PREVENTION

As in all fields, and particularly in those impacted by changing social trends, substance abuse prevention must be concerned with future trends and projections. Proactive rather than reactive approaches to drug and alcohol problems are to be preferred. The authors do not claim expertise as futurists, but believe that certain apparent trends should be considered because of their implications for the design of prevention programs in the United States. This section is primarily intended to stimulate thought and discussion about the social and technological environment in which future prevention programs may operate.

Future Changes in Society

Futurists often portray the future as very different from the present. Because of the slow, incremental nature of most changes, their impact is difficult to gauge. We have lived through 1984 and did not find it as strange as Orwell imagined it. Nevertheless, basic human needs and the structure of society are not likely to change dramatically in the next twenty years. But what kind of world will we create? Many technological advances will free workers for more leisure activities. Americans will enjoy more pursuit of leisure time. Alcohol and drugs have been closely tied to pleasure and leisure in

America. Will the use of drugs and alcohol increase in the future? A number of social factors will be discussed below that could affect patterns of drug usage, beneficially or adversely.

Possible Negative Influences

Americans may need to adjust to a reduced or much less rapidly rising standard of living. Each new generation may not be wealthier than their parents. Despite inflation and reduced productivity, American households today have more money for leisure time activities for several reasons: (a) many households have increased the number of breadwinners (wives working and shared living arrangements with relatives and friends), (b) fewer families have dependents (only 48% of families have children in the home according to the Census Bureau) and those families with children have fewer children, and (c) many families have reduced their basic living expenses by returning to earlier patterns of simpler, more self-sufficient living. Hence, in some respects our lives look more like our grandparents' lives. However, there are several major differences that increase stress and vulnerability to drugs and alcohol.

As life becomes more and more complex, choices increase. Many people are not equipped by temperament to deal with the complexity and fast pace of this society, and fewer slower-paced islands of retreat are available. Fewer people live on small farms, ranches, in small towns, or in religious or mental health retreats—monasteries or mental hospitals. Stress and disillusionment are increasing because the gap is increasing between people's expectations for the good life as portrayed on television and in magazines, and the realities of their everyday lives. If economic conditions should worsen significantly in the next twenty years—and it's hard to believe that Americans can continue to finance their prosperity on borrowed money forever—it will be extremely difficult for Americans (conditioned to thinking of themselves as number one) to make the transition to a lower standard of living. People unhappy with their external environment often find in drugs an effective way to alter their internal perceptions and responses.

Despite recent difficulties in selling and buying residences,

Americans have in general been increasingly mobile, seeking job opportunities wherever they occur. This transiency means decreased commitment and ties to any community or group of friends. The lack of social support networks and family ties and a breakdown in informal social controls have contributed to increased substance abuse. As discussed in the Wallack article, television and mass media have a great influence on children and youth because of the large amount of time children spend watching TV. Children are partly left to the socializing influences of peers and mass media because working parents have less time to spend with their children. Although the amount of time has been shown not to be the most important variable in child rearing, the amount of quality or instructional time is important. Responsible parents are now attempting to set aside some time to assure that their children's education in values and social skills is not left to others. Parents must be careful not to abdicate their role as the primary socializing agent by assuming that their children will learn all that they need to know in school or church.

Schools are facing funding and enrollment crises of increasing proportions. Teachers have less and less time to be concerned with socialization of children. It is possible that schools will not devote the necessary time or money to deliver well-designed drug abuse prevention programs. This easy avenue to a large number of children may not be open in the future. The Department of Education has recently decided that teachers are not responsible for the socialization of children or for their alcohol and drug education. Since this is true, parents may in fact need to spend more time with their children in order to counter the negative values communicated by television, movies, and comic books, as well as by their children's peer groups.

The number of preadolescent and early adolescent criminal offenders is increasing rapidly and faster than the criminal justice system knows how to handle. Will the youthful violence portrayed in "A Clockwork Orange" be the most accurate picture of the future? Crime and drug and alcohol abuse are clearly linked in a deviant lifestyle (R. Jessor & S. L. Jessor, 1977). Many young adults of today foresaw the current economic realities as teenagers and decided that they must get a decent job to survive. The drug culture decreased somewhat and use of legitimate, traditional chemicals (prescription and nonprescription medications) has partially replaced their parents' or older siblings' use of drugs of the 1960s or 1970s—marijuana, hashish, and hallucinogens (Johnston et al., 1985). Perhaps the small number of preteenagers who are engaging in violence, child molestation, satan worship, and drugs do not see a positive future for themselves, even if they work hard. This upsurge in teen violence could be the product of a society that seems to condone violence (as depicted on television and in movies).

Finally, the age distribution of the nation's population is shifting. In the first decade of the twenty-first century, the baby boom generation will constitute a population of senior adults unprecedented in number. Little attention has been given to the drug and alcohol abuse problems of the elderly, but the data that are available suggest that misuse of prescription drugs, alcohol abuse, and instances of drug and alcohol/drug interaction are fairly widespread in this population. Moreover, there are currently few prevention programs specifically designed to address the substance abuse problem of the elderly. Clearly, more basic research and program development work will be needed in order to meet the future substance abuse prevention needs of this rapidly growing segment of society.

Positive Influences

There are some very healthy trends in society upon which prevention planners could capitalize. Mainly, middle-class youth are becoming increasingly concerned with healthy lifestyles. They are interested in staying young, and hence to the degree that the abuse of alcohol and drugs can be portrayed as detrimental to health and sexual attractiveness, young people may listen to prevention messages and decrease their consumption. Unfortunately, the bulk of alcohol and prescription drug advertising attempts to counter this trend by associating substance abuse with a young, healthy, and sexual lifestyle.

Another positive influence is that there has been a slight return and reaffirmation of the value of the family—in whatever form it takes. People realize that they need others to survive and have a meaningful life. Communities are mobilizing against all forms of social problems and are providing more supportive and preventive services. At the same time there is a concern for personal liberty and ethical interventions. "Public right to know" or public information and labeling are generally considered more ethical than public control tactics that limit personal choice.

Trends in Drug and Alcohol Usage

Drug and alcohol use and abuse have a long history. Societal and religious traditions surround the ritualistic use of alcohol and drugs. Although these traditions rarely sanction abuse, they generally sanction use of alcohol as well as other psychoactive drugs. One interesting property of alcohol and drugs is that it does not take any particular talent for their use. Youths who want to increase their social standing in a group need to have money, talent, sexual appeal, personality, social graces, or imagination. But a youth needs few skills to use drugs. Drugs and alcohol serve different functions on different occasions. Drinking or drug use can have symbolic meaning for a particular group, e.g., they can be used to reduce stress or to elevate mood, or to loosen up and be more comfortable at a party. They can be used to disinhibit oneself, or instrumentally to disinhibit another (e.g., to get a date or deliver sexual favors). Understanding the functions of drug use may be essential for designing more effective prevention programs like alternatives (Schaps et al., 1984; Murray & Perry, 1985) or drug education (Moskowitz, 1983).

Increased Health Concerns

Since 1978 more and more high school seniors have expressed concern about the potential harm of using marijuana as well as other drugs (Johnston et al., 1985). A major decrease has occured for "regular" marijuana use, whereas a minor decrease has occured for "occasional" marijuana use, heavy drinking (4-5 drinks a day) and party drinking (at least 5 drinks per weekend). However, increased knowledge of the health risks of drug use does not appear to be only factor in decreased drug use in the last few years. High school seniors recently reported slight increases in cocaine and other drug usage, despite increased awareness of the health risks associated with this use (Johnston et al., 1985). As more medical research links substance abuse to a number of health problems, some youths and adults may moderate their use. In addition, as suggested earlier, some youths appear to respond to warnings about the short-term physical and social consequences of cigarette smoking (Polich et al., 1984). Current trends toward decreases in smoking, drinking, and marijuana use are encouraging. Furthermore, some drinkers are switching to drinks with decreased alcohol content and also fewer calories. These trends may be due largely to lifestyle changes occurring predominantly among the white, middle-class. However, young adults, a group that has been heavily targeted by the alcohol industry, are still consuming large amounts of alcohol. Perhaps the movement toward a uniform minimum drinking age of 21, in conjunction with political pressures on the alcoholic bevarage industry to curtail their marketing and promotional practices will have major effects.

New Drugs

As more people move away from harmful drugs and alcohol for health reasons, there will be an increasing market for new, unscheduled drugs—like "designer drugs," which often are more harmful. It is likely that with increased chemical technology, this society will see a proliferation of new drugs developed that have a variety of effects, more specific time duration, and fewer harmful side effects. It will be difficult for the Federal Drug Administration to keep up with the development of new psychotropics and pain killers, some of which may be manufactured by youth at home with an introductory knowledge of chemistry. Already youth are dying because of the side effects and impurities of homemade drugs.

Advocacy for a free market approach to drugs is increasing even in very conservative circles (spearheaded by William Buckley). Common arguments for free competition in drug production and marketing are that pharmaceutical companies are more likely to produce quality drugs with less harmful side effects; adequate research and control would be possible; the costs of crime control would be decreased; and criminal activity to raise money for purchasing drugs would decrease. Society has always had certain drugs that it considers accept- able, such as caffeine, and nicotine. It does seem somewhat ironic that caffeine, a potent stimulant, found in most cola drinks as well as other soft drinks, is considered acceptable for use by children who are already quite active.

Free market advocates argue that given increased access to drugs, people are not likely to use them excessively. This argument is not terribly compelling, however, given our soci- ety's record to date in controlling alcohol and tobacco abuse, which in 1980 claimed some 585,000 lives (Ravenholt, 1984).

Polydrug Abuse

Another drug trend that is noticeable in the last ten years is polydrug use. It is becoming increasingly difficult to study or treat alcoholics as opposed to drug abusers, because most young abusers—particularly women—use both. Polydrug use increases the potential for alcohol and drug interactions and cross tolerances. In a review of women's alcohol and drug abuse, Kumpfer and Holman (1985) could find little research on the extent of polydrug use or drug interaction effects. Obviously, more monitoring of polydrug use patterns and re- search and education on the health hazards of interaction effects is needed.

Prescription Drug Abuse

Youth are more likely than their elders to use prescription drugs medically and nonmedically as well as over-the-counter (OTC) medications (Labenta, Kumpfer & Binyon, 1984). New generations of youth appear to believe that there is a pill to cure almost any pain, discomfort, or unwanted mood. Chil- dren are brought up to be pain-phobic. As mentioned earlier in the Kumpfer/DeMarsh article, the human body has its own natural opiodes for dealing with pain, which could be dimin- ished by the use of external pain killers. Prescription drug abuse appears to be the final stage in the progression of drug abuse of youth. Yamaguchi and Kandel (1984) have recently reported that only about 25% of those who used "street" drugs as youth continued this use beyond 23 years of age; of the young adults who continue to use drugs, many switched to prescription psychotropics.

Recommendations and Promising Prevention Approaches

Future alcohol and drug abuse prevention programs should be tailored more specifically to the intended audience in terms of their cognitive capacity or developmental stage (Inhelder & Piaget, 1958) and proximal life circumstances. Pro-drug influences existing in the family and peer groups must be considered in developing prevention interventions. It will be easier to design effective programs given adequate knowledge about function and meaning of drug use among youth exposed to different cultural and environmental contexts. More research is needed to identify factors that contribute to abstinence or cessation of use in youth to determine whether these factors can be incorporated into prevention programs. In the same vein, high-risk youth who do not become abusers need to be studied for possible protective factors.

Once researchers better understand the etiology of youthful drug abuse, improved theoretical frameworks can be developed that may provide empirically derived goals for prevention programs. Improved behavior change theories and technologies should be incorporated into future prevention strategies to enhance their effectiveness. Prevention efforts could also be far more effective if they had equal access to the resources employed to promote consumption of alcohol and prescription drugs in this country. Given that this is unlikely, restrictions on the advertising and promotion of alcohol and OTC drugs may be essential, if prevention programs are ever to become cost-effective. Cost-effective programs will most likely include the following elements: community volunteers working with youth in community settings; strategies that target high risk children and youth; messages that stress healthy lifestyles and focus on short-term health consequences; and integrated programs with enduring, coordinated, and pervasive strategies that address the many domains of environmental influence on youth.

Communities or agencies considering the development and/ or funding of prevention programs for substance abuse should consider the following in their choice of a preferred prevention strategy.

1. Coordinated, Local Community Involvement

Programs that involve large numbers of volunteers from the local community and integrate media, community, school, and family strategies into coordinated campaign are more likely to be successful. Coordinated prevention approaches that fit with community norms and have locally approved prevention goals are more likely to endure.

Community programs should be coordinated with community policies. Availability of alcohol to youth should be limited to family or religious settings. Minimum age laws should be rigorously enforced by increasing the resources of regulatory agencies to monitor violations. Training of commercial servers in conjunction with more responsible management policies and practices will facilitate compliance. Adults can be brought into compliance by extending their liability for purchasing or serving alcohol to minors. Recently, some communities have made parents liable for teenage drinking that occurs in their homes, even when the parents are not present. Other communities have begun to employ zoning policies and practices as a means of reducing local alcohol problems.

2. Messages That Stress Healthy Lifestyles

The increased interest by youth and adults in physical fitness and disease prevention has created a climate in which smoking is no longer acceptable public behavior. Increasing concern about the adverse health consequences of breathing secondhand smoke, in conjunction with the noxious odor of smoke-filled air, has motivated nonsmokers to become more vocal even to organize. Now, both informal social influences and formal social controls (i.e., public policies to restrict smoking in public places or work sites) put pressure on smokers to stop. If substance abuse prevention programs can capitalize on this emerging health consciousness, they may be able to influence children's and youth's norms towards the use of other drugs. Methods need to be found to decrease the association of drugs and alcohol with good times, relaxation and celebration. Messages aimed at youth need to stress the negative, short-term social and health consequences of alcohol and drugs.

3. Target High-Risk Youth

More preventive interventions need to be developed and tested that are appropriate for the developmental level, cultural lifestyle, and type of use/abuse pattern of the targeted youth. Increased programming is needed for children of chemically dependent parents because of their higher risk status. This programming should be based on empirical knowledge of those family factors that contribute to drug use.

4. Enduring, Naturalistic Prevention Programs

Because of the multitude of environmental factors promoting alcohol and drug use in youth, it may not be possible to substantially decrease use until prevention messages are pervasive and enduring. Youth are not likely to be inoculated against substance use, by a one-shot, short-term prevention program. Children learn more about healthy lifestyles from their daily contacts with adults than from short-term special programs. Hence, adults need to consider what messages they give children when they use and abuse drugs, model inappropriate use (Bandura, 1977), or condone use at social functions and parties. By allowing an excessive amount of positive portrayals of alcohol and drug use in the mass media, we are as a society sanctioning use and contributing to abuse. Adults should become aware of the pro-alcohol and drug use messages that they communicate to children and youth through their own behaviors or statements. Parents and professionals who come in contact with high risk children and youth need not only to eliminate these pro-use message but need to incorporate nonuse messages in their interactions with children whenever appropriate opportunities arise.

Adults who discuss drug and alcohol use with an adolescent should be empathetic and aware of the context and function of drug use for a particular youth. Youth may experiment with drugs and alcohol to fulfill certain social and emotional needs, including maturity, risk-taking and competence. Youth should be encouraged to consider alternative activities that could fulfill the functions of drug use—mountain climbing, bicycling, running, or dancing. Unfortunately, many alternate activities, as pointed out earlier, require hard work, dedication, and sometimes talents that not all youth possess. Hence, finding alternatives will be a challenging task.

Possibly, some youth may be more vulnerable to drugs because of the pronounced physical, hormonal, and personality changes that they undergo during adolescence. Endocrine system changes may make adolescents more sensitive emotionally to any unbalancing stimulus, similar to women during menopause. In addition, during adolescence youth enter a new cognitive development stage that allows them to consider universal ethical principles (Inhelder & Piaget, 1958; Kohlberg & Gillighan, 1972). When a new cognitive skill is acquired, the developing child tends to repeatedly practice the new skill. Some have hypothesized that this is the reason that adolescents tend to be dreamers who are disappointed in their parents, critical of the hypocrisies they see around them, and occasionally are rejecting of the adult world. Not all youth reach the stage of formal operations, but this disappointment in the adult world could contribute to drug abuse in those brighter youth who do.

Prevention specialists should examine the environmental factors that contribute to alcohol or drug abuse in the children or youth of their community. Analysis of the weakest link in the chain of factors leading to substance use could provide practitioners with some clues as to where and how to intervene. This analysis should include the social and cultural context of the youth. What is a youth's motivation to refuse drugs if the only peer group willing to accept the child uses alcohol or drugs as a criterion for membership? Perhaps the peer group's norms and behaviors can be affected by organizing their parents into a concerned parent group. If not, can other alternative strategies for acceptance be developed for this youth? Possibly, if they have a car, they could be the sober or nondrugged member of the group who drives the others home safely. This may sound like a strange type of alternative to drug use, but it does take into consideration the social reward milieu in which youth operate.

Some youth do not have the option of having "straight" friends of whom their parents approve. Often their only option to drug-using friends may be no friends at all. Consider this real case: A young child of a drug dealer lost her mother at two years of age and has been socially and emotionally neglected ever since. She arrives in junior high school with no friends, no particular social competence, but a vast knowledge about drugs and access to drugs. She is rejected by all of the popular groups in school because of her poor language and inappropriate, demanding interaction style. If she discovers that her knowledge and access to drugs gains her social points in a drug using clique, what is the likelihood that she will be motivated to refuse drugs? Some youth may be motivated to refuse drugs, but lack the skill. But what is their number compared to the number of youth who simply lack the motivation to refuse drugs?

Prevention programs that teach drug resistance skills may be effective primarily because they help to change the school or peer group norms about drug and alcohol use. Several researchers argue that adolescent drug use is not deviant, but represents a social adaptation to the peer group norms (Baumrind, 1985; Suchman, 1968; Segal, Huba & Singer, 1980). In many schools in this country, knowledge and use of drugs is considered one of the signs of social competency. Among preschool children, social status can be obtained through knowledge and acquisition of brand name consumer products, e.g. My Ponies, Care Bears, Transformers, Barbie dolls, and the ultimate Cabbage Patch dolls. Likewise, in junior and senior high school, to have tried many different drugs may have great social value. In many peer groups, boasting about one's latest drug or alcohol-related experience may be a valued activity. Hence, until drug and alcohol use is not normative, and it is no longer considered "cool" to have drug experiences, youth will have little motivation to resist peer drug pressure. Besides, where does the pressure really occur? Do youth really taunt and tease peer group members to use drugs? Or is the pressure more subtle? More research needs to be conducted on how group drug use norms and behaviors are established as well as youth's changing attitudes towards alcohol and drugs.

The vast amount of knowledge needed to help inform choices about the most effective prevention strategies should not deter planners and funders. The knowledge contained in this volume will help to promote at least educated guesses as to the best prevention approaches for a particular population of children or youth. In the past few years we have witnessed a considerable decline in the prevalence of teenage use of marijuana, particularly more frequent use (Johnston et al., 1985). To maintain this advance and to increase the fight against new drugs of abuse, Americans must continue their commitment to decreasing the consumption of drugs and alcohol in youth. A good place to start is by decreasing their own consumption of alcohol and drugs (even prescription drugs) and modeling healthful lifestyles for the children of America.

REFERENCES

Bandura, A. (1977). *Social learning theory.* Englewood Cliffs: Prentice-Hall.

Baumrind, D. (1985). Familial antecedents of adolescent drug use: A developmental perspective. In C. L. Jones, & R. J. Battejes (Eds.), *Etiology of drug abuse: Implications for prevention,* (National Institute on Drug Abuse Research Monograph 56, DHHS Publication No. ADM 85-1335, pp. 13-44). Washington, DC: U. S. Government Printing Office.

Beauchamp, D. (1976, Fall). Exploring new ethics for public health: Developing a fair alcohol policy. *The Journal of Health Politics, Policy and Law, 1,* 338-354.

Bell, C. S., & Levy, S. M. (1984). Public policy and smoking prevention: Implications for research. In J. D. Matarazzo, S. M. Weiss, J. A. Herd, & N. E. Miller (Eds.), *Behavioral health* (pp. 775-785). New York: John Wiley.

Biglan, A., Severson, H. H., Ary, D. V., Faller, C., Thompson, R., Nautel, C., Lichtenstein, E., & Weissman, W. W. (1985). *Refusal skills training and the prevention of adolescent cigarette smoking.* Manuscript submitted for publication.

Botvin, G. J., & Eng, A. (1980). A comprehensive school-based smoking prevention program. *Journal of School Health, 50,* 209-213.

Botvin, G. J., & Eng, A. (1982). The efficacy of a multicomponent approach to the prevention of cigarette smoking. *Preventive Medicine, 11,* 199-211.

Bukoski, W. (1979). *Drug Abuse prevention evaluation: A meta-evaluation process.* Paper presented at the Annual Meeting of the American Public Health Association, New York.

Cook, R., Lawrence, H., Morse, C., & Roehl, J. (1984). An evaluation of the alternative approach to drug abuse prevention. *The International Journal of the Addictions, 19* (7), 767-787.

Dielman, T. E., Horvath, W. J., Leach, S. L., & Lorenger, A. L. (1984). *Peer pressure in recruitment to smoking.* Final report to NIDA, University of Michigan.

Dielman, T. E., Leach, S. L., Lyons, A. C., Lorenger, A. T., Klos, D. M., & Horvath, W. J. (1984). Resisting pressures to smoke: Fifteen-month follow-up results of an elementary school based smoking prevention project. *International Journal of Health Education.*

Evans, R. I., Rozelle, R. M., Maxwell, S. E., Raines, B. E., Dill, C. A., Guthrie, T. J., Henderson, A. H., & Hill, P. C. (1981). Social modeling films to deter smoking in adolescents: Results of a three-year field investigation. *Journal of Applied Psychology, 66,* 399-414.

Evans, R. I., Rozelle, R. M., Mittelmark, M., Hansen, W. B., Bane, A., & Havis, J. (1978). Deterring the onset of smoking in children: Knowledge of immediate physiological effects and coping with peer pressure, media pressure, and parent modeling. *Journal of Applied Social Psychology, 8* (2), 126-135.

Fisher, D. A., Armstrong, B. K., & de Klerk, N. H. (1983, July). A randomized-controlled trial of education for prevention of smoking in 12-year-old children. Presented at 5th World Conference on Smoking and Health, Winnipeg, Canada.

Flay, B. R. (in press-a). Efficacy and effectiveness of health promotion programs. *Preventive Medicine.*

Flay, B. R. (in press-b). Psychosocial approaches to smoking prevention: A review of the findings. *Health Psychology.*

Flay, B. R., d'Avernas, J. R., Best, J. A., Kersell, M. W., & Ryan, K. B. (1983a). Cigarette smoking: Why young people do it and ways of preventing it. In P. McGrath & P. Firestone (Eds.), *Pediatric and Adolescent Behavioral Medicine.* New York: Springer-Verlag.

Flay, B. R., Hansen, W. B., Johnson, C. A., & Sobel, J. L. (1983b, August). *Involvement of children in motivating smoking parents to quit smoking with a television program.* Paper presented at the 5th World Conference on Smoking and Health, Winnipeg, Canada, July, and the 91st Annual Convention of the American Psychological Association, Anaheim, California.

Flay, B. R., Johnson, C. A., Hansen, W. B., Grossman, L. M., Sobel, J. L., & Collins, L. M. (1983c, October). *Evaluation of a school-based, family-oriented, television-enhanced smoking prevention and cessation program: The importance of implementation evaluation.* Paper presented at the Joint Meeting of Evaluation Network and the Evaluation Research Society, Chicago.

Flay, B. R., Johnson, C. A., Hansen, W. B., Ulene, A., Grossman, L. M., Alvarez, L., Sobel, D. F., Hochstein, G., & Sobel, J. L. (1982). Evaluation of a mass media enhanced smoking prevention and cessation program. In J. P. Baggaley & P. Tanega (Eds.), *Experimental research in televised instruction* (Vol. V.) Montreal: Concordia University Press.

Flay, B. R., Ryan, K. B., Best, J. A., Brown, K. S., Kersell, M. W., d'Avernas, J. R., & Zanna, M. P. (1985). Are social psychological smoking prevention programs effective? The Waterloo Study. *Journal of Behavioral Medicine,* 8,(1), 37-59.

Goodstadt, M. (1980). Drug education: A turnon or a turnoff. *Journal of Drug Education, 10,* 89-99.

Goodstadt, M., Sheppard, M., Crawford, S., Cook, G., McCready, J., & Leonard, J. (1979). *Alcohol education: A comparison of three alternative approaches.* Toronto: Addiction Research Foundation.

Grossman, M., Coate, D., & Arluck, G. M. (1984, October 7-10). *Price sensitivity of alcoholic beverages in the United States.* Paper presented at conference on Control Issues in Alcohol Abuse Prevention II: Impacting Communities, co-sponsored by the South Carolina Commission on Alcohol and Drug Abuse, et al., Charleston, South Carolina.

Hooper, F. J. (1983, November 16). *The relationship between alcohol control policies and cirrhosis mortality in United States counties.* Paper presented at American Public Health Association annual meeting, Dallas, Texas.

Inhelder, B., & Piaget, J. (1958). *The growth of logical thinking from childhood to adolescence.* New York: Basic Books.

Institute of Medicine. (1984, October). *Research on mental illness and addictive disorders: Progress and prospects,* (IOM Report).

Jessor, R., & Jessor, S. L. (1978). *Problem behavior and psychosocial development: A longitudinal study.* New York: Academic Press.

Johnson, C. A., Hansen, W. B., Collins, L. M., & Graham, J. W. (1984). *Final report: The high school anti-smoking project* (Report to National Institute on Drug Abuse). University of Southern California.

Johnston, L. D., O'Malley, P. M., & Bachman, J. G. (1985). *Use of licit and illicit drugs by America's high school students, 1975-1984.* Rockville, MD: NIDA, (ADM) 85-1394.

Kohlberg, L., & Gillighan, C. (1972). The adolescent as a philosopher: The discovery of the self in a post-conventional world. In J. Kagan & R. Coles (Eds.), *Twelve to sixteen: Early adolescence.* New York: Norton.

Kumpfer, K. L., & DeMarsh, J. (1984, February). *Prevention services to children of substance-abusing parents: Project rationale, description and research plan.* Technical report submitted to National Institute on Drug Abuse, Rockville, MD.

Kumpfer, K. L., & Holman, A. (1985, September). *Women and substance abuse treatment: A review of the literature.* Social Research Institute report submitted to the Utah State Division of Alcoholism and Drugs, Salt Lake City, UT.

Labenta, D., Kumpfer, K., & Binyon, J. (1984). Findings of the Utah 1983 incidence and prevalence survey. Utah State Division of Alcoholism and Drugs Report.

Lauzon, R. R. J. (1977). An epidemiological approach to health promotion. *Canadian Journal of Public Health, 68,* 311-317.

MacDonald, S., & Whitehead, P. (1983). Availability of outlets and consumption of alcoholic beverages. *Journal of Drug Issues* (Fall), 477-486.

Malvin, J. H., Moskowitz, J. M., Schaps, E., & Schaeffer, G. A. (1985). Evaluation of two school-based alternatives programs. *Journal of Alcohol and Drug Education, 30,* 98-108.

McAlister, A. L., Perry, C., Killen, J., Slinkard, L. A., & Maccoby, N. (1980). Pilot study of smoking, alcohol, and drug abuse prevention. *American Journal of Public Health, 70,* 719-721.

McAlister, A. L., Perry, C., & Maccoby, N. (1979). Adolescent smoking: Onset and prevention. *Pediatrics, 63,* 650-658.

Merrill, R. M., & Boswell, B. N. (1975). *Study No. 5: Volunteers in the Cottage Program.* Salt Lake City, UT: Cottage Program International.

Moore, M. H., & Gerstein, D. R. (Eds.) (1981). *Alcohol and public policy: Beyond the shadow of prohibition.* Washington, DC: National Academy Press.

Mosher, J. F. (1982). Federal tax law and public health policy: The case of alcohol-related tax expenditures. *Journal of Public Health Policy, 3* (3), 260-283.

Mosher, J. F. (1983). Server intervention: A new approach for preventing drinking driving. *Accident Analysis and Prevention, 15* (6), 483-497.

Mosher, J. F., & Wallack, L. M. (1981). Government regulation of alcohol advertising: Protecting industry profits versus promoting the public health. *Journal of Public Health Policy, 2* (4), 333-353.

Moskowitz, J. M. (1983). Preventing adolescent substance abuse through drug education. In T. J. Glynn, C. G. Leukefeld & J. P. Ludford (Eds.). *Preventing adolescent drug abuse: Intervention strategies.* Rockville, MD: National Institute on Drug Abuse Research Monograph 47, 233-249. (ADM) 83-1280.

Murray, D. M., & Perry, C. L. (1985). The prevention of adolescent drug abuse: Implications of etioligical, developmental, behavioral, and environmental models. In C. L. Jones & R. J. Battjes, (Eds.), *Etiology of Drug Abuse: Implications for Prevention* (National Institute on Drug Abuse Research Monograph 56, DHHS Publication No. ADM 85-1335). Washington, DC: U.S. Government Printing Office.

Nathan, P. E. (1983). Failures in prevention: Why we can't prevent the devastating effect of alcoholism and drug abuse. *American Psychologist, 38,* 459-467.

National Institute on Alcohol Abuse and Alcoholism. (1984). *Preventing alcohol problems through a student assistance program: A manual for implementation based on the Washington County New York model.* Rockville, MD: Author, (ADM) 84-1344.

Patton, M. Q. (1980). *Qualitative evaluation methods.* Beverly Hills, CA: Sage Publications.

Pentz, M. A. (1982). *Social skills training: A preventive intervention for drug use in adolescents.* Paper presented at American Psychological Association meeting, Washington, DC.

Pentz, M. A. (1983). Prevention of adolescent substance abuse through social skill development. In T. J. Glynn, C. G. Leukefeld, & J. P. Ludford (Eds.) *Preventing adolescent drug abuse: Intervention strategies* (National Institute on Drug Abuse Research Monograph 47, DHHS Publication No. ADM 83-1280). Washington, DC: U. S. Government Printing Office.

Perry, C., Killen, J., Slinkard, L. A., & McAlister, A. L. (1980a). Peer teaching and smoking prevention among junior high students. *Adolescence, 9* (58), 277-281.

Perry, C., Killen, J., Telch, M., Slinkard, L. A., & Danaher, B. G. (1980b). Modifying smoking behavior of teenagers: A school-based intervention. *American Journal of Public Health, 70* (7), 722-725.

Peters, J. (1985). Director, Intermission, Ltd., 56 Main Street, Northampton, Massachusetts 01060.

Polich, J. M., Ellickson, P. L., Reuter, P., & Kahan, J. P. (1984, February). *Strategies for controlling adolescent drug use.* Santa Monica, CA: The Rand Corporation.

Ravenholt, R. T. (1984). Addiction mortality in the United States, 1980: Tobacco, alcohol, and other substances. *Population and Developmental Review, 10* (4), 697-724.

Roffman, R. A. (1982). *Marijuana as medicine.* Seattle: Madrona.

Ryan, W. (1972). *Blaming the victim.* New York: Vintage Press.

Schaps, E., Moskowitz, J. M., Malvin, J. H., & Schaeffer, G. A. (1984). *The Napa drug abuse prevention project: Research findings.* Rockville, MD: National Institute on Drug Abuse Prevention Research Report.

Schinke, S. P., & Gilchrist, L. D. (1983). Primary prevention of tobacco smoking. *Journal of School Health, 53* (7), 416-419.

Schinke, S. P., & Gilchrist, L. D. (in press a). Preventing cigarette smoking with youth. *Journal of Primary Prevention.*

Schinke, S. P., & Gilchrist, L. D. (in press b). Preventing substance abuse with children and adolescents. *Journal of Consulting and Clinical Psychology.*

Schlegal, R., Manske, S., & Page, A. (1984). A guided decision making program for elementary school students: A field experiment in alcohol education. In P. Miller & T. Nirenberg (Eds.), *Prevention of alcohol abuse,* pp. 407-439. New York: Plenum Press.

Segal, B., Huba, G. J., & Singer, J. L. (1980). *Drugs, daydreaming and personality: A study of college youth.* Hillsdale, NJ: Erlbaum.

Stein, J. A., Swisher, J. D., Hu, T., & McDonnell, N. (1984). Cost-effectiveness evaluation of a Channel One program. *Journal of Drug Education, 14,* 251-269.

Suchman, E. A. (1968). The "hang-loose" ethic and the spirit on drug use. *Journal of Health and Social Behavior; 9,* 146-155.

Tell, G. S., Klepp, K. I., Vellar, O. D., & McAlister, A. (1984). Preventing the onset of cigarette smoking Norwegian adolescents: The Oslo youth study. *Preventive Medicine, 13,* 256-275.

Vartiainen, E., Pallonen, U., McAlister, A., Koskela, K., & Puska, P. (1983). Effect of two years of educational intervention in adolescent smoking (The North Karelia Youth Project). *Bulletin of the World Health Organization, 61* (3), 529-532.

Vingilis, E. R., & DeGenova, K. (1984). Youth and the forbidden fruit: Experiences with changes in legal drinking age in North America. *Journal of Criminal Justice, 12,* 161-172.

Wagenaar, A. C. (1981). Effects of an increase in the legal minimum drinking age. *Journal of Public Health Policy, Inc., 2* (3), 206-223.

Wagenaar, A. C. (1982). Aggregate beer and wine consumption: Effect of changes in the minimum legal drinking age and a mandatory beverage container deposit law in Michigan. *Journal of Studies on Alcohol, 43* (5), 469-487.

Wagenaar, A. C. (in press). Effects of minimum drinking age on alcohol-related traffic crashes: The Michigan experience five years later. Forthcoming in H. Holder (Ed.), *Control Issues in Alcohol Abuse Prevention: Impacting Communities.* Greenwich, CN: JAI Press.

Wallack, L. M. (1984). *The prevention of alcohol-related problems: Recommendations for public policy initiatives.* Berkeley, CA: Prevention Research Center.

Wepner, S. (1979). Which way drug education? *Journal of Drug Education, 9,* 93-103.

Williams, T. P., & Lillis, R. P. (1985, April 18-21). *Changes in alcohol consumption by eighteen year olds following an increase in New York State's purchase age to nineteen.* Paper presented at the National Council on Alcoholism, National Alcoholism Forum, Washington, DC.

Wittman, F. D. (1985). *Reducing environmental risk of alcohol problems.* Berkeley, CA: Prevention Research Center.

Yamaguchi, K., & Kandel, D. B. (1984). Patterns of drug use from adolescence to young adulthood: III. Predictors of progression. *American Journal of Public Health, 74,* 673-681.

SELECTED READINGS

ERIC Documents
and Journal Articles

ERIC DOCUMENTS

COGNITIVE FACTORS IN SUBSTANCE ABUSE: THE CASE FOR EARLY LEARNING. Robert B. Noll and others. (ED 249 445, 1984, 12p.)

Reports two studies in which preschool children from families with alcoholic and nonalcoholic fathers performed Piagetian tasks to determine their cognitions about alcohol and its uses. Findings suggest that learning about alcoholic beverages could begin early in a child's life and that educational programs could appropriately be introduced in kindergarten.

COMMUNITIES: WHAT YOU CAN DO ABOUT DRUG AND ALCOHOL ABUSE. Gardner, Stephen E. (ED 250 599, 1983, 17p.)

Identifies four critical areas for alcohol and drug abuse prevention strategies: communities, parents and families, schools, and the workplace. Suggests strategies appropriate for intervention in each area, and includes a list of resource organizations.

EVALUATION OF AN ALCOHOL EDUCATION PROGRAM FOR TEACHERS: A CASE STUDY. Genevieve Fitzpatrick. (ED 249 191, 1983, 60p.)

Describes the effects of a 14-week alcohol education program on the knowledge and attitudes of a self-selected group of teachers in one Massachusetts school system. The assumption underlying the program was that, with appropriate knowledge about problem drinking, teachers might intervene early with students affected with drinking problems.

KINDERGARTEN CHILDREN AND DRUGS: BELIEFS, USE AND EXPECTED USE. Michael Young and Doug Williamson. (ED 242 669, 1983, 21p.)

As part of a statewide drug education project, 112 kindergarten children from five elementary schools were interviewed individually. Data indicated significant relationships between personal use of drugs and race, living arrangement, beliefs about drugs, and expected use of drugs. Children exhibited much misinformation about drugs.

PARENTS, PEERS, AND POT—II: PARENTS IN ACTION. Marsha Manatt. (ED 247 498, 1983, 172p.)

Contains nine chapters describing the progress of the parent movement for drug-free youth, detailing the efforts of programs in Atlanta, Georgia; Florida; Connecticut; rural Indiana; Omaha, Nebraska; Nassau County, New York; inner-city Washington, D.C.: and California.

ROLE OF THE MEDIA IN DRUG ABUSE PREVENTION AND EDUCATION. HEARING BEFORE THE SUBCOMMITTEE ON ALCOHOLISM AND DRUG ABUSE OF THE COMMITTEE ON LABOR AND HUMAN RESOURCES. UNITED STATES SENATE, NINETY-EIGHTH CONGRESS, SECOND SESSION ON EXAMINING THE ROLE WHICH THE MEDIA COULD PLAY IN HELPING TO PUT AN END TO THE RAVAGING EFFECTS WHICH DRUGS HAVE COME TO HAVE ON THE YOUNG PEOPLE OF THIS NATION. (ED 248 415, 1984, 67p.)

Includes statements by members of the communications industry concerning the effects of television viewing of drug and alcohol use, abuse, and rehabilitation. Testimony by government officials and consultants is also provided.

JOURNAL ARTICLES

THE ADE PROGRAM: AN APPROACH TO THE REALI-
TIES OF ALCOHOL AND DRUG EDUCATION. Richard
E. Sherman and others. *Journal of Alcohol and Drug Educa-
tion*, 1984, *29* (2), 23-33.

Describes the development of the Alcohol and Drug Education (ADE) in the schools program, emphasizing problems
encountered prior to and during implementation of program
activities.

DYADS AT RISK: METHADONE-MAINTAINED WOM-
EN AND THEIR FOUR-MONTH-OLD INFANTS. Rita
Jeruchimowicz Jeremy and Victor J. Bernstein. *Child Devel-
opment*, 1984, *55* (4), 1141-54.

Compares methodone-exposed and control 4-month-old infants in interactions with their mothers. Results indicate that
methodone is only one of several risk factors affecting interaction: Mothers rated poor in communication exhibited poor psychosocial and psychological resources, and infants rated poor in
communication showed problematic motor functioning.

ECONOMICS OF PREVENTION. John D. Swisher. *Journal of Drug Education*, 1984, *14* (3), 249-92.

Discusses two recent studies sponsored by the National Institute on Drug Abuse which focused on the cost-effectiveness
of prevention programs for adolescents. Results showed that
the alternatives program (Channel One) produced increased
drug use at one site, while the affective education program
reduced drug use and was judged cost-effective.

FETAL ALCOHOL SYNDROME (FAS)—A REVIEW.
Ian R. Holzman. *Journal of Children in Contemporary Society*, 1982 *15* (1), 13-19.

Suggests that at least 30 percent of newborn children of
alcoholic mothers are affected severly by the fetal alcohol
syndrome and that 40-45 percent show some stigmata.

RELATIONSHIPS BETWEEN ADOLESCENT DRUG USE AND PARENTAL DRUG BEHAVIORS. Glenn M. Johnson and others. *Adolescence,* 1984, *19* (74), 293-99.

Reports findings suggesting that relationships between parental use of drugs and adolescent use of the same drugs are moderate and roughly equivalent across drugs. Parental use of marijuana was found to be strongly related to adolescent use of harder drugs.

SUBSTANCE ABUSE AND THE FAMILY. *Journal for Specialists in Group Work,* 1984 9 (2), 106-12.

Examines the effect that a substance abuser may have on the family system and the maladaptive role sometimes assumed by family members. Discusses dysfunctional family phases and therapeutic issues, presenting 11 guidelines for counselors working with chemically dependent families.

ABOUT ERIC

ERIC, the Educational Resources Information Center, is funded by the National Institute of Education. Included in the ERIC system are 16 separate clearinghouses, each responsible for collecting and disseminating information on a specific subject area in education. The ERIC Clearinghouse on Elementary and Early Childhood Education (ERIC/EECE) deals with information relating to the education and development of children from birth through age 12.

ERIC DOCUMENTS are cited and abstracted in the monthly index *Resources in Education (RIE).* Most ERIC documents may be read on microfiche in libraries and information centers. In addition, the majority can be ordered in paper copy and/or on microfiche from the ERIC Document Reproduction Service, 3900 Wheeler Ave., Alexandria, VA 22304 (Telephone: 800-227-3742). For complete information on how to order, contact EDRS or consult the most recent issue of *RIE.*

JOURNAL ARTICLES are cited and annotated in the monthly publication *Current Index to Journals in Education*

(CIJE); journals may be read at libaries or ordered through subscription. Selected article reprints are available from University Microfilms International, Article Clearinghouse, 300 N. Zeeb Rd., Ann Arbor, Mi 48106 (Telephone: 800-732-0616). Please contact UMI or see the most recent issue of *CIJE* for ordering details.

Further information about the ERIC network and services of ERIC/EECE is available from ERIC/EECE Information Services, College of Education, University of Illinois, 805 W. Pennsylvania Ave., Urbana, IL 61801 (Telephone: 217-333-1386).

Author Index

Abel, E.L. 52,65
Achenbach, T.M. 68
Ackerman, Robert 72,77,79,110,142, 211
Ackoff, R. 165
Adams, G. 66
Adams, T. 110
Adler, P.T. 18,27,29
Adler, M. 100
Agarwal, D.P. 60
Ageton, S.S. 12,62
Ahmed, S.W. 13,14,30
Ahlgren, A. 30
Ainsworth, M.D.S. 65
Akers, R.L. 27,29,33
Alegre-Jurado, C. 143,144
Alexander, J.F. 141
Alfaro, J. 20
Aliapouluis, M.A. 2,6
Alpert, R. 59
Alister 52
Allen, L. 23
Allen, C. 171
Alterman, A.I. 20,59
Alvry, K.T. 126,127,129
Ames, G.M. 70
Anderson, D. 18
Anderson, Bonnie 49
Andronica, M. 124
Anhalt, H. 25,30
Annis, H.M. 26,61
Aragona, J. 127
Arluck, G.M. 250
Ary, D.V. 196
Atkin, C.K. 167,169,170,185
Auerswald, E.H. 81
Ayers, J. 56

Bachman 12,29,41,100,154,194,257
Bahr, S.J. 33

Baker, E. 104,162
Balch, R.W. 25,26
Bandura, A. 33,34,103,121,186,271
Barnes, G.E. 18,20,24,27,29,30
Barrows, D. 177
Barry, H. III 65
Bartlome, Jeffrey 49
Battjes, B. 99,101,105,106,124
Baumrind, D. 18,19,20,36,76,81,82, 273
Bavolek, S.J. 126,134
Bavry, J. 196
Beauchamp, D. 163,254
Beck, A.T. 68
Begleiter, H. 59
Behling, D.W. 52
Bein, N.Z. 123
Beletsis, S. 73,78,80
Bell, C.S. 251
Bell, C. 99
Bell, D.S. 21
Bell, R. 68
Bennett, C. 27
Bentler, P.M. 27,50,102
Berberian, R.M. 119
Bernstein, L.T. 59
Berg, B. 144
Bergin, A. 133
Berkanovic, E. 185
Bernstein, Victor J. 281
Berrett, R.D. 131
Berry, K.L. 18,76,101,119
Beschner, George 201,231,250
Best, J.A. 185
Bey, E. 141
Biglan, A. 196,256
Bihari, B. 59
Binyon, J. 268
Black, A. 30
Black, C. 69,72,73,76,77,80
Blackburn, H. 182

Subject Index